IN A LEAGUE
OF THEIR OWN
100 Cricket Legends Select Their World XI

'Mixing eras is very hard but that's the beauty of this. It's hypothetical but we are able to indulge ourselves and weave a little magic.'
Richie Benaud, taken from his *Greatest XI*

DEDICATION

This book has taken a long time getting to this stage and I want to dedicate it to those who have always supported me, in all my endeavours – Mum, Dad, Deborah, Jeff, Donna and Kiely and my newborn son Isaac, who I hope will pick this up one day and come to the conclusion that sports writing is for fools and enter a highly-paid career in medicine or law!

Richard Sydenham

RICHARD SYDENHAM

IN A LEAGUE OF THEIR OWN

100 Cricket Legends Select Their World XI

Forewords by
Sir Garfield Sobers & Dickie Bird CBE

About the Author:

RICHARD SYDENHAM was born in Birmingham in 1974 and began a sports journalism career in 1994 by writing on cricket and football for a weekly newspaper in Birmingham, predominantly covering Warwickshire and Aston Villa. He went on to work for Gulf News in Dubai, Bloomberg News in London and freelance for *The Sunday Telegraph* and news agencies Reuters and the Associated Press. He founded Bigstarcricket.com and client and event management company Big Star Creations. This is his fourth book after *In the Line of Fire* (1999) on the great opening batsmen of Test cricket, *Inside Out* (2006), an autobiography of Mushtaq Mohammed, and an as yet unpublished biography on the movie career of Steve McQueen.

First published in Great Britain in 2010 by The Derby Books Publishing Company Limited, 3 The Parker Centre, Derby, DE21 4SZ.

A catalogue record for this book is available from the British Library.

ISBN 978-1-85983-802-0

Printed and bound by OZGraf, Poland.

CONTENTS

ACKNOWLEDGEMENTS

Obviously the first acknowledgment has to be to all the current and former cricketers who have kindly and generously agreed to contribute their World XI to this book. None have been paid and all have given up their time to consider their input to these pages. So a huge thank you must go out to those guys. And I must express an additional appreciation to the ex-players who contributed but have since passed away. I hope their families, friends and supporters will enjoy their words of wisdom and thoughts expressed.

I must thank DB Publishing and in particular publishing manager Alex Morton and managing director Steve Caron, and the chief designer Matt Limbert; thanks for believing in this project. I am also grateful for the help of Susan Kelly, who has provided photographs taken by her late father, Ken Kelly. I used to speak with Ken now and again at the Edgbaston Cricket Ground museum, and though he was a man of few words I was always impressed by his photographic collection and I am pleased to include some of them here – it was pleasing to see so many fresh-looking images that I had never seen in other publications. Roger Wootton also kindly helped out with images, while the efficient Jo Miller from the Surrey County Cricket Club Archive provided photos for this book. Michael Temple at Nottinghamshire CCC also contributed. I also wish to thank my good friend (mera bahut acha dost he) Mirza Iqbal Baig in Karachi for assisting with Mohammed Yousuf's XI. Last but not least, I want to thank Dickie Bird for his entertaining foreword and agreeing to contribute without too much deliberation. And especially to Sir Garfield Sobers, whose foreword I think is worthy of the cover price alone. I couldn't persuade Sir Garfield to select his World XI, but I am happy that he instead agreed to discuss the many great players before, during and after his career for the good of a foreword. I probably got lucky there.

Richard Sydenham, April 2010

AUTHOR'S NOTE

With a sport so rich in history, one which has been blessed with a multitude of great achievers, entertainers and ambassadors over the years, it is understandable that followers of the game, from fanatics to those with a more casual association with cricket, indulge themselves and wonder: 'Which players would make it into my Greatest XI?' Many a passionate discussion will have been had over the years as folk have donned their selectors' hats and exchanged views on their favourite or most respected cricketers. These debates might have taken place in the school playground, the office, on the factory floor, during a dominoes match in Jamaica or over chi in Asia. Ultimately, a World XI or Select XI is meaningless and those not picked are not suddenly to be deemed unworthy of greatness. It's more about the fun of the discussion or debate and the intricacies or reasoning involved in reaching a certain selection.

Naming a World XI isn't an original subject, but actually putting together an elite group of 100 people and asking them all to pick their greatest side is. The only guidelines I gave were that I asked players to select their team on the basis of Test cricket, good enough to beat any opposition in any conditions. I encouraged voting players to consider cricketers from the start of the 20th century and beyond. Some were happy to do that and some were not, preferring to judge from their own experiences. Who am I to dictate to them how they should arrive at their World XI? This is the beauty of the debate. Every player has their own idea about how this model should be achieved and, while I personally could never ignore the exploits of Bradman and Sobers, despite not having seen them play, others insisted they could not pick them. So this is a book full of personal selections, which is what I strived to achieve. And the resulting Greatest XI of all time suggests that a cross-section of eras have been well represented, with only the finest players rising to the top of the voting charts.

The majority of voters were from generations after the 1930s. This of course means contributions by legends such as Wilfred Rhodes, Victor Trumper, Bill Ponsford, Harold Larwood, Bill O'Reilly, Clarrie Grimmett and Learie Constantine were not possible, and thus players from this era may not be recognised as fairly as they would have been if this book had been produced in the 1950s, but that is unavoidable. It is only natural that most cricketers will hold in higher regard those whom they saw or played with or against. However, the names of Barnes, Bradman, Headley and Hobbs have still featured prominently despite being from pre-war times.

There are many aspects of these selections that should answer age-old curiosities as well as recent ones. For example, Sunil Gavaskar, the most prolific opening batsman in Test history and a master at playing quick bowling: which fast bowlers from his era did he include? Those he selected are paid the ultimate tribute by Test cricket's highest-scoring opener. Jeffrey Dujon kept wicket to a succession of greatly feared bowling attacks in Test history, with Roberts, Holding, Garner, Croft, Marshall, Walsh and Ambrose among them. As he was the man that kept to all of them for such a long time his selection is perhaps the most accurate judgement of that elite group. Furthermore, teams from older generations appear to include a nucleus of players. There are always going to be a few more unusual names mentioned – like Alec Bedser's intriguing inclusion of Australia leg-spinner Bruce Dooland – but the likes of Lindwall, Bradman, Sobers, Harvey, Hutton, Miller, Compton, Laker and Weekes are players that feature with a regularity that can only signal their greatness.

Nearly every player who has contributed his XI for this book has endured considerable difficulty in streamlining such a vast collection of talent. Some arrived at their selections with relative ease, believing their team almost picked itself, but most agonised over a countless number of formidable cricketers that have graced the sport at some point. The great Barry Richards suggested that even after selecting his seemingly invincible unit, his team could still be defeated by not one, but two different sides comprising players he omitted. I could not disagree with that notion. However, my feeling is that selecting a team that is certain to win a fairytale match and one which will never ever happen is not the vital issue; the idea is to see the personal selections by great players of those whom they most respect(ed) and regard(ed) as the best. I would surmise that the most frequently asked questions of cricketers of whatever generation are along the lines of: Who was the best fast bowler you ever faced? Who was the best spinner you ever faced? Who did you feel were the best opening batsmen you ever bowled to? Who was the best wicketkeeper you have ever seen? These are common but understandable curiosities, and I hope this publication answers many of them.

It has been painstaking yet satisfying to put this book together. It has taken years, as you will note from the teams of players like Malcolm Marshall and Bert Sutcliffe who have long since passed away. The reasons for the length of time taken are varied: several publishers initially rejected the project; it took time to reach hard-to-contact players; and there are other commitments in one's life that make it hard for an author to dedicate himself to a book that is not backed by a publisher. Prior to eventual publication most players were offered the opportunity to reconfirm their selection if it was made some time ago – this game evolves at such a rate that new greats are forever surfacing. The project has not been without its rewards, however. One of the more satisfying memories was sitting on the players' balcony at Hampshire's former ground Northlands Road as then Hampshire coach Malcolm Marshall explained his choices to me. This was the same day on which I had asked him to contribute. He was so conscientious he had scribbled down teams with and without West Indians, who were so dominant during his era. I appreciated his professionalism and generosity. Another good memory is the time I telephoned the late Fred Trueman. After I presented my pitch to him about the book – when most would either say 'no thanks' or ask that I call back in a week after they had had time to think – Fred just said: 'Right, number one has to be Gavaskar.' And that was it, he was away. We spent about 45 minutes on the phone discussing his side, which he thought of there and then. That was the great Fred Trueman for you. Famously upfront, honest and blunt maybe, but what I will never forget is his generosity. I met him in the committee room at Headingley a couple of years later when he still didn't know me that well, yet he would have been happy to talk about cricket all day long.

I had plenty of other memorable experiences putting this book together, including the half-hour telephone chat with Gordon Greenidge, after he thought about his team for a week (I pretended to be Gordon Greenidge countless times in backyard cricket in the mid-eighties). Another team I was pleased to have 'in the bag' was that of Ian Botham. He was a boyhood hero of mine who always made the most mundane cricket matches exciting. Ian reeled off his side to me while pacing the television gantry at Edgbaston during a Test match he was commentating on. A couple of years later, it was no surprise when he changed Alan Knott for Adam Gilchrist, a batsman from the Botham School of Batting.

There are great players whose teams do not feature in these pages, but that is due to their decision not to be involved as opposed to my failure to recognise them as a great. Any player that declined to partake – and there were a few, including Everton Weekes, Alan Knott, Dennis Lillee, Javed Miandad and Desmond Haynes – had his own reasons, which I naturally respected, knowing full well that players generally try to avoid picking World XI teams as it is such a difficult task. Lord Colin Cowdrey kindly replied to my typed invitation letter with 50 names he had pencilled in at the bottom and a note saying, 'How could I possibly separate these players?' Imran Khan's reason was a typical, understandable one, as he said, 'You must excuse me from this as too many people will get upset.' The response from one of Australia's finest openers, Arthur Morris, was eloquent if not accurate, when he said: 'Stan McCabe once told me that Bradman is up here (pointing to the sky) and the rest of us are down there (pointing to the floor) and I pretty much agree with that.' It was a poignant quip and one that reflected the difficulty of choosing a Greatest XI. And because I put so many legends in such a quandary, I thought it only fair to put myself through the same process, so my own Greatest XI appears below.

RICHARD SYDENHAM'S XI

I tried to include a blend of those who simply couldn't be omitted due to their records, some personal favourites and some I felt must be included based on the opinions of others. Although I was born in 1974 and have therefore missed out on seeing many greats in action, I am a keen student of the game and didn't want to ignore performances from years past. However, my most vivid memories and personal recollections are from more modern times and thus there is a bias to this era. I offer few apologies to those I omitted, purely because there is not enough space to accommodate so many of them.

1) Leonard Hutton
It was tough leaving out Gavaskar, Hobbs and Sutcliffe, but the opinions of those who played with and against Len are just so overwhelming in his favour. He had a model technique and scored a mountain of runs against such quality bowlers as Lindwall, Miller, Davidson, Benaud, Ramadhin and Valentine – all on uncovered wickets. He averaged just 20 in his last 15 innings for England but still maintained a Test average of 56.67!

2) Gordon Greenidge
I considered another favourite, Desmond Haynes, as well as Graham Gooch and Barry Richards, but this is a sentimental choice. It was the exploits of Greenidge and Haynes

that infected me with the cricket bug. Gordon was such an exhilarating player with his power-hitting, but he also had a wonderful technique to play deft shots against the spinners: I can recall him reverse sweeping Abdul Qadir in the Lord's Bicentenary Test. Purists may question whether he could bat on the wet wickets of years gone by, but some of his best innings for Hampshire were on damp tracks.

3) Donald Bradman

His Test average of 99.94 sets him out like a Titan among minnows. I hear negatives like 'Cricket wasn't as good in those days' and, one nearer the truth, 'The fielding wasn't as strong in his time.' My feeling is that whatever the standard of the fielding and bowling, it was the same for everyone and I don't see evidence of others emulating his spectacular feats. His superiority over every other batsman in Test cricket is freakish and one that shouldn't be undermined – just admired and respected accordingly.

4) Brian Lara

It was tempting to go for Viv Richards, Sachin Tendulkar or an old favourite like the elegant Dilip Vengsarkar, but Lara is another personal choice. He is famous for taking bowling attacks apart, but I remember him saving a match for my team, Warwickshire, against Leicestershire in 1994 with a resilient century – his second of the match. He was not credited enough for his tenacity (this was his last innings at Edgbaston before his world record 501).

5) Steve Waugh

A man who has broken many a bowler's heart with his unyielding resolve. He shades it over two boyhood favourites of mine, Allan Border and Javed Miandad, but all three are legendary for their fighting qualities. I've never seen a more determined player than the aptly named Waugh, who excelled in the heat of battle. He revelled in adverse situations – I lost count of the times he rescued Australia from early strife.

6) Garfield Sobers

I didn't see him, and have only ever viewed black and white footage of his famous six sixes against Glamorgan. It would be remiss of me to ignore so many great players who insisted Sobers was always the best player on the ground bar none. He represented Barbados at cricket, golf, basketball and football, and rejected the chance to play tabletennis, such was his natural sporting prowess.

7) Adam Gilchrist

Ten years ago I would have selected Ian Healy for his immaculate keeping and dogged, combative batting. Although Gilchrist was a world-class, destructive Test batsman, I also cannot remember all that many mistakes with the gloves, and this while keeping to one of the trickiest bowlers of all time, Shane Warne.

8) Ian Botham

A spectator's dream. I would accept shouts of bias, as Imran Khan, Keith Miller, Jacques Kallis, Kapil Dev and Mike Procter were all qualified to take this place, but Botham is a personal favourite. He was not as consistent as some of the previously mentioned all-rounders, but in terms of producing the seemingly impossible and turning a match on its head, Botham was unique.

9) Richard Hadlee

I thought about Ray Lindwall because of the esteem in which he is held by so many from his era, but Hadlee is another personal choice. He had such a rhythmic action and the ability to bowl almost any kind of delivery at will, plus the capacity to be a danger with the bat. The fact he didn't have another high-class bowler to support him to maintain pressure on batsmen gives him the edge over Lindwall, who had Miller and Johnston.

10) Shane Warne

Like Marshall, I expected a wicket every ball with Warne. I enjoyed the theatre of Abdul Qadir's bowling in the 1980s, but Warne was something else. That huge drift into the right-hander before a ripping leg-break – how do you play that? Warne embodies much that has become synonymous with Australian cricket: the pride to wear the baggy green cap, the positive outlook, the fierce will to win, skill in abundance and the desire to extend friendship to opponents after a match, usually over a cold beer.

11) Malcolm Marshall

I remember watching him in 1984 against England and expecting a wicket to fall every ball, such was his threat. He was just so quick, which was unique in that he was several inches shorter than his fellow West Indies pace bowlers. I could have opted for Curtly Ambrose, Joel Garner, Michael Holding or Glenn McGrath, but Marshall was tops for me.

FOREWORD

By Sir Garfield Sobers

This book is an exciting concept and cricket lovers should find it interesting to observe all these teams picked by so many excellent players. I personally find it too difficult to select my greatest XI because I have seen so many great players before, during and after my career – not to mention those I didn't see: players like Bradman, Headley, Ponsford, McCabe, Larwood and Voce. It's one long stretch from era to era and, instead, I would prefer to discuss some of those greats whom I have seen in my lifetime. Many of them will no doubt feature throughout the book.

As a youngster growing up, I never used to follow cricket to the extent that I used to run everywhere that cricket was being played, because I was too keen to play cricket myself. I must have visited the Kensington Oval once or twice to watch cricket in my early years as I always preferred to play. I used to listen to a lot about the game though, as I found that you could pick up many interesting things that can help you improve as a player, and the player I used to idolise was Everton Weekes. He would have to be one of the greats of all time. He was my hero because he played the game the way I have always expected it to be played; he was a very attacking player, very correct, never seemed to be tied down by any bowler and I thought that was what cricket was all about.

As I grew up and started to travel and play at Test level, Sir Frank Worrell and I became very close. After we played together on the 1957 tour of England I then went back to play for Radcliffe in the Central Lancashire League the year after and he was living in Radcliffe. It was wonderful to have a friend like Frank Worrell and to be able to go to his house. He was a captain, a great man and a great player too, but in my own view I thought Everton was the better player. The difference between the two was that Everton seemed to handle the real quicks a lot better than Frank did in those days. I remember Frank telling me once that because he had a lot of muscle under his left arm, he was able to cover his face and he didn't mind if he got hit on his arm with a short-pitched ball, so long as he never got hit in the face. Everton, though, would get inside the line and dispatch the short-pitched ball to the boundary because he was a great hooker; so that would be the main difference between the two.

As for the Australians, I came into Test cricket towards the end of Keith Miller's and Ray Lindwall's careers. They were still pretty good bowlers, but it is hard for me to make any great comment on them because they were on their way out. However, I still feel privileged to have played against them. I was more of a bowler in those days and so batted down the order, but I did open the innings in one Test match in that 1954–55 series and I can tell you that it was a lot different facing Keith and Ray at the top of the order than lower down. I can only echo the words of many others that Keith Miller was a great all-rounder, if not the greatest. Neil Harvey, Arthur Morris and Bill Johnston were other greats from that Australian team. I always liked to watch Arthur bat; I thought that if I had to model myself on any batsman, I would like it to be Arthur, because of his movements and the way he got behind the ball. Neil was a brilliant player too, very exciting and could be a destroyer in the middle order. I was lucky to see those players. As I got older and continued to play Test and Sheffield Shield cricket, I saw guys like Richie Benaud, Alan Davidson and Bobby Simpson, who were all very good players. In fact, apart from Keith Miller and possibly myself, there's been no better all-rounder than Alan.

With the Englishmen, I still think the best English player I have seen is Len Hutton, and he was on the way out when I saw him in 1954 in my first Test match, but he still scored 205. He was so good that I can't imagine what he must have been like in his prime – he was magnificent and has always stood out in my estimation as one of the greats. The beautiful thing about Len was that for an Englishman he was a back-foot player, which made him stand out so much because you don't see many Englishmen play that way. It's harder to be a back-foot player because when you play on the front foot the ball can hit you on the pad and there is a good chance you will be given not out; but if you get hit on the pad on the back foot there is a much greater chance of you being given out. Colin Cowdrey was a far better player than he showed in Test matches. We batted together in India for a Commonwealth team and we both scored hundreds. I went down to him after he registered his century and said, 'Well played Colin, that's one of the finest hundreds I've ever seen you play. Why don't you bat like that all the time?' Typically, he just said, 'Oh, it was because I was watching you at the other end.' He batted magnificently, but in Test matches Colin would sometimes get hit on the pad more times than he hit the ball with his bat. When English players played shots and got out, they were told that it wasn't good enough and that the idea was to stay there for as long as they could. So what English batsmen often did was to get on the front foot and use their pad as their second, sometimes first, line of defence to make sure that they stayed there. Kenny Barrington once told me what an attractive batsman he used to be, but he scored a quick 30 in one match and was dropped. It took him a long time to get back in the England team, so when he got another chance he scored 40 in three hours and was picked for the next Test and the next after that. Kenny wanted to play for England and that was what he had to do to play.

On the other hand, Ted Dexter was one of the best English batsmen I have ever seen because he never used to stick his pad out. He didn't get as many runs as some of them, but what a player – he was always in control and dictated the game to bowlers. In my mind that is what a great player is all about. Tom Graveney is one of the best front-foot players I have ever seen; he was one of the best but he also had some rough days. Peter May was very, very good but was limited and great players shouldn't be limited. Peter wasn't a hooker, he played in the 'v' and on the on-side, and when he got a short ball he wasn't too clever. The short ball didn't bother him, but he never took advantage of it and to be a great player you should be able to play all of the shots. People say he was a great player, but he couldn't hook; well how can he be a great player if he couldn't hook? Geoffrey (Boycott) was a great player in his own style. He played within his limitations and didn't take too many chances with good balls or even half good balls. Great players have to take good balls and turn them into bad balls, but Geoff never seemed to be able to do that. Maybe he would do it once or twice, but not consistently, so that took the greatness away from Geoff, but he was great in his own right. He batted well in difficult situations and although he wasn't a talented or gifted player, he made himself into what he was, which was a batsman who was very hard to get out. I have always admired him for that. Another Yorkshireman, Freddie Trueman, was a great bowler and certainly one of the greatest fast bowlers that I ever played against. I don't like to compare eras too much, but I have no doubts that Fred would have destroyed batsmen from the 1980s or any era. I know he kept telling people that he was a great bowler, but he actually was. Other people who think they're great or thought they were great are more diplomatic, but that was Fred for you and we should honour his achievements.

Pakistan's Hanif Mohammed was a class player. I saw every run of his 337 in Barbados in 1958. He was a very patient player and played within his limitations. He was always calculating and a very correct player who didn't take advantage of good balls, as he waited for the loose ones, but he was still one hell of a class player and certainly one of the greats from his era. One man who was never classed as a great player but whom I used to admire was Imtiaz Ahmed of that same Pakistan side. He never worried about anything. We had Roy Gilchrist who was very quick, but Imtiaz just stood up and smashed him. Saeed Ahmed was also very good and Fazal (Mahmood) was a great bowler who carried the bowling department virtually on his own.

There were some very good Indian spinners, particularly the four from the 1960s and 1970s: Bedi, Prasanna, Chandra and Venkat. The two that stood out from that famous quartet were Bishan (Bedi) and Prasanna – they were head and shoulders above the others. Venkat was a tight bowler who bowled a good length, but he didn't have the variety like Prasanna, who was a great bowler. Chandrasekhar, in his own era and in his own style, was a top bowler. There are greats from different eras and he was certainly one of the best in his. But when it comes to a man called Subhash Gupte, who played in the 1950s, we are talking about a great, great bowler. He is the best leg-spinner I have ever seen and in my opinion the greatest leg-spinner of all time. India had other very good players in those days. I never really played much against Vinoo (Mankad) when he first started but I believe, at his best, he was classed as a very good all-rounder. I also saw people like Vijay Hazare, who was a class batsman, but I only really saw him at the end of his career. The same goes for Vijay Merchant, whom I played against when he was on his way out. Other good players from that side, along with Subhash Gupte, were Polly Umrigar and Vijay Manjrekar – they weren't greats but they were very good players. They had fielders like Gaekwad and Gadkari at cover and cover point – two of the best I've ever seen in those positions – I had never seen fielding like that at Kensington (Oval). In later years, I saw Sunil Gavaskar come to the West Indies in 1971 and do very well, but you couldn't call him a great in those days because you did have flash-in-the-pan cricketers. However, he went on to become a great player in the true sense of greatness. From what I have seen he would have to be the best Indian batsman there has been, because he played in all types of conditions and made runs in the West Indies, in England; in fact he made a lot of his runs outside of India. Sachin Tendulkar would obviously push him close.

Things have changed over the years. I can't make comparisons between players of today and players of yesterday because cricket has changed so much. There are helmets, arm pads, chest pads; they're bowling with a front-foot rule; the field placing has changed, the bouncer rule has changed – everything has changed. When I was playing, batsmen used to get four or five bouncers an over, which you don't get today; we used to get bowlers bowling at you from 20 yards with the back-foot rule so bowlers got much closer to you; there could be any field setting with four men behind square – now you can only have two; we didn't bat with helmets, chest pads or arm guards; bat-pad fielders didn't wear shin guards. It was completely different from what it is like today. With that said I have still admired many cricketers from the modern era.

Those four great all-rounders Ian Botham, Imran Khan, Kapil Dev and Richard Hadlee I admired in particular. It's very difficult to separate them but I've always felt that Ian had so much ability that he could easily have been one of the greatest ever, but he never used his ability to the full extent. He is one of the most gifted cricketers I've seen – as bowler, batsman and fielder – and he was a lovely hitter of the ball, but he never seemed to make things happen when he batted. He just took chances and if it came off it came off, but if it didn't – that was it. I can't class great batsmen on that attitude. Great batsmen go in and make things happen and once they are in they don't get out, whereas with Ian if he came off he was marvellous but often he didn't. I felt Ian had more ability than the others, but these people have to be judged in context. Take Kapil Dev, for him to get the amount of wickets that he did (434) bowling on slow wickets in India is really fantastic. He played a lot of Test matches to get his wickets but you could also say that because he played more Tests than the others he should have been more tired, but that never appeared to be the case. He was obviously very, very fit and very good. Imran was a great influence on Pakistani cricket and a great influence on cricket in general: a great fast bowler with plenty of pace, a man who could bat well and who came in to bat in situations when things were tight and put it together and pulled his team around – he was a good leader. When he was in control of the team, Pakistan always seemed to play a lot better. Richard Hadlee is one of the best bowlers that I've seen. He and Dennis Lillee are two of the best ever, but I've always admired Richard more. I had a chance to see a lot of him when I was coach of Sri Lanka and I just thought he was so good. If you're at an advanced level in cricket you could read his mind and actually tell what ball he was going to bowl next. I would tell the Sri Lankan boys what he was going to bowl; he set batsmen up and usually dismissed them that way.

From South Africa, players like Barry Richards, Mike Procter and Graeme Pollock were unlucky not to have had the Test careers they deserved. Sadly for those boys players are remembered by what they did at Test level, not by how many runs they scored in county cricket or any other type of cricket. Barry and Procky were greats in their own right, but when you look at the record books they can only really be known as potential greats who were cheated because they weren't able to play the amount of Tests that they should have played. Graeme was slightly different because he played a few more Tests and has been classed as a great player, but I still don't think that he can be in that category either because he didn't play enough Test cricket (23 Tests). If Jimmy Adams had retired when he had an average of 84 he would have been statistically the second-best player to Bradman – how false would that have been? Lawrence Rowe (West Indies) to me was a great player or potentially great. He was brilliant, absolutely brilliant, possibly the best we've ever produced, but again he didn't play enough Test matches to be a true great, but he was certainly class.

Someone who is called 'great' from today's game is Shane Warne, but I have got my reservations about Shane. I think he is a great bowler, but I'm not sure how well he compares with spinners overall. I think people get carried away with this man's ability, as he hardly ever bowled a good googly. To me Shane Warne is a great turner of the ball, and I like his aggressive attitude, I love the way he attacks batsmen and I give him 100 per cent for that, as not enough spinners bowl with that approach, but in my estimation Subhash Gupte was a better leg-spinner. I can never understand, given the amount of turn he gets, why he bowls around the wicket into the rough. If he is that great why does he need the rough? Jimmy Adams bowled over the wicket into the rough and caused a lot of problems, but was he a great bowler? I accept that Shane Warne is a great of his era, but I'm not sure about overall. I don't think someone apparently so great should rely on the rough as much as he does. People obviously rate great players differently.

Sachin Tendulkar *is* a great, great player. People say that he will go on to break all the records in the future, but records are not important. If you go out there and do a job for your team or help your team to win and break a record at the same time then that's good. If anybody plays just to break records or for personal accolades it's pure hopelessness. But I don't think that is the case with Sachin. I think Sachin's innings have always been for his team, as India has not always had the strongest of batting line-ups where other people could come in and make big runs, so Sachin has had to do quite a lot of it himself. Viv Richards was a great player in his era, so too Brian Lara, there's no doubt about that. Rohan Kanhai is the same and another very good player, but one who never gets much of a mention is Seymour Nurse – who played in my era. He was a class act and actually scored 258 in his last Test match – how many people have scored that in their last Test?

Not long after I retired (in 1974) the West Indies discovered a battery of great pace bowlers. People like Michael Holding, Andy Roberts, Colin Croft, Joel Garner, Malcolm Marshall and later on Courtney Walsh and Curtly Ambrose. They made a very big impact because there had never been anything like it. They certainly shocked the world and the world has not recovered for nearly 20 years. It has done a lot of good for West Indies cricket with all the success it helped bring, but it has also done a lot of harm too because today we seem to concentrate mainly on pace, even when some of those bowlers are not good enough. We feel that we still produce those top-quality fast bowlers, but we don't.

We're fortunate that we're playing against opposition that is probably not good enough, because if they were our latest crop would be made to look like nothing. We still believe that fast bowling is the trend even now, because we had that run of producing great fast bowlers – and they were great. We had about seven greats from which you could pick four or five that would beat the world. It's very unfortunate for some that they all came along together, because the likes of Wayne Daniel, Franklyn Stephenson and Sylvester Clarke – who were very quick and very good – didn't get much of a chance. Because of that strength in previous years we've since had fellas walking into the team just because they are fast bowlers and that's the way things have changed over the years.

Finally, I see that I'm the most popular choice in players' teams. All I will say is I played the game because I loved it and I played for my country because I tried to help them, and if in doing so I have achieved these things I am very grateful and proud. But I certainly didn't start out in my career looking for any accolades. My whole idea was to be good enough to play for Barbados and then the West Indies and to try and hold my place in the team and support my team.

FOREWORD

BY DICKIE BIRD CBE

Cricket evokes so many different points of discussion and selecting a World XI is certainly one of the more interesting ones. Admittedly, it is a subject that can cause a lot of anguish, as I discovered in selecting my team, as there have been so many great cricketers throughout the various eras. Not just great players, though, but great characters too. Something that disappoints me about cricket in the modern era is the lack of characters. Not as many players nowadays look as though they enjoy their cricket, like in previous eras. I used to love the camaraderie that I had with people like Ian Botham, Allan Lamb and David Gower. Don't get me wrong, although they used to enjoy a laugh and a joke, they were also fierce competitors and always out to win. I think the influx of vast amounts of money coming into the game is largely responsible for the significant loss of characters and entertainers that cricket was once able to boast plenty of. Why that is I'm not sure. But you can't keep mourning the past; times change and although it is sad we have to accept the way the game is now and appreciate what we have as opposed to what we don't have.

There are many household names in the book that have picked teams and it was very interesting to learn that my choice of opening bowlers – Andy Roberts and Dennis Lillee – are the same as those picked by Sunil Gavaskar and Barry Richards. They are two of the best opening batsmen of all time and there can be no better judges of quick bowlers of their generation. I have limited my selection to players I saw as an umpire. However, I am not ignoring other greats that have played through the years. I suppose Bradman – on his figures alone – would have to be the best batsman that has ever played the game. Likewise, Wally Hammond was another legend. As a lad I thought Hammond was the best batsman around as he could play comfortably on any kind of pitch that he was confronted with. Others, like Ray Lindwall, Keith Miller, Fred Trueman and Brian Statham, were also great players and no doubt there are more that I haven't mentioned. One Englishman, though, to whom I would like to pay a special tribute, is Peter May. I still believe he is the best batsman England has produced since the war; he really was a marvellous player.

Before I explain my Greatest XI I would like to mention a few players who came very close: Malcolm Marshall – he would be in the squad as he was a tremendous all-round cricketer and particularly a great fast bowler; Joel Garner – another great fast bowler I rated highly; Javed Miandad – a terrific batsman; Allan Border and Steve Waugh – both were considered for my team; Ian Botham – I'd have selected Ian had it not been for the genius of Sobers; Ian Healy – the next best keeper to Knotty; Imran Khan, Kapil Dev and Wasim Akram – three great all-rounders and all masters of fast bowling; Shane Warne

– another legend; and Gordon Greenidge and Desmond Haynes. I apologise to anybody I have left out, but please understand how difficult it is to streamline such a vast group of talent. Michael Holding would be in the XII and would play at the expense of Abdul Qadir if the pitch suited seam bowling as opposed to spin. Michael was a super-fast bowler and had that great model action. In all my years as an umpire I can't remember having to no-ball him, which tells you how smooth he was.

DICKIE BIRD'S XI

1) Sunil Gavaskar
One of the best opening batsmen of all time who scored runs all around the world. His runs against the West Indies in particular proved his undoubted class.

2) Barry Richards
Not only the best opening batsman I have ever seen, but also the best batsman, along with his namesake Viv.

3) Viv Richards
As I mentioned above, the best batsman I have ever seen along with Barry. He was such a powerful and destructive player.

4) Greg Chappell
Another great batsman and probably the classiest player of them all with his elegance and style.

5) Graeme Pollock
It is close between him and Sobers, but Pollock is probably the best left-hander I have ever seen.

6) Garfield Sobers
The best all-round cricketer that has ever played the game and I find it hard to think there has ever been a better player than him in any generation.

7) Alan Knott
A great wicketkeeper who made a difficult job look easy. I also saw him make some very important runs when his side was in trouble.

8) Richard Hadlee
I rated him as a fine all-rounder. With the ball, he could bowl any kind of delivery and at a good pace too.

9) Dennis Lillee

The greatest fast bowler that ever lived. There have been some fine quicks down the years, but I cannot believe there has been one better than this man; he had everything.

10) Abdul Qadir

It might surprise a few people that I have opted for Qadir and not Warne, but Qadir had the best control that I have ever seen from a spin bowler. Whether he was bowling leg-spinners, googlies or top-spinners, they were all controlled expertly.

11) Andy Roberts

He was lethal with a cricket ball in his hand. Batsmen could never relax because he had a great injection of pace from nowhere and an abundance of skill.

100 CRICKET LEGENDS SELECT THEIR WORLD XI

ABDUL QADIR'S XI

This is the best team in my opinion, from players that I have seen. I would like to make a special mention for Kapil Dev, whom I desperately wanted to include, but sadly I can only name 11. Kapil was a fantastic all-rounder and a great competitor. I also considered Dennis Lillee, Shane Warne, Waqar Younis, Arjuna Ranatunga – a brave batsman and captain – Richard Hadlee, Martin Crowe, Malcolm Marshall, Zaheer Abbas, Desmond Haynes, Gordon Greenidge…they were all equally good players. But I would like Aravinda De Silva in the 12.

1) Sunil Gavaskar

He was a player who had depth in his batting. He was a book of a batsman, who had a terrific, model-like technique.

2) Brian Lara

My first thought was for Desmond Haynes as he really liked to dominate bowlers. But Lara proved so many times he's the greatest player the West Indies has ever produced by weight of runs: 400, 500 in county cricket, so many runs. He also made runs against the best spinners like Muralitharan and Warne. Lara was also my last Test wicket!

3) Sachin Tendulkar

Sachin has broken so many records in the game, how can you ignore him? His attitude is first-class. I wanted to select Zaheer Abbas, who was so stylish, but I personally feel Sachin is best.

4) Viv Richards

He used to play like a king and didn't mind who he attacked when he was batting. Viv never bothered about who was bowling or how good their reputations were; he just wanted to dominate. He never played like Gavaskar or Haynes, who wanted to stay there even if they weren't scoring. He always had to be scoring while he was at the crease.

5) Allan Border

He was a great player who could either attack the bowlers or just stay there and be a difficult man to remove. If his side needed quick runs though, he was able to raise the tempo of the innings.

6) Javed Miandad

Javed was a fighter and understood and observed the game better than anyone else, but most of all he was the original fighter in world cricket; a very good fielder too.

7) Adam Gilchrist

I was also a massive fan of Alan Knott, Ian Healy, Rodney Marsh, Syed Kirmani and Wasim Bari, but I feel Gilchrist brings more to this team with his batting ability as well as being a very good wicketkeeper. He can bat well anywhere, whether opening or lower down.

8) Ian Botham

I was a great fan of Ian Botham and I consider myself lucky that I played against him and watched him up close in his career. He had a big heart and was like a tiger on the cricket field. When he was facing the fastest bowlers in the world, he never showed any fear and he always took them on, like against Australia in 1981. That was the difference between him and the other great all-rounders of his era.

9) Imran Khan

He was a very good planner and tactician as a captain and was also a fine batsman and bowler. He could build an innings and be very solid with the bat or play in an attacking manner when the situation called for it. As for his bowling, he was the most dangerous fast bowler of his generation. He showed the way for the likes of Wasim, Waqar and Shoaib Akhtar. Imran is a dictionary of Pakistani cricket.

10) Wasim Akram

Another great all rounder, though clearly a better bowler. Since the mid-nineties I haven't seen a bowler like him or a better match-winner; he deserves credit for what he has done for his country.

11) Abdul Qadir

Shane Warne is a good friend of mine and I have respect for Shane and other great spinners like Murali and Underwood. I am not conceited or saying I am better than all of them, but I do not think I am inferior to them. I had a full command of this art we call leg-spin and feel that if I was playing in these days I would also take this many wickets (700). I had a gift from God. I would have loved to play in the Twenty20 era and would attack batsmen with mid-on and mid-off up and a slip. I enjoyed the challenge of big games against the best batsmen.

ABDUL QADIR played 67 Test matches for Pakistan between 1977–78 and 1990–91 and claimed 236 wickets at an average of 32.80. He is widely regarded as one of the greatest leg-spin bowlers of all time. His most notable triumph in Test cricket came against England in 1987–88 at Lahore when he took nine for 56 in an innings.

NEIL ADCOCK'S XI

I have kept my selections to the period that I played Test cricket (1953 to 1962) and also the cricketers that I performed with and against. This meant that I could not choose anyone from India, Pakistan and the West Indies, as during that period we were prevented from playing against those countries. Because of this, there are many great players left out, such as Wesley Hall, Garfield Sobers, Everton Weekes, Sonny Ramadhin, Hanif Mohammed and Sunil Gavaskar later on. I did not have the good fortune to play against these guys or even have the chance to even watch them. This left my selections to come from Australia, England and South Africa. Still, I have to leave out some very fine cricketers including: McDonald, Simpson, Barlow, Dexter, Barrington, McLean, Evans, Lock, Tyson, Statham and Laker, who was a great off-spinner but was never able to be as successful outside of England.

1) Jackie McGlew
A fearless opener who scored seven Test hundreds, including that marathon 255 not out against the New Zealanders.

2) Colin Cowdrey
One of England's truly great batsmen. In order to accommodate him in my team – and I had to have him in – he would open the innings, which he sometimes did for England in Test matches.

3) Neil Harvey
The finest left-hander of his time, who also played over three decades and never showed any evidence of inconsistency.

4) Peter May
The most complete batsman of the fifties and sixties. On our tour of England in 1955 he made two hundreds and was always a threat.

5) Denis Compton
This man was a genius with a bat in his hand; a free-scoring batsman over four decades. He always looked quality.

6) John Waite
The finest wicketkeeper of his time and also a top-class run-scorer. I remember two fine centuries he scored in a home series against Australia with Richie Benaud and Alan Davidson bowling.

7) Richie Benaud
Australia's finest all-rounder, who would be captain of this team because of his astute knowledge of the game.

8) Alan Davidson

There has been no finer left-handed bowler for Australia. He was also an extremely accomplished batsman, making him a more than useful all-rounder, and one of the best there has been.

9) Hugh Tayfield

An off-spinner who took many wickets in every country he played. It is for his ability to bowl in all types of conditions that I have selected him ahead of Jim Laker, who was also a great bowler.

10) Fred Trueman

'Fiery Fred' was England's leading fast bowler of the 1950s, and he had great pace and terrific strength and stamina.

11) Neil Adcock

I was the first South African bowler to take 100 Test match wickets; I like to think I always attacked with pace and bounce.

NEIL ADCOCK played 26 Tests for South Africa between 1953–54 and 1961–62, claiming 104 wickets at an average of 21.10. In all first-class cricket, he took 405 wickets at 17.25. In 1960, during an England tour, he took 108 wickets at 14.02 and became one of Wisden's Five Cricketers of the Year. He was one of the most fearsome quick bowlers of his era.

* * * * *

BOB APPLEYARD'S XI

It was difficult selecting from all the various generations, so I picked my side mainly from those I played with and against. I'd also like to mention: Peter May — he could easily have been in ahead of Cowdrey as Peter was the best on-side player I ever saw; Denis Compton — he was a great player, but personally I never had that many problems against him. I always felt that I could get him out because he played unorthodox, risky shots; Alec Bedser — he was a master of the leg cutter and could bowl forever. The reason I left him out is that Sydney Barnes could do a similar role for the team; Wilfred Rhodes — his record is unbelievable, but Verity is my left-arm spinner; Johnny Wardle — one of my personal favourites. He used to compete with another great bowler in Tony Lock. Whereas Tony was the best orthodox left-armer, Johnny was better on good batting pitches that needed something extra from the bowler. He could bowl chinamen and googlies; Ray Lindwall and Keith Miller — two terrific Australians. I would bring one of these into the side on a quick pitch; Frank Tyson — the quickest bowler I ever saw, especially in 1954–55. I opted for Fred ahead of Tyson because he played more. In the right conditions, such as at Old Trafford, I would bring in Jim Laker. There are other greats I haven't mentioned because I never played against them — like the West Indians, and the likes of Botham and Boycott from the modern day.

1) Leonard Hutton

He was the best batsman I ever saw on all types of pitch. Some people thought of him as being a slow player, but he was only slow when things were difficult. I remember after the war, when Len was batting at Headingley, Brian Close commented to Norman Yardley what a great player Len was. Norman said, 'It's a pity you didn't see him before the war, when he was at his best!'

2) Herbert Sutcliffe

His record, averaging 60 from 55 Tests, speaks volumes. Herbert was successful opening with Hobbs, Holmes and Hutton, which goes to show what he was like to bat with. When Herbert and Len were batting, us bowlers didn't bother to get changed.

3) Donald Bradman

I only saw him as a schoolboy, but he left a massive impression on me. We travelled from our school in Bradford to Headingley and we just missed the first wicket of the day. Ponsford and Bradman were batting when we arrived. We left at five to six and Ponsford and Bradman were still batting! Bradman went on to score 304 and he was just amazing. I met him at a later date and told him my tale.

4) Neil Harvey

There's no way I could leave this man out. He was brilliant against Tyson in 1954–55 and almost won Australia the match on his own in Sydney.

5) Colin Cowdrey

He had an extremely good defence and plenty of guts. The other thing that struck me about Colin was the amount of time he appeared to have against the quick bowlers.

6) Wally Hammond

I didn't see much of Wally, but from talking to pre-war players such as Hutton, Yardley, Rhodes and my old coach George Hirst, they all said the only player who really stood out as an all-time great was Hammond. There couldn't have been many better than him.

7) Godfrey Evans

He was the best wicketkeeper that I ever came across. He was an England regular for such a long time. Godfrey was tremendously enthusiastic from behind the stumps and if we had been in the field for a long time, he used to keep everybody going.

8) Shane Warne

He's from a different era but I couldn't ignore him. A great leg-spinner; it would have been interesting to see him bowl on the uncovered wickets of a few years ago. He might not have been able to turn it as much, but his control was so good that he still wouldn't concede many runs.

9) Fred Trueman

There has never been a more consistent bowler, day in and day out, than Fred. He used to bowl a lot of overs and hardly ever broke down.

10) Sydney Barnes

Sydney was a bit like Alec Bedser, but he was a lot more successful in his Test career, which is saying something. I met him once when he was very old at Staffordshire, when I was playing for the Second XI. It was nice to meet him and I tried to pick his brains.

11) Hedley Verity

I saw him as a schoolboy and remember how Bill Bowes spoke so highly of him. His record is excellent with 1,956 wickets at 14.87 and he could have had more if he hadn't died in the war.

BOB APPLEYARD played nine Test matches for England from 1954 to 1956, taking 31 wickets at a miserly average of 17.87. The Yorkshire off-spinner would have played many more Tests had he not suffered health problems throughout his career. His first-class record of 708 wickets at 15.48 proves his class. In his first full season of first-class cricket in 1951 he took 200 wickets at 14.14 and headed the averages.

* * * * *

ASIF IQBAL'S XI

My team has been selected from players I have seen, which discounts many greats such as Bradman, Hutton, Larwood and many more. Of the modern-day players that haven't made my team I would like to apologise to Richard Hadlee, Imran Khan, Desmond Haynes, Greg Chappell, Adam Gilchrist, Virender Sehwag, Rahul Dravid, Ricky Ponting and Muttiah Muralitharan, who all came close.

1) Sunil Gavaskar

Technically, he is the best and the most correct batsman that I have ever seen. He always performed against the strongest bowling attacks all around the world – and not only in India, as many sub-continental players are often accused of doing.

2) Gordon Greenidge

He is the ideal partner for Gavaskar. Greenidge was always looking to attack and to be aggressive in order to gain the initiative – over opening bowlers particularly.

3) Viv Richards

The best number three in the world, who could take any bowling attack apart when he wanted to. Bowlers genuinely feared bowling to him. Viv was also a more than useful off-spin bowler.

4) Sachin Tendulkar

In this entire list of such great batsmen, I consider Tendulkar to be the best of them all. He has all the qualities one needs to be a great batsman. He can also do a good job with the ball.

5) Brian Lara

A genius. There may be better batsmen in terms of concentration and technical ability, but there is no one like him who can turn a match around single-handedly in such an emphatic way.

6) Javed Miandad

If you ever needed someone to bat for your life you would want Miandad out there. A real determined character who could bat in any situation.

7) Garfield Sobers

A complete all-rounder. I cannot say whether he was a better batsman or bowler – he was just so good at both, and a tremendous fielder.

8) Alan Knott

Gilchrist is the best keeper-batsman ever, but Knott is a specialist wicketkeeper. I saw a great deal of Knotty in my days at Kent and he's the best glove-man ever, be it standing up on a bad wicket to Derek Underwood or standing back on a green top to the quicks.

9) Shane Warne

I had the chance to pick from many wonderful spin bowlers from the sub-continent with the likes of Bedi, Prasanna and Qadir, but I have to say that Warne comes out on top of them all. He's an amazing leg-spinner.

10) Michael Holding

The finest new-ball bowler I saw and he was rightly known as 'Silent Death'. His performance against England at the Oval in 1976, when he took 14 wickets on a dead pitch, was one of the best exhibitions of fast bowling I have ever had the privilege of seeing.

11) Dennis Lillee

A tremendous, aggressive, all-action character. To come back after a serious back injury the way he did, and with such devastating results, proved what he was about as a bowler, and just how determined he was to succeed.

ASIF IQBAL played 58 Tests for Pakistan between 1964–65 and 1979–80, scoring 3,575 runs at an average of 38.85. He began as an opening bowler and number-10 batsman, but his 41 runs (and 36 at number three in the second innings), showed there was much more batting potential in the stylish right-hander, which he later proved in Pakistan's middle-order. Asif played county cricket for Kent from 1968 to 1982.

MOHAMMAD AZHARUDDIN'S XI

I only know about the players that I have seen, so this is how I have selected my side. I realise this means many greats have been left out but I am sticking to my policy.

1) Gordon Greenidge
His defence was very good and his attacking ability was even better. His 200 at Lord's in 1984, which helped the West Indies to victory, was a magnificent innings that many will never forget.

2) Sunil Gavaskar
He was a great influence on me for the way he conducted his innings. He's in this team for his faultless technique and will to stay at the wicket. The way in which he used to take on the West Indian quick bowlers was enough for him to get in to this side alone.

3) Greg Chappell
Tremendous grace and style. He played very straight and correct and he always caught my eye when he was at the wicket because his batting was so elegant.

4) Viv Richards
The bowlers were scared when he came to the wicket. It never mattered what position his team was in, he would always bat the same way. He was a very good player of all types of bowling, particularly pace. The quicker people bowled to him, the quicker it reached the boundary! He'd be captain.

5) Sachin Tendulkar
He is simply tremendous; a very entertaining batsman. Sachin is also a good player of both spin and pace.

6) Kapil Dev
An excellent striker of the ball and a fearsome pace bowler. He was very fit and strong and always played according to the situation of the game. Undoubtedly, he's the greatest all-round cricketer that India has ever produced.

7) Syed Kirmani
His keeping was very safe. He could keep well to fast bowlers and to spin bowlers. In fact his keeping to the leg-spin of Chandrasekhar was just brilliant.

8) Richard Hadlee
A very accurate bowler. He was always trying to get you out. He was a great trier and had the ability to think the batsman out. You felt he was always trying to work you out.

9) Malcolm Marshall

He was very fast and got big movement. He also used to think batsmen out all the time and was very good at knowing where the batsman was going wrong and how to put him under pressure.

10) Wasim Akram

He's left arm and has good variety. You were never at ease with him because he has so much variety: he could bowl quick, slow, move it both ways and had a very good bouncer.

11) Shane Warne

He is the best spinner that I ever faced. I have never played against a bowler with so much variety. He has a beautiful action and makes bowling look easy.

MOHAMMAD AZHARUDDIN played 99 Tests for India from 1984–85 to 2000 and scored 6,215 runs at an average of 45.03, with 22 centuries. A majestic and wristy stroke-player, Azhar's baptism in Test cricket was an overwhelming success when he scored three centuries in his first three Tests against David Gower's England team. He was also an excellent fielder anywhere, particularly close to the wicket.

* * * * *

TREVOR BAILEY'S XI

I'm confident this team would be unbeatable given the strength in the batting, while the bowling attack is also superior and well balanced. There are other greats I could have gone for, like Keith Miller and Ray Lindwall, but I could only select 11. I'd like to point out that Jack Hobbs, Don Bradman, Wally Hammond and Sydney Barnes's records could have been even better had it not been for war.

1) Jack Hobbs

He obviously scored a few runs (61,237 first-class) and could play well on bad wickets. Was aptly nicknamed 'The Master'.

2) Sachin Tendulkar

Comfortably the best batsman I've seen of late and I'm sure his great achievements will continue as he matures further as a batsman. It's difficult to see his records being broken.

3) Donald Bradman

The best batsman there has ever been and probably ever likely to be. Could anybody doubt such a choice?

4) Walter Hammond

An excellent batsman who would also play his part with the ball too, as he'd certainly make a more than handy fourth seamer. His fielding was also exceptional (110 Test catches).

5) Viv Richards

A superb player who just destroyed bowling attacks. It didn't matter what the situation of the game was – he always played in the same manner. Could be unorthodox but that was part of his genius.

6) Garfield Sobers

He is undoubtedly the best all-rounder ever to play the game. He dismissed me on his Test debut in 1954, though he went on to enjoy greater highlights than that, of course.

7) Ian Healy

The best wicketkeeper I have seen, although his successor Adam Gilchrist is clearly a better batsman.

8) Michael Holding

He was a very fine fast bowler and in my opinion the pick of the great West Indian quicks of recent times, which is some tribute given the quality.

9) Shane Warne

The greatest leg-spinner of all time, possessing good variety and able to turn the ball a great deal more than his rivals, and for that reason his position in this team is assured.

10) Sydney Barnes

Two West Indian batsmen were asked who they thought was the best bowler they faced on the 1928 tour of England and both said Sydney Barnes. Remember, there were some rather useful bowlers around at the time, such as Larwood and Voce. And Barnes was 54 years old! Imagine what he must have been like in his heyday.

11) Jim Laker

The best off-spinner there has ever been in my opinion. Give him the right wicket and he was unplayable; he turned the ball a very long way.

TREVOR BAILEY played 61 Test matches for England between 1949 and 1958–59, taking 132 wickets at an average of 29.21 and scoring 2,290 runs at 29.74. In all first-class cricket, he took 2,082 wickets at 23.14 and scored 28,642 runs at 33.42. Bailey, a famously dependable batsman and right-arm fast-medium pace bowler, was England's premier all-rounder during his England career. He played 482 matches for Essex.

BISHAN BEDI'S XI

I think you have to go on figures really as there are so many great cricketers that I never got to see play and I don't think you can ignore their records. It is a very difficult task to select such a side given all the varying conditions that people have played in throughout the generations, but I am sure these selections would perform admirably. I would have loved to have picked Shane Warne also, especially from his peak years, but it is a competitive world and he is up against two greats with special records in Laker and Rhodes. However, Warney would be in my 12 and would play if the conditions called for another spinner.

1) Jack Hobbs
The man had a hundred centuries by the age of 47 and then got another 97 hundreds after that, and all on uncovered wickets. It's a phenomenal record that I can't imagine will ever be beaten.

2) Leonard Hutton
He was a great player of all types of bowling on uncovered wickets. He was solid, dependable and was the rock at the top of England's batting order for some time, and through three decades.

3) Donald Bradman
Is there any doubt about this selection? I don't think so. I would have enjoyed the challenge of bowling to the great man.

4) Garfield Sobers
Like Bradman, there will never be another like Sobers. He is the greatest cricketer I've ever seen and am ever likely to see.

5) Sachin Tendulkar
Considering that Bradman himself reckons Tendulkar is a bit like him is a compliment in itself. I don't think there are so many 'great' bowlers around today like in other generations, but I feel he would still have been as successful in another era. I'm not sure though, how he would have adjusted to play on uncovered wickets.

6) Wilfred Rhodes
Another with a phenomenal record with bat and ball. He could bat anywhere and bowl at any time in a match situation.

7) Alan Knott
It's close between him and Wasim Bari, but Knotty was a very upstanding team man, a useful batsman and was tough to dislodge. He was unorthodox and made it hard for bowlers to work him out.

8) Richard Hadlee

He could rise to any occasion when such an effort from him was needed. He was a superb fast bowler and a good attacking batsman.

9) Dennis Lillee

He had a very big heart, never gave up, and was a real tough competitor with an enormous will to win. He would make any team stronger.

10) Jim Laker

There are others around who have taken more wickets, but with suspect actions. In my opinion, Jim Laker is the best off-spinner ever, just ahead of Pras(sana) and Gibbsy. We may never see a spinner take 19 wickets in a Test match again as he did in 1956.

11) Alec Bedser

A tremendous swing bowler and one of the bowlers who troubled Bradman the most, which is no mean feat.

BISHAN BEDI played 67 Test matches for India between 1966–67 and 1979, taking 266 wickets at an average of 28.71. In first-class cricket he took 1,560 wickets at 21.69. Bishan, an eternal student of the game with great cricket knowledge, was a cunning left-arm spin bowler whose clever use of flight often accounted for his victims. He would often applaud batsmen after they hit him for a six because he knew he had more chance of dismissing them if they attacked him.

✳ ✳ ✳ ✳ ✳

SIR ALEC BEDSER'S XI

I only considered those I played with or against. That excludes all the modern players and the likes of Botham, Boycott and Willis and anyone else that has played since 1955 when I retired from Tests. Modesty prevents me from considering myself. As for the selection of Dooland, which will probably surprise, he might have only played three Tests, but I felt he was a neglected leg-spinner and batsman.

1) Leonard Hutton

He was a fine player, a great technician of a batsman who knew his own game inside out. He was an ordinary captain but very methodical.

2) Arthur Morris

Arthur was a totally different player to Len. He liked to attack, was very strong off the back foot and was good against spin when he would like to use his feet. We enjoyed our battles and have stayed in touch ever since our playing days and remained close friends.

3) Donald Bradman

He'd be captain. Can't say much about him as he was simply the best ever. When the ball was moving I obviously felt I had a chance against him, but if there was no movement… I wouldn't say I felt helpless, but it was considerably harder.

4) Denis Compton

He was a good attacking player and a good improviser. Denis was a difficult man to bowl at when he was set.

5) Everton Weekes

Another very fine player and particularly on the back foot – he was a phenomenal square cutter. He liked to dominate bowlers and on a good wicket he could be devastating.

6) Keith Miller

He was a fine all-rounder, strong in all capacities. He was a mood player and, depending on how he felt, he could be as good as anyone when batting or bowling. Keith was a reliable fielder as well.

7) Garfield Sobers

He's the best all-rounder I have ever seen and I don't think there would ever be another as good as him. He could bowl spinners, could bowl fast and was an awesome attacking batsman. He had everything. Even more than 50 years after his Test debut there hasn't been another anywhere near as good as him.

8) Bruce Dooland

I thought he was a very fine leg-spin bowler and useful lower-order batsman. I felt he should have been on the 1948 and 1953 Ashes tours to England, but others were preferred to him and I don't know why that was. I thought he was the best leg-spinner of that era. In his first season of county cricket for Nottinghamshire he took something like 165 wickets and scored around 1,300 runs. I think that form would make him a pretty useful overseas player nowadays.

9) Godfrey Evans

I selected Godfrey because he stood up to the wickets better than anyone else. He stood up to me all the time and I always bowled better when the keeper stood up.

10) Ray Lindwall

He's the best fast bowler I've ever seen because he swung the ball more than anyone else, was quick with it and was handy with the bat. Ray was the ultimate master of his craft.

11) Jim Laker

His record speaks for itself (the only person to take 19 wickets in a Test). He was unplayable on a helpful pitch. South Africa's Hugh Tayfield was probably better on hard pitches, but Laker was more destructive when conditions suited. He was extremely accurate.

SIR ALEC BEDSER played 51 Test matches for England between 1946 and 1955 and took 236 wickets at an average of 24.89. In first-class cricket he claimed 1,924 wickets at 20.42. In his first two Tests his figures against India were 11 for 145 and 11 for 93. Bedser was a master of swing, and leg-cutters in particular. He had terrific stamina that allowed captains to bowl him for lengthy spells. He was one of few bowlers to trouble the great Don Bradman on a consistent basis.

[This team was received before Sir Alec passed away in 2010]

* * * * *

RICHIE BENAUD'S XI

This is my greatest team of the 20th century. It was no easy task and the selection criteria were skill, that they were undeniable champions, and would have been outstanding in any era. Mixing eras is very hard, but that's the beauty of this. It's hypothetical but we are able to indulge ourselves and weave a little magic. My 12th man would be Keith Miller, and Frank Worrell the manager.

1) Jack Hobbs

Two of the innings Hobbs played on treacherous pitches against Australia, Bradman says, provided some of the finest batting he ever saw.

2) Sunil Gavaskar

I always had a lot of time for him. Sunil was a tough cricketer and a fine opening batsman.

3) Donald Bradman

I once said to Keith Miller over a beer in Adelaide how unlucky I felt not to get the chance to bowl at Bradman – he retired when I came into the game. Keith replied, 'Son, we all have a lucky break in our lives and that was yours'.

4) Viv Richards

I suspect he is the most quelling sight for any bowler running in.

5) Sachin Tendulkar

I haven't seen a better middle-order player of his type.

6) Garfield Sobers
He was the greatest all-rounder the world has ever seen. He also finished up being one of the greatest batsman the world has seen.

7) Imran Khan
There were four fine all-rounders over a period through the 1970s and 1980s. Imran just had the edge on them in flair.

8) Adam Gilchrist
I have never seen a cleaner hitter. He revolutionised the position of number 7 batsman and wicketkeeper.

9) Shane Warne
He is the best leg-spin bowler ever to play the game.

10) Dennis Lillee
The best fast bowler I have seen and I doubt we will see anyone better. He was the complete fast bowler, for control of swing both ways, movement off the seam and ability to come back after injury.

11) Sydney Barnes
He was a phenomenon. He went straight from league cricket to the England Test side.

RICHIE BENAUD played 63 Tests for Australia between 1951–52 and 1963–64. He was the first Test cricketer to reach the 'double' of 2,000 runs and 200 wickets (at the 'Gabba, 1963 v South Africa) and the first Sheffield Shield cricketer to reach the double of 2,000 runs and 200 wickets (at the MCG, 1961 v Victoria). He was a highly respected captain, is a journalist and an outstanding television commentator.

This team was published courtesy of Richie Benaud and In The Box Media, taken from *Richie Benaud's Greatest XI*.

* * * * *

COLIN BLAND'S XI

Unfortunately, due to circumstances in South Africa, there are quite a few talented players that I have not had the chance to see and, therefore, I have selected my team from players I've seen a fair bit of – with the obvious exception of Bradman, and Lindwall to a lesser extent. There are some other great cricketers that have not made the 11 and these include: Neil Adcock, Tom Graveney, Ted Dexter, Jim Laker, Bobby Simpson, Mike Procter and Kenny Barrington.

1) Barry Richards
Probably one of the most gifted players the game has ever seen. His problem was that he got bored. Things became too easy for him out there when he was batting and, consequently, he

got himself out a lot. There were times when he came to the crease and the umpire would ask him if he wanted a guard and he would say, 'No thanks, I've played here before.'

2) Sunil Gavaskar
He has to be in this team, I think, purely because of the number of centuries he scored against all-comers, particularly a very strong West Indies attack.

3) Donald Bradman
What does one need to say about Don Bradman? He must have been an absolutely superb player. His average alone is enough to guarantee him a place in this side.

4) Graeme Pollock
A tremendous player who hit the ball very hard. His cover drive was exquisite and when he played the shot there was never any need to chase it because it would bounce back to mid-off from the boundary fence! He rarely gave his wicket away when he was set, which was an amazing strength for a shot player like him.

5) Colin Cowdrey
A magnificent timer of the ball and he was particularly strong against the quicks. I remember in 1965 in a Test match, Peter Pollock was working up a head of steam and had hit John Edrich on the side of the head, but when Cowdrey came in he played him as nonchalantly as he would an off-spinner.

6) Garfield Sobers
If there has ever been a better all-rounder than this man then I would like to know of him. One of my greatest claims to fame is that I bowled him in Australia once, although it was off his outside edge and he had 152 to his name by then!

7) Alan Davidson
A magnificent controller of swing bowling, and his left-arm style gives variety to the bowling attack. He is also a genuine all-rounder, who gave the Australian team terrific strength in batting depth along with Richie Benaud.

8) Ian Healy
He must be the most complete keeper there has ever been. He kept well to the quicks, while standing up to Shane Warne showed him to be a superb keeper in those conditions. He wasn't really tested against a top quality off-spinner, but I'm sure he would still have done a good job. His keeping ability puts him ahead of Adam Gilchrist. I never saw much of Alan Knott, and my old teammate John Waite was a good, no-nonsense keeper, but not in Healy's class.

9) Shane Warne
Probably the best match-winner the game has seen for decades; in fact I can't think of another more dominant and consistent match-winner than him; simply a wonderful leg-spinner.

10) Ray Lindwall

I saw him when I was a kid in 1953 and though I was young, I could tell he was something special by the reaction of the crowd, who were 'ooohing' and 'ahhhing' when he bowled. He had a beautiful action and a magnificent record also.

11) Hugh Tayfield

It's close between him and Jim Laker, but I feel Tayfield was better on all types of wickets. He was a superb competitor and always felt every wicket had his name on it; he never gave up.

COLIN BLAND played 21 Test matches for South Africa between 1961–62 and 1966–67, scoring 1,669 runs at an average of 49.08, a remarkable statistic when compared with his average of 37.95 in first-class cricket. Although a reliable middle-order batsman, Bland was better known for his outstanding fielding displays, which help rank him with Jonty Rhodes as one of the greatest fieldsmen the game has ever seen.

* * * * *

DAVID BOON'S XI

You could pick this side three times over. However, of the players I have seen – with the exception of Bradman – here are the best in my opinion. I found it difficult, though, to leave out the likes of Brian Lara, Sachin Tendulkar, Steve Waugh, Ian Botham, Michael Holding, Curtly Ambrose, Graham Gooch, Javed Miandad, Imran Khan and Wasim Akram. Unfortunately, I can only name 11!

1) Gordon Greenidge, 2) Sunil Gavaskar, 3) Donald Bradman, 4) Viv Richards, 5) Allan Border, 6) Garfield Sobers, 7) Ian Healy, 8) Shane Warne, 9) Malcolm Marshall, 10) Richard Hadlee, 11) Dennis Lillee

DAVID BOON played 107 Test matches for Australia between 1984–85 and 1995–96, scoring 7,422 runs at an average of 43.65. He plundered 21 Test centuries – the best being 200 versus New Zealand. His consistent run-scoring and reliability at number three was a key ingredient for his country's success during his international career.

* * * * *

SIR IAN BOTHAM'S XI

The only basis on which I can pick a World XI is selecting from those who I played with and against in Test cricket – with the exception of Warne. That's the true test of a player in my opinion.

1) Sunil Gavaskar

Sunny's the finest opener I ever bowled to. He was the complete player, possessing enormous powers of concentration and had every shot in the book. His tremendous record against all countries, especially the West Indies, speaks for itself.

2) Gordon Greenidge

He had a wonderful eye. The power of some of his shots was frightening. He was a good player when fit and devastating with a limp, because he was only interested in hitting boundaries.

3) Viv Richards

Simply the best of my era and I cannot believe there has ever been a better batsman. Whatever the conditions, the match situation, the opposition or the type of cricket, he was the man you would back to score runs for your life. Watching him smash me and the rest of the England attack for that century in Antigua in 1986 (the fastest Test hundred in balls faced) was one of the most extraordinary experiences of my career. That day I felt helpless and in the presence of greatness.

4) Javed Miandad

He had the confidence and arrogance that all great players possess and it rubbed off on his colleagues. A master improviser, immensely competitive and able to conjure runs out of nothing.

5) Greg Chappell

Very stylish and could pace an innings to perfection. Was as stubborn in defence as he was punishing in attack.

6) Allan Border

A real tough competitor and an equally uncompromising teammate. Never gave up on a situation. It physically hurt him to lose and he demanded the same commitment from everyone he played with. AB was the ultimate pro' and I respected him greatly.

7) Adam Gilchrist

Before the emergence of Gilchrist I would have plumped for Alan Knott, who was just slightly better as a keeper than Bob Taylor and Rodney Marsh. Knotty shades it on batting with those two, though his batting was not in the same class as Gilchrist's. Knotty's keeping was world-class, but Gilchrist was a good keeper and a destructive batsman who altered the course of matches, as Viv did.

8) Wasim Akram

He's a left-armer, which gives the bowling attack useful variation, and his batting ability adds depth to the order. He had the ability to bowl unplayable deliveries on a regular basis.

9) Shane Warne

A magnificent leg-spinner and a great competitor. He gets in just ahead of Abdul Qadir, who was the best spinner in my era.

10) Joel Garner

His most deadly delivery was a fast yorker. Joel hated conceding runs and would get very upset about a nick through the slips for four. If the wicket was doing a bit, his pace and bounce made him as near to unplayable as you can get.

11) Dennis Lillee

He's a good mate of mine but there's no bias here as DK was simply the best fast bowler I ever played against. He was a wonderful craftsman and had everything you would want from a pace bowler: he had speed, aggression, movement and a massive heart. He would bowl through the pain barrier.

IAN BOTHAM played 102 Tests for England between 1977 and 1992, scoring 5,200 runs at an average of 33.54 as well as claiming 383 wickets at 28.40. He also took 120 catches, mostly at second slip. He is one of the greatest all-rounders of all time, famous for the entertaining and competitive manner in which he played. He was a player always more interested in the plight of the team than personal accolades or statistics.

* * * * *

GEOFFREY BOYCOTT'S XI

To try and name a team to play against all opposition in all parts of the world is an impossible task...it all comes down to personal opinion about who would be successful in the various conditions found in Test-playing countries. In my squad there are seven who would play in every match (Hobbs, Hutton, Bradman, Headley, Sobers, Knott and Barnes), with the others coming into the team to match the conditions in various parts of the world. In the sub-continent I would look to bring in Imran Khan for his reverse swing; Wilfred Rhodes, a left-arm spinner who can also make a lot of runs; Jim Laker, who took wickets on wet and dry pitches; and probably Malcolm Marshall. In India Malcolm's ability to swing it, bowl cutters, up his pace and skid it through would get the vote.

1) Jack Hobbs

You can't fail to be impressed by some of the tributes to him from some of the greatest players of all time. Wilfred Rhodes said: 'He was the greatest batsman of my time...He could have scored thousands more runs...'

2) Leonard Hutton

Len was one of the most complete batsmen ever to play the game and I meet many, many people who say he was their boyhood idol. There's not much argument that he was England's best since World War Two.

3) Donald Bradman

When you look at his performances this man is twice as good as anyone else. He averages just under 100 in Test cricket while others are around the 50 mark.

4) George Headley

His mastery of Clarrie Grimmett led the Aussies to dub him 'the Black Bradman' and it stuck, although at home he was better known as 'Atlas' because he carried the rest of the side on his shoulders...He was revered in the Caribbean and widely respected throughout the cricket world.

5) Everton Weekes

He was short and stocky with quick feet, and when you think he batted at number three against the new ball his record is fantastic.

6) Garfield Sobers

Blessed with so much natural talent, gifted beyond imagination, a natural genius, he allied all that to concentration, determination and great stamina, which allowed him to play long innings and make big scores. If you're picking any side he's got to be number one because he can win you the game with his batting or bowling.

7) Alan Knott

The quality of the keeping is paramount for me and Alan Knott was fantastic. I roomed with him in St Lucia in 1968 and I told him then, 'You're going to be a legend in your own lifetime'. I would say Knotty was a genius of a cricketer and I don't think there is any argument that he is the best ever seen, a top professional.

8) Shane Warne

The reason he was so good is he bowled so few bad balls...Accurate with huge spin – and I mean huge, enough to pitch well outside leg and miss off...When it comes to the spinners everyone would go for Shane Warne and so would I. But not in India, where he took wickets very expensively (34 at 43.11). I'd have no hesitation in telling Shane, 'You're not playing in India, Pakistan or Sri Lanka' and though he probably wouldn't speak to me for a week, if I explained why I'd pick Jim Laker in front of him he might just calm down – but I doubt it!

9) Fred Trueman

Fred was my favourite bowler, one of the best I've ever seen or played against and blessed with the most perfect action you could ever wish to see. Poetry in motion...He bowled the most gorgeous out-swinger at a real nasty pace.

10) Dennis Lillee

Lillee is a must in my team...Dennis and Jeff Thomson were only partners in crime on 26 occasions, but my word what a fearsome combination they were. Just the names – Lillee and Thomson – were enough to have most batsmen quaking in their boots.

11) Sydney Barnes

He has got to be the greatest bowler of all time, with figures to back up that claim...He has got to be the number one pick among the bowlers...Barnes was accepted by all his peers in Australia and England as the best and reading about him only reinforces those opinions.

GEOFFREY BOYCOTT played 108 Tests for England from 1964 to 1981–82 and scored 8,114 runs at an average of 47.72. He was one of the world's best opening batsmen, certainly one of England's finest, and was known for a steely determination and unrelenting concentration that enabled him to compile long innings. He scored 48,426 first-class runs at 56.83 and with 151 first-class centuries is the fifth-highest centurion. Geoffrey later became a leading pundit in world cricket.

This team was published courtesy of Geoffrey Boycott and Penguin Books, edited from his 2008 book *Geoffrey Boycott: The Best XI*.

SIR DONALD BRADMAN'S XI

Bradman hated being in the news — and his fame — with a passion...On average Bradman received 400 letters a day and his mail would have gone through the roof if his 'World Best Ever' or 'Dream Team' were made public. I felt that as a professional selector he might have liked thinking through such a team on paper. But any private sense of enjoyment would be eclipsed by the huge mailbags of complaint and opinion arriving on his doorstep, and the subsequent criticism and speculation in the media...His understandable reticence to stir up more publicity made a book on his best team untenable, so I suggested that the team only be made public posthumously. I sent him a pool of players to choose from...I received a letter from Bradman [with his XI] soon afterwards...When I expressed surprise that he had chosen just five batsmen, he remarked: 'If they couldn't make 500 then who could?' [His 12th man was Wally Hammond].

[from Roland Perry, author of *Bradman's Best*]

1) Barry Richards

He was one of the best players of the short ball, opener or otherwise, ever. He was always aggressive and fearless and had all the shots. He played spin and speed with equal ability...His limited opportunities at Test level were a pity and one of the biggest disappointments for exceptional talent unfulfilled in Test history.

2) Arthur Morris

What I saw in 1948 was enough for me. Towards the end of that tour he was playing the best cricket of any left-hander I'd seen. Since then I've had to modify my view considering performances of Harvey, Sobers and Lara. Yet Arthur was still the best left-hand option to open an innings.

3) Donald Bradman

[Author Roland Perry:] Bradman's attitude was that batsmen should score runs as quickly as possible in order to dismiss an opponent twice. He wanted batsmen to go for a win from the start, not concern themselves with staying at the wicket. 'It is not sufficient to keep the ball out of the stumps and not give a catch,' Bradman said. 'There is a need to attack, take the initiative from the bowlers and set up conditions for the batsmen to follow.'

4) Sachin Tendulkar

Lara and Tendulkar proved to be the two best batsmen of the 1990s. Tendulkar has a very strong defence. He's very tight. But he can be very aggressive, as he showed in the one-day and Test series against Australia in early 1998. On balance, however, Lara has probably proved more aggressive, though more mercurial. Tendulkar is proving more consistent.

5) Garfield Sobers

Garry would be in my team for his batting alone...Garry was by far the best player of short-pitched fast bowlers I ever saw. He was absolutely murderous, miraculous. He mastered anyone who tried to bounce him…If you consider that he could bowl left-hand fast-medium and spin with equal facility and great effect, he would also make any team as a bowler.

6) Don Tallon

He was tall and the most agile keeper I've ever seen. He was at his best when keeping to speed. [Bradman rated Ian Healy the best of the 1990s and said Adam Gilchrist could prove to be the most valuable keeper-batsman in history the way his average was soaring. Bradman didn't rank Gilchrist a better keeper than Tallon].

7) Ray Lindwall

There are several exceptional right-arm speedsters. None could bat as well as Lindwall…With such a list of talent you have to look for a characteristic that allows you to select one fellow over the others. He had scored Test centuries.

8) Dennis Lillee

[Considered Ambrose, Hadlee, McGrath, Marshall, Holding, Roberts, Walsh and S.F. Barnes] Lillee was marginally better in delivering most aspects of the speedster's armoury. He had a superb leg-cutter…Lillee also relied less on the short ball than the others. These are all great players who would perform in any era. They were capable of destroying an opposition, but Lillee was capable of the most devastation, at least from what I saw, and against the best batsmen in the world.

9) Alec Bedser

Bedser was particularly accurate. He could swing the ball either way and had a prodigious leg-cutter. Alec had a nice, quiet, deceptive change of pace, but never sacrificed accuracy when applying it. He also had heart and determination. He never gave up.

10) Bill O'Reilly

He was the best bowler I ever saw or played against. (Warne) is the best in the past 50 years and history might place him above the others. But I can't go past O'Reilly and Grimmett.

11) Clarrie Grimmett

O'Reilly relied on pace and bounce, whereas Grimmett at his best spun his leg-break further…Clarrie never liked to give a run away. I think he liked to bowl a maiden as much as take a wicket…The differences (between Warne and Grimmett) are marginal and very much in the beholder's subjective eye and experience.

DONALD BRADMAN played 52 Tests for Australia between 1928–29 and 1948, scoring 6,996 runs at an average of 99.94 – almost 40 runs an innings better than his nearest rival. This statistic and others, like his 29 Test centuries, mean he is widely regarded as the best batsman ever. His cricket intelligence and ability to read games and situations, or to identify trends in the sport, was also greatly respected.

This team was published courtesy of Random House, publisher of *Bradman's Best*, from which this team was edited.

BILL BROWN'S XI

I have picked my team from those that I played with and against.

1) Arthur Morris
Had a great tour of England in 1948 (where he averaged 86 in the Test series). He was an ideal opening batsman who had a sound defence and all the shots.

2) Leonard Hutton
Had a wonderful technique and tremendous powers of concentration, which he proved in 1938 when he scored his record 364 against Australia.

3) Donald Bradman
No explanation needed here. The Don just had everything. I consider myself privileged to have played in his team.

4) Stan McCabe
When Stan was in full flight, he was unsurpassed. A match situation always brought out the best in him.

5) Walter Hammond
A lovely driver of the ball and was just great to watch when he was at the wicket, even if you were his opponent!

6) Keith Miller
The best all-rounder I have ever seen. He was simply outstanding at batting, bowling and fielding and always exciting at each.

7) Ray Lindwall
Watching him bowl was poetry in motion. He had everything a bowler could ask for – blinding speed, control and a very fine temperament.

8) Don Tallon
Had wonderful safe hands, speed and smoothness. Just the best wicketkeeper I have ever seen who could also handle a bat.

9) Bill O'Reilly
He never let up, was always hostile on any wicket, and was also capable of delivering the unplayable delivery.

10) Clarrie Grimmett
Had complete control of the art of leg-spin. He bowled differently to different batsmen in order to dismiss them. Most of all, Clarrie had wonderful control over his flight.

11) Alec Bedser

For controlled, sharp in-swing, he was a master. He also developed a great leg-cutter and was capable of bowling the unplayable ball.

BILL BROWN played 22 Tests for Australia between 1934 and 1948, scoring 1,592 runs at an average of 46.82. In first-class cricket he amassed 13,840 runs at a lofty average of 51.44. Mostly an opener, he scored 105 at Lord's in 1934 in only his second Test. On his next Ashes tour, in 1938, he scored 206 not out at Lord's – carrying his bat through an innings of 422 to register Australia's 100th century against England. He was one of the so-called 'Bradman's Invincibles' of 1948.

[This team was received before Bill passed away in 2008]

✳ ✳ ✳ ✳ ✳

BHAGWATH CHANDRASEKHAR'S XI

I have only picked players I played with or against, as it is easier this way for me to make a decision on a World XI, rather than choosing between players I never saw or those who I don't know enough about who came after my career.

1) Sunil Gavaskar

He shone immediately in the Test arena and from the time he went to the West Indies (in 1970–71) he showed that India had a hugely talented opener. He later went on to great things.

2) Gordon Greenidge

How could I ignore Greenidge after his Test debut? He scored 90 (93) and a hundred (107) and was only denied two centuries in the match because of a run out! A wonderful stroke-maker but with a fine technique to open the batting.

3) Colin Cowdrey

Colin scored centuries in the first two Test matches I bowled at him so it was not hard to include him in this team. He played spin bowling very comfortably with his straight bat.

4) Tom Graveney

He was probably a bit more of an attacking player than Colin Cowdrey, but equally comfortable against spin and pace.

5) Clive Lloyd

Lloyd was a very powerful hitter who looked elegant with his long swing of the bat and was rarely troubled by pace or spin bowling. He also went on to become a great leader.

6) Garfield Sobers

I would be surprised if anyone leaves this guy out of their team. A wonderful attacking batsman – was hard to tie down; also a skilful bowler who could bowl anything.

7) Syed Kirmani

I considered the brilliant Alan Knott, my old teammate Farokh Engineer and the agile Rodney Marsh, but Kirmani was a very efficient keeper and a useful contributor with the bat as well.

8) Richard Hadlee

He probably went on to reach his peak after I retired (in 1979) but it was clear that even in the early seventies when he started he had a lot of talent.

9) Graham McKenzie

I believe he was underrated and was comfortably one of the best fast bowlers of his generation. Lillee and Thomson and, years before them, Lindwall and Miller, had each other to support them, but McKenzie, in the years in between, was largely alone in terms of leading the Australian attack.

10) Andy Roberts

There were quite a few West Indies bowlers to consider, but I feel that Roberts was not only quick, but cunning and able to use his many skills to suit whatever conditions he faced.

11) Lance Gibbs

I thought about 'Pras', whom I played a lot with, but have opted for Gibbs because of the number of wickets he took (309). He was an awkward bowler with his height and with the turn and bounce he got.

BHAGWAT CHADRASEKHAR played 58 Tests for India between 1963–64 and 1979, taking 242 wickets at an average of 29.74 with his leg-spin, googlies and top-spinners delivered at near medium pace. 'Chandra' was an awkward bowler for opposition batsmen because of the unusual amount of bounce he extracted, quite unlike most spinners. His six for 38 at the Oval in 1971 steered India to a maiden series win in England and he was also key in their first win in Australia in 1978, when he claimed 12 for 104 at Melbourne.

GREG CHAPPELL'S XI

I have not seen all the players in my team at first-hand, but through talking to several people and observing statistics, I feel certain selections are fairly simple, though it was difficult not finding a place for some players like Lara, Tendulkar and Botham.

1) Sunil Gavaskar

He was a terrific run-scorer for a bloke of short stature. He scored the majority of his Test runs in an era when there were some great fast bowlers around, so that speaks volumes for his ability as an opener. He's a player who always gave his side a start.

2) Gordon Greenidge

Gordon was a very, very good player and perhaps had the advantage of not playing against his own fast bowlers, but I'm sure he would still have done well if he had opposed them.

3) Donald Bradman

I've picked him just because he's Bradman. It's almost unfair because he should be in a team of his own.

4) Viv Richards

He was one of the best that ever played the game. The amount of talent he had was unbelievable. He loved to play with aggression and didn't like to be dictated to by anyone. I have seen him play innings in Australia and England where he took very good bowling attacks apart.

5) Graeme Pollock

A sensational player. He could take an attack of very high quality apart with amazing results. Although he wasn't a classical player, he could cope well with both spin and fast bowling. When it looked like a bowler was going to run through the side, he often played a match-winning innings.

6) Garfield Sobers

He was the best all-round cricketer that I have ever seen and am ever likely to see. He could have played in any team as a fast bowler or as a batsman alone. Garry would walk into any side and be the outstanding player. He is the best batsman I have ever seen.

7) Keith Miller

Through talking to people who saw him play and who have seen a lot of cricket since his generation, he would be the closest all-rounder to Sobers. He was a very punishing batsman and a fierce fast bowler. He had the sort of attitude that you have to admire: Keith Miller played the game to win and relished a battle.

8) Don Tallon

I didn't see him play, but through talking to people that played with and against him, he was apparently outstanding.

9) Shane Warne

He is in a class of his own out of the spinners. A very aggressive bowler with a fine temperament and a good cricket brain. He turns it more than anyone I have ever seen and with incredible accuracy. His tremendous control and cleverness puts him far ahead of any other spinner I have ever seen.

10) Jim Laker

I only saw him at the tail-end of his career as a kid, but the people I've talked to who played against him say he had tremendous ability to really turn the ball and bowl with great control. His record overall was pretty good. He gets in ahead of Underwood and Prasanna for the second spinner's position.

11) Dennis Lillee

He was the type of bowler that felt the better the batsman, the better the challenge was. He took a lot of his wickets on unhelpful pitches just because he rose to the challenge so much.

GREG CHAPPELL played 87 Test matches for Australia between 1970–71 and 1983–84, scoring 7,110 runs at an average of 53.86. In first-class matches he scored 24,535 runs at 52.20. Greg is one of the game's most astute thinkers and famous for the elegance with which he batted.

* * * * *

COLIN CROFT'S XI

To select a World XI of all time is almost impossible. Since I have played with or against some of the best cricketers and have seen so many others, I have given my objective overview. Many serious players had to be left out. I have selected a 'proper' team with balance, including a specialist wicketkeeper. Donald Bradman and George Headley were omitted. I expect this could get me ex-communicated from Australia and the West Indies, but my selections have played extensively around the world. However, these two played in a time when cricket was limited globally. Both have been highly favoured for runs made against England. But I ask you: when has England ever been the world's best cricket team? Never! England may have invented the game and its scribes may have conjured up a few heroes, but overall, England has been very poor indeed. Bradman and Headley were great in their time but, for me, not of all time. These are my honest opinions. I expect, or hope, that my selections will conjure discussions, perhaps even anger.

1) Sunil Gavaskar

Easily the best opener to play cricket, ever. Unlike any other considerations, he has made copious amounts of runs against the two best fast bowling combinations of all time: the West Indies and Australia in the 1970s and 1980s. No one else, from any Test-playing country, has ever done this! It could not have been easy to face the West Indies' Holding, Roberts, Garner, Daniel, Croft, Clarke and Marshall. Australia had Lillee, Thomson, Pascoe, Walker and Gilmour, too. Gavaskar stood up to them all.

2) Sachin Tendulkar

No one seems more focused on batsmanship, and to enjoy the honour of representing his country so much. His efforts have been completed over a 20-year spell when spin had become the most successful bowling around. He made runs against fast bowlers and the two best spinners the world has seen: Warne and Muralitharan.

3) Brian Lara

In my analysis Lara takes the place of Bradman. That is not because Lara is West Indian. It is simply that he has made so many runs against all bowling attacks around the world, especially Australia and Sri Lanka with Warne and Muralitharan respectively. Lara ignited the cricket world with his style and panache that few had.

4) Viv Richards

Sir Viv is my captain as his captaincy record is impeccable. There were other considerations for this spot, with the combative Ian and prolific Greg Chappell; David Gower, one of the coolest, classiest batsmen to grace the crease; Everton Weekes, who seldom hit the ball in the air but made mammoth runs, and Ricky Ponting, who has produced so regularly. However, no cricketer, before, or since, has evoked more fear in opposing bowlers, and teams, than 'Uncle Smokey'. Viv emanated poise and fearlessness, even arrogance, like no one else. He was also destructive and productive.

5) Jacques Kallis

His statistical returns are astounding. Kallis reminds me of a World War Two Panzer tank and Stuka dive-bomber aircraft, rolled into one. Angular, tough, strong and resilient, but sometimes pedestrian, certainly dangerous and productive, Kallis has been one of the best all-rounders to play the game. For over 15 years he has been the mainstay of South Africa's batting and bowling.

6) Garfield Sobers

Sobers is too valuable a cricketer to be left out of any world team; the original cricket prodigy and genius who could have been selected purely as a batsman or bowler. Sobers was at least four cricketers rolled into one. His catching was also magnificent.

7) Alan Knott

He is the best, purest, wicketkeeper ever. While Rodney Marsh, Adam Gilchrist, Jeffrey Dujon and Kumar Sangakkara were considered, their selections would be questionable.

Dujon and Marsh had very little slow bowling. My first consideration is for a proper wicketkeeper, not one that is a batsman first and a keeper afterwards; the modern way. The worst thing for any bowler, fast or slow, is to have his catches dropped by a wicketkeeper! And no one I have ever spoken to could remember a keeping mistake by Knott.

8) Shane Warne

This choice is easy. No spin bowler has made the impact that he has. Warne has bowled against all of the world's greatest contemporary batsmen, from Gooch and Atherton to Lara, Tendulkar and Sangakkara, and he has befuddled them all. He brought spin bowling back into vogue after the plethora of fast bowlers of the 1970s and 1980s.

9) Muttiah Muralitharan

Psychologically no other cricketer has had to overcome efforts to discredit him (for his bowling action) like Murali. His unorthodox delivery style is unique. Murali has taken 792 Test wickets so far, at the truly astonishing 22.71 average. This guy has been the mainstay of Sri Lanka's team for what seems like forever!

10) Joel Garner

I had six candidates for this spot: Garner, Curtly Ambrose, Malcolm Marshall, Richard Hadlee, Ian Botham and Imran Khan. Garner is the meanest bowler that has ever lived! Just look at his averages. His yorkers are remembered 'fondly' by many a batsman who hobbled off LBW to the orthopaedic surgeon!

11) Dennis Lillee

The best fast bowler to have ever played the game. No fast bowler, anywhere, has ever displayed as much determination or ability to both swing and cut the ball, not even the great Marshall. Lillee was always in command of his cricket, despite his several on-field trysts with opponents; psychological warfare at its best.

COLIN CROFT played 27 Test matches for the West Indies between 1976–77 and 1981–82 and claimed 125 wickets at an average of just 23.30. Overall, he managed 428 first-class victims at 24.59. Colin was one of the most fearsome pace bowlers of his generation and helped form possibly the most hostile pace attack in Test history along with Michael Holding, Andy Roberts and Joel Garner. In recent times he has developed a reputation as a straight-speaking pundit on radio and television.

MARTIN CROWE'S XI

It was difficult to leave out Greg Chappell, who had great style, and also Ian Botham, whom I played with at Somerset and was the next best all-rounder to Garry Sobers, but I felt these players are the greatest to ever play the game.

1) Jack Hobbs
The greatest opener pre-war and his superior statistics will be difficult for any player to emulate.

2) Barry Richards
Barry was the greatest opener post-war, who always looked to attack the bowler and dominate.

3) Donald Bradman
Greatest batsman of all time. End of story.

4) Sachin Tendulkar
He is the greatest modern-day player and I'm sure he will go on to even greater things. Who would doubt that his records will never be broken?

5) Viv Richards
Had the greatest power for any batsman. Viv was simply a destroyer of bowling attacks and I witnessed this close up and on too many occasions. He was just demoralising for bowlers.

6) Garfield Sobers
The greatest all-rounder of all time, though I think Ian Botham's heroics and ability to entertain make him a close second.

7) Alan Knott
Knotty is the greatest wicketkeeper I have ever seen, though Adam Gilchrist may be the better wicketkeeper-batsman.

8) Malcolm Marshall
Simply the greatest West Indian bowler of all time and that is saying a lot given the number of quality fast bowlers they have produced in modern times.

9) Shane Warne
The greatest leg-spinner of all time. I never saw the great Bill O'Reilly, whom Bradman rated as the best bowler he saw, but he couldn't have been any better than Shane Warne.

10) Dennis Lillee
The greatest fast bowler post-war. DK was a real whole-hearted performer.

11) Sydney Barnes – The greatest pace bowler pre-war, whose statistics are second to none (189 wickets in 27 Tests).

MARTIN CROWE played 77 Test matches for New Zealand between 1981–82 and 1995–96 and scored 5,444 runs at an average of 45.36. He was a technically correct batsman of high quality who entertained spectators with much grace and style. His highest score in Test cricket was 299 against Sri Lanka in 1990–91 at Wellington, where he linked up in a record third-wicket partnership of 467 with Andrew Jones.

✳ ✳ ✳ ✳ ✳

DANISH KANERIA'S XI

This was tough, selecting from so many greats. The records and stats of all the greats down the years made me think 100 times that I haven't picked someone I should have. In respect to all my seniors and out of respect for cricket history I tried to select my best XI from the different generations. I still had to leave out many greats like Denis Compton, Frank Worrell, Sachin Tendulkar, Allan Border, Muttiah Muralitharan, Joel Garner, Dennis Lillee, Hanif Mohammed, Ian Healy, Brian Lara and many more. I wish that one day my name will be mentioned among these greats too.

1) Sunil Gavaskar
I have gone for him mainly because of the way he played in an era when the West Indies had a fantastic pace attack. He stood up to them and was the best player of his day.

2) Garfield Sobers
I know he didn't open all that much but I hear that he was so good he could bat anywhere, so he allows me to play an extra fast bowler. His ability to bowl left-arm pace or orthodox spin gives another option. Everyone that saw him says he's the best-ever.

3) Donald Bradman
There's no doubt. The stats tell everything about him. With an average of 99, no explanation is needed.

4) Viv Richards
He was one of my favourites. He would play well in any conditions against any type of bowling. Viv was capable of winning a game from any situation.

5) Clive Lloyd
He was a stylish player, and of course was captain of the great West Indies side for a long time. Lloyd scored many runs in all types of conditions, against spin and pace.

6) Adam Gilchrist

I bowled against him a few times and it was a great challenge. I took his wicket a couple of times and that was always rewarding. He played for almost 10 years and the runs he scored and the way he scored them make him a great, while he was also an excellent wicketkeeper. He just gets in ahead of Ian Healy.

7) Wasim Akram

One of the greatest all-rounders Pakistan has produced, along with Imran. Wasim Akram was a brilliant bowler and a match-winner on many occasions. He was dangerous on any wicket.

8) Malcolm Marshall

He was very quick, had a beautiful smooth action and always tried to hit the batsman, whether it was his helmet or the shoulder of his bat. There were never any loose balls from Marshall. I saw quite a bit of him on TV growing up and he seemed to take wickets all the time in every country.

9) Shane Warne

A bowler very close to my heart because of the wonderful things he did as a leg-spinner. I have tried to learn from him every time I have watched him or played against him. It was great to see a leg-spinner take over 700 wickets and I can only hope that I get somewhere near his total by the time I retire.

10) Harold Larwood

I have only seen clips from the Bodyline series, but he must have been a great bowler to have caused the stir that he did. He was by far the quickest, and maybe best, bowler of his era.

11) Wes Hall

I saw impressive footage of him bowling in the Tied Test. He was very fast and fearsome and took lots of wickets. My seniors tell me that batsmen were genuinely scared of facing him.

DANISH KANERIA has so far played 58 Tests for Pakistan since 2000–01. No other Pakistan spinner has taken more Test wickets, after he surpassed Abdul Qadir's tally. Danish, Pakistan's fourth-most prolific Test bowler, currently has 254 Test wickets at an average of 34.27, and 855 first-class victims at 26.15. He is a prodigious turner of his leg-break and also possesses a dangerous googly and flipper. He has played for Essex in county cricket since 2005.

ALAN DAVIDSON'S XI

It's easier for me to select a World XI from my own playing days. That is the fairest way for me to select this kind of team.

1) Leonard Hutton
Technically, the best player I ever played against or saw. He was solid as a rock and you really had to earn his wicket.

2) Arthur Morris
He was the complete player. He could play spin, pace, everything and with ease. People said he was Alec Bedser's bunny, but it was just that Alec was the only one good enough to get him out consistently.

3) Neil Harvey
Not only the best left-hander I have ever seen, he's the best batsman I have ever seen. He was one of few to play Fazal (Mahmood) with any ease on the matting in Pakistan. 'Harv' would be the one bloke who could have played Shane Warne with ease when Warney was in his prime.

4) Peter May
The best on-side player I have ever seen; so complete and so effortless. He was a great batsman.

5) Everton Weekes
He was the Viv Richards of our time. No matter what you bowled, any ball could be smashed to the boundary when you were bowling to this man. A superb player.

6) Keith Miller
I never saw anybody change a game in two or three overs like Keith did, with bat or ball. As a bowler, when he got cranky he was like dynamite. The only time I've been scared on a cricket ground was when he got fired up in a state game against Victoria. He really went after this one batsman and nearly knocked his head off.

7) Garfield Sobers
Probably the most complete all-rounder that I have ever seen, as he could bat, and bowl fast or spin. A magnificent cricketer.

8) Don Tallon
He's miles ahead of any other wicketkeeper that I've ever seen. He was a freak, he was that good. Bradman had a Test batting average of 99.94 – well ahead of everyone – Tallon was the same in keeper's terms. After any stumping attempt he ever made, all that had to be replaced was a bail – he was that tidy. Also a very good batsman.

9) Ray Lindwall

He had the best action I've seen, as well as being a magnificent bowler. Everybody talks about 'that ball' Shane Warne bowled to Gatting, but Ray used to bowl special deliveries like those regularly. It was no surprise to see a batsman attempt a leg glance only to see his off stump knocked back.

10) Alec Bedser

He was the complete bowler and the captain's dream. He could bowl long spells and he was *so* accurate. There was nothing he couldn't bowl. On pitches that were under-prepared, he was unplayable. If the top broke on a particular spot he would then land the ball on that spot and take a divot right out.

11) Jim Laker

Give him a wicket that turned and he was virtually unplayable, as he had great control and could spin the ball a long way. Nowadays they bowl 500 overs a season, but Jim used to bowl a thousand overs and that's another reason why he was so great.

ALAN DAVIDSON played 44 Test matches for Australia between 1953 and 1962–63, taking 186 wickets at an average of 20.53 and scoring 1,328 runs at 24.59. In first-class cricket he claimed 672 wickets at 20.90, while scoring 6,804 runs at 32.86. He is one of the greatest left-arm pace bowlers of all time, and many significant contributions with the bat made him a fine international all-rounder.

* * * * *

ARAVINDA DE SILVA'S XI

I've picked a side from those I played with or against. I was sorry not to find a place for Desmond Haynes or Muttiah Muralitharan, who are players I greatly respect.

1) Sunil Gavaskar

He had a near faultless technique and also possessed amazing powers of concentration, which is the key reason why he scored a record 34 Test centuries.

2) Gordon Greenidge

Along with Haynes, he was an awesome prospect. They were the best opening partnership I have ever seen. Gordon attacked with unbelievable power but also had a nice touch.

3) Viv Richards

He was my idol and definitely the best batsman I have ever seen. I used to watch videos of him to try to emulate the way he played, which was near impossible. He is the perfect number three in any team.

4) Sachin Tendulkar

He is an attacking batsman who really gets on top of the bowling, and I think he is a very talented player who has not surprised me one bit with all the world records he has set.

5) Brian Lara

He's one of the most exciting players the game has seen; he's a real entertainer. I watched him play in Sri Lanka and I am still yet to see anybody play Murali as comfortably as he did.

6) Javed Miandad

He's in for being a fighter. If you lost a few early wickets, he was the type of player who would fight it out whatever the conditions and pull his side out of trouble.

7) Imran Khan

He led from the front and would, therefore, be my captain. Imran was another fighter who really knew the game. He was a superb fast bowler who could swing the ball both ways and was also a reliable batsman.

8) Adam Gilchrist

The best wicketkeeper-batsman I've come across. He's the most phenomenal counter-attacker I've ever seen, while his keeping is good, as he proved by standing up to Shane Warne.

9) Richard Hadlee

He was the best pace and swing bowler that I faced. Also very useful with the bat; a fine all-rounder.

10) Wasim Akram

Wasim gets in just ahead of Michael Holding, who was the Rolls-Royce of fast bowling. This left-armer had the skill to trouble the best batsmen in any conditions.

11) Shane Warne

He is my spinner mainly because of his great variation. He's very accurate, which is an important skill for a spinner; he rarely offered you a loose ball. Murali is unlucky not to get in this team, but Warney shades it for me as the lone spinner.

ARAVINDA DE SILVA played 93 Tests for Sri Lanka between 1984 and 2002, scoring 6,361 runs at an average of 42.97. The diminutive middle-order player was once the most prolific batsman Sri Lanka has ever produced. He was an entertaining player who batted with style, but was also capable of resilience when the situation demanded.

ALLAN DONALD'S XI

I selected my team from players I've seen either in person or on television. I can't judge on players I never saw I'm afraid.

1) Gordon Greenidge

He was the most aggressive batsman I've ever seen. He also had terrific patience and, mixed with his aggression and power, he was a great, great player.

2) Mark Taylor

When I bowled to him I always thought he was a very patient and gutsy player, and the kind who will slog it out all innings. Mark was an expert leaver of the ball and when he was playing really well, he was a hard guy to bowl to.

3) Brian Lara

Everybody in world cricket knows what brilliance he was capable of. He looks so calm at the crease, which makes him a fantastic batsman to come in at number three. He is the kind of player who can dominate any bowling attack on any day. Capable of pure genius.

4) Sachin Tendulkar

The best player of the modern era, just awesome to watch. He has great balance, good technique and showed tremendous experience for his age when achieving great things as a youngster – all qualities which make him a true world-class batsman.

5) Viv Richards

Viv coming in at number five behind Lara and Tendulkar would be enough to deflate most bowling sides. What arrogance; he used to come in with his cap on, which he did all his life, and then usually smash bowlers all over the park. I bowled to him once or twice and that was probably enough. I tried to knock his cap off, but the ball just disappeared! He would be a great leader of this side.

6) Greg Chappell

I remember seeing him on television and he was world-class. He was a fluent, elegant batsman – what we call a sexy player – and he was also a good captain for Australia. When you see him come in at six after that lot, it would be pretty scary.

7) Jeff Dujon

He was the greatest keeper standing back, to guys like Marshall, Holding, Croft and Garner. He'd be the one I would most want behind the stumps to my bowling. He was great to watch.

8) Ian Botham

Watching him in his prime was fantastic. He had this attitude that said, 'You are not going to knock me over.' When he had the ball in his hand he was like a golden arm. He would try anything to get batsmen out: long hops, bouncers. People compare him to Garfield Sobers, and having seen him at the end of his career, I don't think there was much between them.

9) Richard Hadlee
He is the greatest bowler ever in my opinion. Hadlee was my idol. He got more intelligent as his career went on. He adapted very well on any kind of wicket and was also a great batsman down the order who could bat according to the situation of the game.

10) Shane Warne
Many people thought of Abdul Qadir as the best leg-spinner of the modern era, but Warney took the art of leg-spin to another level. He had the ability to bowl four different balls an over, and with fantastic accuracy. The amount of wickets he has taken is phenomenal.

11) Malcolm Marshall
Marshie gets in just ahead of Curtly Ambrose. He was a tremendous bowler and the quickest of his era. Put a ball in his hand and he could bowl out-swing, in-swing, cutters, bouncers, you name it. It was great to see him play in South Africa for Natal before he retired. With his experience he became the best fast bowler in the world. Along with Botham and Hadlee, having Marshall in this side would be an added luxury. He would take the new ball.

ALLAN DONALD played 72 Test matches for South Africa from 1991–92 to 2002 and took 330 wickets at an average of 22.25. He amassed 1,216 first-class victims at 22.76. 'AD' was considered the quickest bowler in the world at the height of his career. His pace, craft, stamina and ability to strike at vital times helped establish South Africa as a leading force in world cricket following the years of isolation. He played county cricket for Warwickshire from 1987 to 2000.

✳ ✳ ✳ ✳ ✳

RAHUL DRAVID'S XI

It was tough having to omit so many greats like Steve Waugh, Imran Khan, Gundappa Viswanath, Richard Hadlee, Virender Sehwag and Anil Kumble. In fact I would include Kumble if the game was played in Asia, as there could be no one better than him in the right conditions.

1) Sunil Gavaskar
Just because he played the best fast bowlers of his era with amazing ease, particularly the West Indian quicks. The fact he scored 10,000 Test runs was another reason for his selection.

2) Brian Lara
I was tempted to go for Jack Hobbs, as I appreciate cricket's history and what he achieved, but I had to have Lara. He's not a regular opener but he has done the job before and is a great cricketer with a phenomenal record. On his day he can win a match single-handedly, and has done so.

3) Donald Bradman

With an average of 99.94 – that's enough reason! He must have been freakishly good to have an average like that.

4) Sachin Tendulkar

An exceptional middle-order batsman. He has tremendous judgement of line and length and he has succeeded in all conditions. It's a real privilege to bat with him for India and share the same dressing room as him. He's another with over 10,000 Test runs (12,000+) to show how talented a player he is.

5) Viv Richards

He was someone who could win a match single-handedly and he would be ideal at number five after this top four; he would break bowlers' hearts with his unrelenting aggression.

6) Garfield Sobers

I never saw him but his record is exceptional. People of his era rate him the best all-rounder ever; that's good enough for me.

7) Adam Gilchrist

Undoubtedly a destructive batsman who could get in to any team just as a batsman. He's also very good behind the stumps as his experience keeping to Shane Warne has proved. He gets in just ahead of Ian Healy and the other great keepers around the world.

8) Kapil Dev

He took so many wickets on lifeless tracks. He was a great out-swing bowler and could also bat brilliantly and change games.

9) Wasim Akram

Being a left-armer he adds balance to the attack. He had so much variety and his use of the old ball was excellent. Wasim was also a more than useful batter down the order.

10) Malcolm Marshall

I was tempted to go for Dennis Lillee or Richard Hadlee, but Marshall was a fearsome competitor. I never played against him, but through talking to the greats of that era who played with or against him, they all said he could swing and seam the ball and at serious pace. He could adapt to any conditions around the world.

11) Shane Warne

A great bowler with tremendous variation. He's one of the finest leg-spin bowlers to have played – if not the best. He drifts the ball so well, which is a great strength for a spinner to have.

RAHUL DRAVID has so far played 139 Tests for India since 1996 and has scored 11,395 runs at an average of 53.87. He began his Test career at number seven, but has since gone on to amass the most runs by a number three in Test history. Dravid is one of the most consistent and resilient batsmen in world cricket, with remarkable levels of concentration.

✳ ✳ ✳ ✳ ✳

JEFFREY DUJON'S XI

Picking this team has been almost impossible, but having selected this XI I wouldn't want to leave any of these guys out. I think it's quite a well balanced team. However, it's very difficult to leave out Greg Chappell, Desmond Haynes, Allan Border, Richard Hadlee, Kapil Dev, Ian Botham, David Gower, Steve Waugh — who I think is a real great player — Michael Holding and Curtly Ambrose.

1) Gordon Greenidge
Technically, and in terms of scoring hundreds and double hundreds, he's one of the best. Desmond Haynes is unlucky as Gordon's success was partly due to his partnership with Desi.

2) Sunil Gavaskar
For the same reasons as Greenidge and for his heavy scoring against everybody he played; a very consistent performer.

3) Viv Richards
For obvious reasons: I don't think there's ever been a better batsman or a more devastating one than Viv.

4) Donald Bradman
Like Viv, he's a player that would have transcended any era. His record is phenomenal.

5) Sachin Tendulkar
Sachin has proved to be unquestionably the ultimate in consistency, longevity and achievement, as well as the epitome of what the game is about — a humbling endeavour that is bigger than us all. I was tempted to pick Greg Chappell, as he is one of the greatest players that Australia has ever produced and was stylish, consistent and real good to watch, but I have to go for Sachin for what he has achieved.

6) Garfield Sobers
The greatest all-rounder that has ever lived.

7) Rodney Marsh
He would always be my sentimental favourite for his keeping to the fast bowlers. He has an incredible record with both the gloves and the bat.

8) Malcolm Marshall

He had everything: stamina, skill, intelligence, pace. He swung the ball at pace and he took wickets on all types of surfaces. He is the best fast bowler that the West Indies has ever produced. Malcolm embodied the best aspects of all the other great quicks we had. His 376 Test wickets prove that.

9) Shane Warne

The best attacking leg-spinner that I have ever seen and probably there has ever been. His strike rate is incredible. No leg-spinner has ever dominated an era like he has. If you are going to include a spinner he has to be it.

10) Dennis Lillee

Like Marshall, he had great pace and a great strike rate. He was a terrific competitor and easily one of the best fast bowlers ever. You always knew you were in a fight against him.

11) Joel Garner – Another brilliant fast bowler who gave the batsman absolutely nothing. He was very quick and very accurate.

JEFFREY DUJON played 81 Tests for the West Indies between 1981–82 and 1991, claiming 272 dismissals as wicketkeeper. He scored 3,322 Test runs at an average of 31.94. For much of his Test career he batted at number seven, but was good enough to bat higher. Dujon is regarded as one of the greatest wicketkeepers to fast bowling, after he kept to the likes of Marshall, Garner, Holding, Walsh and Ambrose.

✴ ✴ ✴ ✴ ✴

JOHN EDRICH'S XI

I have selected my team from players I have seen, from my childhood through to the present day. Consequently, there is no place for the likes of Bradman, Barnes, Hobbs and so on. A few other great players who I have seen, but unfortunately had to leave out, include: Colin Cowdrey, Bobby Simpson, Bill Lawry, Wes Hall, Rohan Kanhai, Steve Waugh, Derek Underwood, Greg Chappell – who I felt was limited to the on-side in his early days – Ian Botham – who, unfortunately for him, is up against Sobers, and Barry Richards and Graeme Pollock – two great batsmen, but they never played Test cricket long enough for me to pick them.

1) Leonard Hutton

He is the best player I have seen on all types of wickets. He had a tremendous technique, which is evident in his fine record.

2) Sunil Gavaskar

His one-time world record 34 Test centuries says it all. Sunny was a big innings player and a great accumulator of runs.

3) Peter May

I played with him at Surrey and, to me, he was a great entertainer. He was the straightest hitter of a cricket ball that I have ever seen, and the best player off the back foot.

4) Denis Compton

A genius. He just took bowling attacks apart with amazing ease, and he had this unorthodox way of playing which added to his unique style of cricket.

5) Walter Hammond

His record says it all. I only saw him at the very end of his career when my father took me to see him, and I would have liked to have seen a lot more of him. He would be my captain.

6) Garfield Sobers

He would have to be the best all-rounder there has ever been. He could do it all: bat, bowl as quick as anyone when he wanted to, and was a great fielder too. Overall, he was a tremendous entertainer. It was never dull playing against him either.

7) Alan Knott

He was a genius and is by far the best wicketkeeper there has ever been. I suppose he was in the Godfrey Evans mould, but I feel that Knotty changed the art of wicketkeeping; he would dive around, take regular one-handed catches and really batted with purpose, like a seventh front-line batsman. It was a pleasure to play with him.

8) Shane Warne

He has to be the best leg-spinner I have ever seen and that there has ever been in the game. Not only does he spin the ball a long way, but he bowls it at such a pace that it makes it hard for the batsman to come down the wicket to him.

9) Jim Laker

The best off-spinner I've seen, though Lance Gibbs is not far behind. I haven't selected him just for his 19 wickets at Manchester; I also felt he was a brilliant off-spin bowler generally.

10) Fred Trueman

Fast, wonderful action, terrific change of pace and was first to take 300 Test wickets. He was able to bowl three or four different types of ball and he could put it where he wanted. There have been many to bowl quick, but few can boast Fred's accuracy and skill.

11) Dennis Lillee

His amazing record proves how good he was – undoubtedly one of the world's best-ever quick bowlers. Like Trueman, he had a lovely action, change of pace, was quick and knew where he wanted to put the ball, usually succeeding with deadly accuracy.

JOHN EDRICH played 77 Test matches for England between 1963 and 1976, scoring 5,138 runs at an average of 43.54. In first-class cricket the opening batsman amassed 39,790 runs at 45.47, including 103 centuries. His 310 not out for England against New Zealand in 1965 set a world record for the most boundaries hit in a Test innings, with 57, and the innings is still the highest by an English left-hander.

* * * * *

JOEL GARNER'S XI

My team has been picked from players that I have seen. I had problems leaving out players such as Gordon Greenidge, Zaheer Abbas, Clive Lloyd, Alan Knott, Abdul Qadir, Shane Warne, Imran Khan, Andy Roberts and John Snow, but I can only select 11. If this team had to play on a turning track then I would leave out one of the players below and bring in Abdul Qadir. The way it is, I just think Lillee, Marshall and Hadlee are so good that you probably wouldn't need to bowl a spinner anyway. The combination of these three fast bowlers would dismiss any batting side in the world. However, Garry Sobers can provide a bit of left-arm spin in this side, and Richards, Border, Miandad and Chappell can all do a job with the ball too.

1) Conrad Hunte
He was an attacking opener until he became more defensive to stabilise the West Indies' batting. I didn't see a lot of him but he and Gavaskar would make a great opening pair.

2) Sunil Gavaskar
A great accumulator of runs. I played against him a few times and I always found him to be a very compact player who hung around, was hard to remove and always thought about what he was doing.

3) Viv Richards
There is not a lot for me to say about this man other than that he could take apart any bowling attack from any team in the world. If he was required to play defensively he could do that too, because his defence was as good as his ability to attack.

4) Allan Border
One of the most difficult batsmen that I ever bowled to because he was such a gutsy and gritty player. He could also hold an end up with the ball.

5) Greg Chappell
He was a very determined batsman who was always ready for a fight out in the middle. However, he didn't just stay there, because he was a fluent shot player and a very elegant one too.

6) Javed Miandad
There is no way I could leave this man out. He was always there battling for his team. He was a player who you could never discount because he was always there taking the fight to you; a real tough competitor.

7) Garfield Sobers

His fantastic record speaks for itself. He could bat, bowl fast, bowl spin, swing the ball and field very well. It would be a wonderful luxury for any team to have this man's excellence and versatility. Not a bad man to come in at number seven!

8) Rodney Marsh

I have chosen him over Knotty for his batting ability. His strengths were in his batting in my opinion. Not only was he an excellent wicketkeeper, but he was also a batsman who could spend vital time at the crease, able to pull his team out of trouble if he needed to.

9) Richard Hadlee

One of the best fast bowlers you will ever see. Had a lovely action, could do everything with the ball and was also a decent batsman as well.

10) Malcolm Marshall

Same as Hadlee. Malcolm was a top bowler who could bowl in any kind of conditions. He bowled as well on the slow pitches in India and Pakistan as he did on the quicker wickets in Australia and the Caribbean, which you cannot say about too many.

11) Dennis Lillee

He would compliment any fast bowling attack. Dennis was not only fast and aggressive, but he also always did something with the ball too.

JOEL GARNER played 58 Tests for the West Indies between 1976–77 and 1986–87, claiming 259 wickets at a miserly average of 20.97. Joel was one of the most respected fast bowlers of his era, linking up with Andy Roberts, Colin Croft, Michael Holding and Malcolm Marshall to form the most fearsome bowling attack of the seventies and eighties, maybe of all time. Garner's height (6ft 8in) made him an awkward opponent for batsmen; when he bowled his yorker he was near unplayable. He served Somerset loyally in county cricket from 1977 to 1986.

Jack Hobbs
'When I think of this guy, I think of him as the father of openers' – Alf Valentine

Harold Larwood
'Without him there wouldn't have been a Bodyline controversy' – Graham McKenzie

Donald Bradman
'The best batsman there has ever been and ever likely to be'
– Trevor Bailey

Alec Bedser
'He was the greatest exponent of the leg-cutter ever. Alec could be unplayable'
– Fred Trueman

Peter May
'PBH is certainly the best batsman England has produced since the war' – Ray Illingworth

Men for a crisis. Len Hutton and Denis Compton are seen going out to resume England's second innings on the fourth day in the Nottingham Test in 1948. At that stage England, with Washbrook and Edrich both out cheaply, required 223 runs to avert an innings defeat. Compton helped Hutton to put on 111 and went on to hit 184 before he trod on his wicket in moving away from a Miller "bumper."

Leonard Hutton and Denis Compton

'The best batsman against all types of bowling and on all types of wickets' – Sonny Ramadhin on Leonard Hutton

'Those two hundreds he scored against us in 1948 were two of the best knocks I've ever seen' – Neil Harvey on Denis Compton

Fred Trueman
'He was genuinely fast and certainly one of the finest bowlers of all time' – Hanif
Mohammed

Frank Worrell (left) and Everton Weekes (right) – Clyde Walcott in centre
'He was the Viv Richards of our time' – Alan Davidson on Everton Weekes

'The greatest captain of all time and not a bad player either' – Deryck Murray on Frank
Worrell

Hanif Mohammed
'Hanif Mohammed was a class player. I saw every run of his
337 in Barbados in 1958' – Sir Garfield Sobers

Sir Garfield Sobers
'Garry would walk into any side and be the outstanding player. He is the best batsman I have ever seen' – Greg Chappell

Lance Gibbs
'Simply the best off-spinner that has ever played the game' – Lawrence Rowe

Graeme Pollock and Alan Knott

'Batting was easy for him… The coolness in which he dominated situations amazed me' – Alvin Kallicharran on Graeme Pollock

'Simply an out and out genius. I consider myself very fortunate in my life that I was able to play in the same Kent and England teams as this man' – Derek Underwood on Alan Knott

Sunil Gavaskar
'On the right pitch he was almost impossible to bowl at' – Andy Roberts

Dennis Lillee
'The best fast bowler to have ever played the game' – Colin Croft

Barry Richards
'He was always aggressive and fearless and had all the shots' – Sir Donald Bradman

Richard Hadlee
'He was what I would call a computer bowler, so perfect' – Kapil Dev

Imran Khan
'He was a source of inspiration on and off the field for so many people' – Hanif
Mohammed

Greg Chappell
'He was a batsman who you would back every time to get a hundred' – Jeff Thomson
(pictured in 2006 when Greg was India's coach)

SUNIL GAVASKAR'S XI

I have not seen all of these players, but through records and what I have heard I have selected a team from all eras. One has to leave out so many great players; some before my time, some during my time and some after my time, but I hope they will understand it is no reflection on their ability – it's just that the constraints are to pick only 11. I should add that if the match were to be played in England or the sub-continent I would play Jim Laker instead of either Roberts or Lillee. With his record, Laker should be finding a place in this team, but I have got Bishan Bedi and also Viv Richards to bowl a bit of off-spin as well as Sobers to do a job. I was particularly sad to have to leave out Everton Weekes and Rohan Kanhai.

1) Jack Hobbs

With his record of 197 first-class hundreds and playing at a time of uncovered pitches, he must have been an amazing player.

2) Leonard Hutton

The same as above. Fast bowlers got closer to you in those days with the no-ball rule, so he must have been some player to handle the likes of Lindwall and Miller.

3) Donald Bradman

What can one say? He was the greatest, and more than 60 years down the road after his retirement from the game, there is nobody who comes remotely close to his record. A champion of one era would be a champion of any era.

4) Viv Richards

He was capable of conquering a bowler mentally with his aggressive batting. Viv was a complete destroyer. There was no such thing as a good ball to him.

5) Sachin Tendulkar

Simply the best batsman of the present day. I always expected him to beat my Test centuries' record and score many more than my Test run aggregate. I told him early in his career, when I could see how talented he was, that if he didn't score 40 Test centuries and 20 centuries in one-day cricket, I would kill him. Thankfully I won't have to!

6) Garfield Sobers

The greatest cricketer ever – he could do anything. He could bat, bowl fast, bowl spin and was a great fielder anywhere. He could have kept wicket if he wanted to, and would have made a good job of it too. When you consider he batted at number six for most of his career and still got 26 hundreds, took over 200 Test wickets and over a hundred catches, you couldn't find a better all-round cricketer than him.

7) Alan Knott

Knotty was as safe as a bank as a wicketkeeper. He was also a very good help to bowlers with his observations of batsmen. He was brilliant keeping to spinners and the quicks. As a batsman, you could rely on him to score runs, particularly when the chips were down.

8) Andy Roberts

The best fast bowler that I faced. He had the ability to surprise you, even when you were well past a century. You could never relax against him. With a lot of bowlers, as soon as you had seen off their first few overs, you knew you were okay – but not against this man.

9) Dennis Lillee

The same as Roberts, because he had the ability to produce the unplayable delivery, even to a batsman who was well past a hundred. There were many bowlers that were dangerous in their initial spell, but once past that stage only over-confidence could get you out. Against Lillee and Roberts you always had to watch out.

10) Fred Trueman

I didn't see Fred Trueman at all, but to have been the first fast bowler to reach 300 Test wickets is an indication of how good a fast bowler he was. Being a character he would be ideal in the dressing room to brighten a tense moment, which of course this great team would not have too many of.

11) Bishan Bedi

He was a fantastic bowler who had great variety and a super action – he was poetry in motion. He could bowl six different balls in an over if he wanted to.

SUNIL GAVASKAR played 125 Test matches for India between 1970–71 and 1986–87, scoring 10,122 runs at an average of 51.12, including a then world-record 34 Test centuries. He was a hugely consistent and prolific opening batsman and an excellent judge of where his off stump was and so was able to leave the ball expertly. He was the first player to reach 10,000 runs in Tests and had a highest score of 236 not out – then an Indian Test record.

* * * * *

HERSCHELLE GIBBS'S XI

I wanted my team to be entertaining. My players are, apart from Sobers, ones I have seen or played with or against. I would like to have found room for Courtney Walsh, Gordon Greenidge, Glenn McGrath, Ian Botham – but I wanted specialists rather than all-rounders (Sobers could be in here either as a batsman or bowler) – and Michael Slater. I was a big fan of the way he batted. Sachin Tendulkar is another great player; I just feel he had it easier than some playing so much on batsman-friendly surfaces in India. None of these players hung around if they were struggling for timing, or with the conditions or anything like that, they just went for it. I've never been big on stats and although these players have great stats, the way they played the game meant more to them; my kind of cricket.

1) Desmond Haynes

When people speak of great opening partners Haynes and Greenidge are always mentioned. I played with Desi at Western Province when I was a youngster and I learned a lot from him; he was a gentleman and we became really good friends. He didn't talk that much and led by example – I learned just by watching him in the nets. His stats proved he could do it at the very top with over 8,000 one-day runs and more than 7,000 Test runs.

2) Matthew Hayden

A huge presence at the wicket, you knew he was going to come at you. I can't imagine what goes through bowlers' heads when he's coming at them. He played the game hard but was a good guy off the field.

3) Ricky Ponting

He's a genuine attacking batter, more interested in taking the game forward and not interested in stats. He has always played the game hard.

4) Brian Lara

Your best batsman has to bat at four. Lara could hit the ball to strange areas and therefore he was awkward to bowl to. He played shots to balls that others would leave and that enabled him to create more run-scoring opportunities.

5) Viv Richards

My personal favourite for his confidence, maybe a bit of arrogance, his physical presence. He murdered bowling attacks and is the only guy I have seen hit away swingers over square leg; I haven't seen another guy do that all my life, so you must have to be very special to do that. Most of us would go over point.

6) Garfield Sobers

I didn't see him but he had exceptional skill, could bowl seam or spin. He looked to move the game forward at a quick pace whether as a batsman, bowler or as captain.

7) Adam Gilchrist

If you thought this wicketkeeper was a part-time batter you would soon be proven completely wrong. He batted as well as the top of the order and against an old ball or a new ball. Often when keepers come out they have to face the second new ball, but it never worried Gilchrist. He never changed his style. He also had safe hands.

8) Shane Warne

Home and away his record is better than his nearest rival (Muttiah) Muralitharan. Murali's pitches were prepared for him at home but Warney didn't have that. He is simply a legendary leg-spinner. He told me he bowled his second-best delivery ever to me (at Edgbaston in the 1999 World Cup). It remains the best ball I ever faced: it pitched outside leg stump and clipped the off bail. Gilly [Gilchrist] went mad and I thought he'd tried to stump me, but then I realised…

9) Malcolm Marshall

For his great ability. My first limited-over 100 was against Marshall's Natal side, which meant a lot to me. Duncan Fletcher told me Marshall was the most skilful fast bowler he had seen as he could swing the ball both ways. Even a great bowler like Shaun Pollock could only swing the ball away. But Marshall did both at serious pace, and he was smaller than the other big quicks.

10) Wasim Akram

He adds variety, and was an amazing batsman at number 10 as he was good enough to bat above Warne. He initiated reverse swing and had no big jump in his delivery stride, which made him awkward when he bowled his bouncer. Wasim just bowled great spells. He didn't bowl a lot of bouncers, so when he did it took you by surprise. He felt quicker than he looked – he was an incredible athlete.

11) Allan Donald

AD is a good friend of mine. He was never short on rhythm, swung the ball into right-handers so you had to play him – if you didn't know where your off stump was he would find you out. I remember my first net against him, he was bowling with a new ball and he hit me in the gap between my thigh pad and leg pad. I didn't walk for three days! He was seriously quick. I liked the fact he was never short of a refreshment at the end of play, and how he would take a pint with him into team meetings. Great guy.

HERSCHELLE GIBBS has played 90 Test matches for South Africa from 1996–97, scoring 6,167 runs at an average of 41.95, including 14 centuries. He has been one of the most electrifying batsmen in world cricket throughout his career and a similarly exciting fielder. Gibbs, who excelled as an opener and in the middle-order, was the first player to hit six sixes in an over in one-day internationals, at the 2007 World Cup.

LANCE GIBBS'S XI

I would have included S.F. Barnes in the 12, as he is considered by many to be the best bowler ever.

1) Jack Hobbs
Had war not interrupted his career, I'm sure Hobbs would have been a strong candidate for the undisputed greatest batsman ever.

2) Sunil Gavaskar
One of the most complete of opening batsmen. He combined a rock solid defence with the ability to dispatch the bad ball for four, and scored more Test centuries than any other batsman; at least until Sachin and Co. came along!

3) Donald Bradman
The greatest batsman ever and his selection comes without any question.

4) George Headley
A batsman surpassed only by Bradman. He succeeded in a weak West Indies team, which is even more impressive.

5) Viv Richards
A destroyer of any type of bowling, and the holder of the fastest century in Test cricket.

6) Garfield Sobers
Simply the world's greatest all-rounder of all time. I was privileged to play in the same team as him for most of my career.

7) Alan Knott
In my opinion he is the best wicketkeeper the game has seen. He made a minimal amount of fuss and got the job done. There might be better batting-keepers like Adam Gilchrist or Rod Marsh, but Knotty was the best glove-man you could wish to see.

8) Malcolm Marshall
The best of the great West Indies' fast bowlers with a strike rate in the forties. This is some achievement given the competition.

9) Dennis Lillee
One of the greatest fast bowlers of the 20th century. A bad back forced him to reduce his pace, but he was still very effective after recovering from the injury.

10) Shane Warne
The best leg-spinner ever. There were others, like Grimmett, O'Reilly and Qadir, but I can't believe they could be any better than this man.

11) Lance Gibbs

The best off-spinner. I am going on the fact that I was the first spinner to reach 300 Test wickets. And I would relish the chance to bowl after Lillee, Marshall and Sobers and in tandem with Warne.

LANCE GIBBS played 79 Tests for the West Indies from 1957–58 to 1975–76 and claimed 309 wickets at an average of 29.09. In first-class cricket he took 1,024 wickets at 27.22, helped by the 338 wickets he took while playing with Warwickshire from 1967 to 1972. Gibbs was a prodigious spinner of the ball and used his height to extract awkward bounce.

* * * * *

TREVOR GODDARD'S XI

Graeme Pollock and Ian Botham just narrowly miss out, along with a few other greats, due to the brilliance of those listed below. Bradman would be my captain.

1) Jack Hobbs, 2) Leonard Hutton, 3) Donald Bradman, 4) Denis Compton, 5) Garfield Sobers, 6) Viv Richards, 7) Shane Warne, 8) Godfrey Evans, 9) Ray Lindwall, 10) Sydney Barnes, 11) Dennis Lillee

TREVOR GODDARD played 41 Test matches for South Africa between 1955 and 1969–70. He scored 2,516 Test runs at an average of 34.46 and took 123 wickets at 26.22. In first-class cricket Trevor made 11,279 runs at an average of 40.57 and took 534 wickets at 21.65. He was one of the best all-rounders of his era and indeed was the first South African to score 10,000 runs *and* take 500 wickets in first-class cricket.

* * * * *

GRAHAM GOOCH'S XI

My side has been picked from players I've played with and against. I feel that's the fairest method by which to select this kind of team.

1) Barry Richards

The best opening batsman I have ever seen and there are a lot to choose from! He's also one of my personal favourites.

2) Sunil Gavaskar

Another true great and the next-best opener to Barry Richards. I admired his patience and ability to apply himself very much.

3) Viv Richards

The best attacking batsman I have ever seen. He was awesome and almost impossible to stop when he was in the groove, like during his rapid century in Antigua against us in 1986.

4) Allan Border

A wonderful professional who was extremely difficult to get out. I saw him from both sides of the fence; as an opponent with England and as a teammate at Essex. He hated to lose anything.

5) Sachin Tendulkar

I was tempted to pick Greg Chappell as he was very stylish, elegant and very prolific, but Sachin has achieved so much over a 20-year period, which is quite incredible. I first played against him in 1990 when he scored his first Test hundred at Old Trafford and then again in India in 1993. You could see he had a great talent even then.

6) Ian Botham

A match-winner with great all-round talent. He made things happen when the game could sometimes be drifting.

7) Alan Knott

Knotty had safe hands, was very tidy with his glove work, had good agility and was more than useful with the bat.

8) Malcolm Marshall

The best bowler that I ever faced, who could swing it and move it off the seam at great pace. Every good innings I played against Marshall gave me a great deal of satisfaction. I always felt that runs against top-quality attacks meant a lot more.

9) Shane Warne

I enjoyed batting against him; it was a tremendous challenge. Some batsmen are pleased when the best bowlers are not playing against them, but I always got more satisfaction out of doing well against the very best, as Shane Warne undoubtedly is, if not 'the' best.

10) Wasim Akram

Wasim had tremendous variety, not only as a left-arm bowler, but also with the different types of delivery he was capable of.

11) Dennis Lillee

A great bowler who gave me a few problems early in my career. He was always at you.

GRAHAM GOOCH played 118 Tests for England between 1975 and 1994–95 and scored 8,900 runs at an average of 42.58. In first-class cricket, Graham amassed 44,841 runs at 49.11, including 128 centuries – the best being his 333 in the Lord's Test of 1990 against India. He was an opener that loved to drive the ball, especially through mid-on, and a player who thrived on a challenge, whether against the quickest bowlers, the best spinners, in a run-chase situation or maybe saving a game.

* * * * *

DARREN GOUGH'S XI

All of my players, with the exception of Boycott, took the attack to the opposition and made things happen. That's nothing against Geoffrey; the reason he still gets in is that you need balance in a side. The fact he's from Yorkshire also helps! I considered Imran Khan because of the great things he did for Pakistan; Murali, but he's not as strong a character as Shane Warne; Brian Lara, a genius but I couldn't find room; Glenn McGrath, but he misses out to Lillee; Waqar Younis, whom I almost picked but opted for his strike partner Wasim Akram instead; Allan Donald, for his blistering pace, and Fred Trueman, for what he achieved as a whole-hearted pace bowler.

1) Geoffrey Boycott
I've got to have a Yorkshireman in there. If I wanted anyone to bat for my life it would be Geoffrey. He got a lot of stick for the way he batted but most of it was unfair because he scored so many runs for his country. He's a terrific character and I'm a huge fan of the way he batted and of him as a person.

2) Sachin Tendulkar
He doesn't get in the team in the middle-order but his technique is good enough for him to open, and it was the only way I could get him in. He has scored runs all around the world against pace and spin and out of the present-day batsmen he would be the best, though Lara runs him close. I found that the main difference between the two of them was on a flat wicket; you just felt helpless against Sachin and could not see how you would get him out. You would always want a bit in the wicket when bowling to him.

3) Donald Bradman
Anybody who averages 99 in Test cricket cannot be left out. The way he's remembered for his greatness and knowledge and how everybody speaks so highly of him is proof that he was something special. Nobody will ever achieve what he did again.

4) Vivian Richards
The next four are players who I would be happy to pay to watch and see them entertain. What Viv did for the game was amazing. He had such unbelievable confidence in his own ability and rightly so, because he could smash any bowling attack on any day. He was also a useful off-spinner and slip fielder. I got him out a couple of times when he played for

Glamorgan – bowled and leg-before – but I'm honest enough to admit that he was at the end of his career.

5) Garfield Sobers
I didn't really see him play but anybody that could score 365 in a Test innings as well as hit six sixes in an over, and bowl left-arm spin or seam, must have been a remarkable talent.

6) Ian Botham
Beefy was my hero. Watching what he did in the Ashes in '81 when I was just 11 was enough to make me follow the game. A terrific cricketer with bat or ball; he was a partnership breaker with the ball and a heartbreaker with the bat. I played against him once when he was with Durham but I didn't bowl at him.

7) Adam Gilchrist
If you asked me for the best wicketkeeper of all time I would say Alan Knott, but as batting is a huge part of the game nowadays I had to go for Gilchrist. He opened the batting in one-dayers and batted seven in Tests, which is a crucial position. You think you're into the tail when you have five wickets, but I've forgotten the number of times he came in and smashed a hundred. He would take matches away from teams; it's always a challenge bowling at him.

8) Shane Warne
This guy has changed the face of world cricket and must be given credit for what he has done for the game. Anywhere you go in the world, kids are running in and trying to bowl like him. People copy his earring, his fashion sense, his haircut; Warney just has a charisma that has been a breath of fresh air for the game. He's a good friend of mine and another one of my cricket heroes, who all tend to be guys who can change a game with a spark of brilliance.

9) Malcolm Marshall
The fact that I have chosen Marshall instead of any of his great teammates like Croft, Holding, Roberts, Garner, Walsh or Ambrose, shows how highly I rate him. I played against him when I was at the start of my career and it was an education to see him swing the ball both ways at 90 mph. He impressed me greatly; not many people can swing the ball both ways at that speed.

10) Wasim Akram
He remains the king of reverse swing. Actually I also considered Waqar Younis and there was not much between the two of them, but the fact that Wasim was a left-armer just gives the team something different. He was another, like Marshall, who could swing the ball both ways and at speed.

11) Dennis Lillee

It was very close between him and Glenn McGrath but because I played against Glenn throughout my career it probably takes the mystery element away as far as he's concerned. The images of Lillee running in with his head band on and hair flowing and shirt open are still fresh in my mind and he was another character who influenced me to take up cricket as a lad.

DARREN GOUGH played 58 Test matches for England from 1994 to 2003 and claimed 229 wickets at an average of 28.39. The right-arm paceman was renowned for his commitment and whole-heartedness, which his captains always appreciated. He swung the ball away from the right-hander expertly, while his in-swinging yorker was one of his most dangerous deliveries, particularly early in his career.

* * * * *

TOM GRAVENEY'S XI

I picked a side from players I played with and against, obviously at a time when they were all at their best. Sadly I had to leave out some great cricketers such as Arthur Morris, Fred Trueman, Brian Statham, Peter May, Mike Procter, Graeme Pollock and Alan Davidson.

1) Leonard Hutton

The best of the lot. The main job of any opener is to lay the foundations for an innings and it was a job that Len did better than anybody else. The fact he averaged 56.67 in his 79 Tests provides all the evidence that is necessary to prove his remarkable consistency.

2) Frank Worrell

Although usually a middle-order player, he opened in 1957 against us and he scored a big hundred (191 not out). He was a great player, who could also bowl useful medium pace too.

3) Neil Harvey

One of the finest left-handers ever and also a great fielder. I remember him scoring 92 not out against us in Sydney in 1954–55. It was a glittering performance, made all the more memorable because his teammates were getting into all sorts of trouble against Frank Tyson, who bowled faster than anybody I have ever seen. He was the only Australian batsman who offered any resistance, but he ran out of partners before he could reach a deserved ton.

4) Denis Compton

A batting genius. There's not much more that I can say: he was pure class and his place in this side is guaranteed.

5) Everton Weekes

A real terrific player, especially coming in at number five. I saw a lot of him on England's 1953–54 tour of the West Indies and he was quite superb.

6) Garfield Sobers

Simply the greatest all-rounder ever. I find it hard to believe that there will ever be a better all-round cricketer than Garry.

7) Keith Miller

There was never a dull moment when Keith was involved, whether as bowler or batsman. 'Nugget' was a fine all-rounder who is up there just below Sobers as the best all-rounder of all time. As a bowler, he was best when partnered by Ray Lindwall.

8) Ray Lindwall

My best new-ball bowler. For me, Ray Lindwall is the world's number one fast bowler of the post-war era. He had genuine pace and even when at top speed had full control of the ball. He was always beautifully balanced at delivery, could swing the ball both ways and was a marvellously competitive player. He was a determined but sporting opponent who went about his job without fuss.

9) Godfrey Evans

Just brilliant; he was never down. He was a great man to have in your team. For sheer exuberance, enthusiasm and match-winning brilliance, Godders was a one-off. They threw away the mould when they made this man. He was acrobatic, extremely agile and he kept all his teammates on their toes with his competitive drive and good humour. He was, for me, the tops as a keeper.

10) Jim Laker

A superb off-spinner. Jim's 19 wickets for 90 runs in the 1956 Old Trafford Test against the Australians will stand for all time as a monument to his genius. He was the greatest off-spinner of them all: model action; made the ball turn sharply and was deadly accurate.

11) Derek Underwood

He was almost unplayable on a helpful pitch. Derek was fittingly nicknamed 'Deadly' because of his uncanny accuracy. He could stifle the most adventurous batsmen on good wickets and trick the finest technicians on any surface that offered him any encouragement. He would be my number one left-arm spinner of all time.

TOM GRAVENEY played 79 Tests for England between 1951 and 1969 and scored 4,882 runs at an average of 44.38, even though he was not always in favour with the selectors. In first-class cricket he scored 47,793 runs at 44.92, including 122 centuries. Tom was the first player to score 30,000 runs and 100 centuries in purely post-war cricket.

GORDON GREENIDGE'S XI

I opted for a balanced side that has been injury-free consistently. I was reluctant to pick players I have not seen myself, though I've huge respect for the achievements of people like Don Bradman, George Headley, Everton Weekes and Clyde Walcott, who all played before my time. It's a pity I can't pick 20 players – there are so many greats to pick from. Those not in my team shouldn't feel slighted. I'm sure they will feature in many other sides in the book. Those who came close were: Hadlee, Garner, Roberts, Holding, Walsh, McGrath, Ambrose, Botham, Greg Chappell, Barry Richards, Imran Khan, Kapil Dev, Miandad and Donald, and Boycott and Redpath, who were not exciting but you had to admire their technique and determination.

1) Sunil Gavaskar
A great accumulator. He had great patience in his batting and he could be stubborn at the crease. Not being one of the most robust players, and because of his height, he was well suited to opening.

2) Desmond Haynes
A player who preferred to dominate. He looked to set the pace of how he wanted to play and in doing so he was quite forceful in his approach.

3) Allan Border
A player, like Gavaskar, who you didn't really associate with big hitting; but when you looked up at the scoreboard when he was at the crease, he'd often have 30 or 40 to his name and it was difficult to remember an attacking shot that he had played. He wasn't a big puller or cutter, he worked the ball around very well.

4) Viv Richards
Well, what can I say? Viv was a player who always punished anything wayward. And even good bowling could have a similar result. He really was a dominator of the game. He liked to take the game forward. Viv was never afraid to play his own game as he knew that in order for him to dominate a match, he had to play his own positive way, whether batting, bowling, fielding or as captain.

5) Garfield Sobers
A terrific player who I didn't see enough of sadly; probably the greatest all-rounder ever. Like Viv, when Sobers was playing, the game never drifted along. He always excited people. When he came in to bat there was always a feeling of anticipation and you felt something great was about to happen – he brought the game to life. Another aspect I loved about playing with him in my early days with Barbados was the knowledge he gave you. I would sit in the dressing room when he talked cricket, along with people like Clyde Walcott, Everton Weekes and Conrad Hunte, and I would just marvel at what they had to say. You dare not speak while they were talking cricket. These were enlightening

and gratifying times for me, I don't know if that happens today but I would hope so for the sake of the young players.

6) Clive Lloyd
Clive was a tremendous father figure to us when he captained the West Indies. He knew how to handle us all and how to get the best out of everyone. As a batsman, he was another dominating figure. When he came to the crease fielders took five steps back. If you can imagine this 6ft 5in guy carrying a 3lb bat, when he struck that cricket ball, it flew; he was such a powerful player and an accomplished all-round cricketer. He was an excellent fielder who may not have dived around like they do today, but he made tough stops look easy.

7) Shaun Pollock
He would fit in well. He performed superbly well in Test cricket and is maybe South Africa's greatest-ever bowler. It was close between him, Botham, Hadlee, Kapil and particularly Imran, but as second-change bowler and as a hard-hitting batsman he gets the vote.

8) Alan Knott
He would have to be the greatest keeper I have ever seen. Although, when I came into county cricket I thought Roy Swetman was unbelievable: Hampshire were playing Gloucestershire and I saw him stump Barry Richards off a full toss down the leg side – he was one of the quickest keepers I'd ever seen. However, Knotty was even better. He kept brilliantly to pace and spin – particularly Derek Underwood, though they had the advantage of gaining an understanding at Kent. Knotty was also a very useful batsman who got runs when his team really needed them.

9) Malcolm Marshall
It was a very difficult choice between him and all the other great West Indian quicks of that era. Malcolm was always at the batsman, whether he was changing his field or changing his line. He always thought deeply about dismissing the batsman.

10) Shane Warne
Leg-break bowling is an art. We had people like Qadir and Hirwani who were great exponents, but I think Warney took it to new heights. He had his shoulder problems, but I feel that as long as he was fit he was always a very difficult customer for batting sides.

11) Dennis Lillee
I'm not selecting him because he was my biggest downfall in my career, I just feel that Dennis, along with Michael Holding, had the best action that a fast bowler could ask for: he was so rhythmic from his run-up through to his follow-through. As an opponent, I always looked at him and admired.

GORDON GREENIDGE played 108 Tests for the West Indies between 1974–75 and 1990–91, scoring 7,558 runs at an average of 44.72. In first-class cricket he amassed 37,354 runs at 45.88 – the most by a West Indian. Gordon was a destructive batsman in Test cricket, but immensely stylish and technically sound at the same time. He and Desmond Haynes shared the record in Tests for the most runs as an opening partnership. From 1970 to 1987 he loyally represented Hampshire in county cricket.

* * * * *

CHARLIE GRIFFITH'S XI

I felt the only way that I could choose a World XI was from those who I played with and against in my career and still I've had to leave out some great talent, such as: Ted Dexter, Colin Cowdrey, Tom Graveney, Bobby Simpson, Fred Trueman, Brian Statham, Alan Knott, Keith Andrew – who I cannot believe only played two Test matches, he was a victim of poor selection in my view – Intikhab Alam – who was a useful leggie, Graeme Pollock – you could tell he had everything as a batsman but he never played that much Test cricket, and Colin Bland, whom I saw in Australia. In fact, I was overwhelmed by Bland's fielding; he was incredible when throwing at the stumps. Obviously, there are greats such as Headley, Bradman and Viv Richards, but I have stuck to my policy of only picking those that played during my career.

1) Conrad Hunte
He played for the West Indies when we didn't have a solid batsman and when we used to go through the motions a little. Connie then changed his game and became a less flamboyant player for the sake of the team. He really was a solid and dependable batsman for us.

2) Bill Lawry
He was one of the most difficult batsman to dislodge that I ever bowled to. He never gave you a chance; he was so dependable. In fact I've never seen a better judge of a ball than Bill Lawry; he rarely played the wrong shot.

3) Ian Chappell
Another very reliable player who played good strokes all round the wicket, though he probably preferred it on his legs. He was solid but was never afraid to play his shots.

4) Everton Weekes
He was unbelievable. I was fortunate to play with him at the start of my career when he was captain of Barbados, and he guided me while I was young. I could soon see why he was called the 'Little Maestro'. I have a lot of time for this man.

5) Ken Barrington
Not everyone appreciated the way he batted, but I just thought that Kenny was such a solid player, and someone who I would always want in my team. He was certainly not

the kind of flamboyant batsman who I would take my son to watch, but he was so dependable. He would get to a hundred and you would struggle to remember one of his shots – he was a nudger of the ball, a steady accumulator. I rate Ted Dexter as a better attacking player, but he wasn't as consistent as Kenny.

6) Garfield Sobers
I played with Garry for Barbados and the West Indies and he's a real knowledgeable chap, a great batsman and a very good left-arm bowler. There was certainly no better all-rounder than Garry during my time, possibly ever.

7) Wally Grout
A very good keeper. It was close between him and Jackie Hendriks, because I thought they were both excellent keeping to pace and to spin. I saw Wally take a magnificent catch down the leg side once off an inside edge, which has always stayed with me, and anybody that pulls off that sort of catch has to be a little special.

8) Graham McKenzie
Better known as Garth; he played for Australia when they were in transition and because of this he never got the recognition that he deserved. Whenever I played against him, I was always very impressed with him. He really thought about what he was trying to do; he was quite sharp and was a very dependable bowler for Australia, shown clearly in his record (246 Test wickets).

9) Wes Hall
It's hard to find words to describe Wes. We were a partnership and are still very close friends now. He had carried the West Indies' pace bowling responsibilities for a long time before I came into the side. In 1960–61 in Australia he was the only genuine fast bowler on the trip. Wes had a beautiful action, was very fast and always fully committed.

10) Lance Gibbs
Lancelot was the best slow bowler or off-spinner that I ever played with or against. The only one who came close was Prasanna of India. I would like youngsters to emulate Lance because he worked very hard at his game, and was a very hard taskmaster, but has the results to show for his efforts. He was also a fine gully fielder.

11) Bhagwath Chandrasekhar
The mystery man! I remember playing against him in India and we were always wondering what he was going to bowl next. He was so unorthodox as leg-spinners go that he would bowl bouncers. My teammates used to talk a lot about him and say how much they struggled to pick him. I think we came to the conclusion that it was best to play for his googly, as he didn't turn his leggie that much.

CHARLIE GRIFFITH played 28 Tests for the West Indies between 1959–60 and 1968–69, taking 94 wickets at 28.54. In first-class cricket he claimed 332 wickets at 21.60. Charlie was one of the fastest and most fearsome quick bowlers of his era, famous for the opening partnership he shared with fellow Barbadian, Wes Hall. On tour in England in 1963 he took 119 wickets at 12.83, including a career best eight for 23 against Gloucestershire.

✳ ✳ ✳ ✳ ✳

SUBHASH GUPTE'S XI

I have selected my side from players I know from my own era, with the exception of Gavaskar and Knott. Sobers was the best of the lot bar none, while I cannot see a better new-ball attack than Lindwall and Miller. This team has everything: reliability and solidity in the shape of Sunny, Hanif and Rohan, mixed with the flair of Weekes, Garry, Peter May and Frank Worrell.

1) **Sunil Gavaskar,** 2) **Hanif Mohammed,** 3) **Rohan Kanhai,** 4) **Peter May,** 5) **Everton Weekes,** 6) **Frank Worrell,** 7) **Garfield Sobers,** 8) **Keith Miller,** 9) **Alan Knott,** 10) **Ray Lindwall,** 11) **Jim Laker**

SUBHASH GUPTE played 36 Tests for India between 1951–52 and 1961–62, taking 149 wickets at an average of 29.55. In total he gleaned 530 first-class wickets at 23.71. Gupte, nicknamed 'Fergie', is regarded as the best exponent of leg-spin of all time by West Indies great Sir Garfield Sobers. He was the first Indian to take all 10 wickets in a first-class innings when he achieved figures of 10 for 78 for Bombay against Pakistan Services in 1954–55. He also claimed nine for 102 against the West Indies at Kanpur in 1958–59.

[This team was received before Subhash passed away in 2002]

✳ ✳ ✳ ✳ ✳

SIR RICHARD HADLEE'S XI

World XIs are purely subjective. Players' fitness and expectations have changed dramatically from the early 1900s. My team mainly comes over a 40-year period from when I was able to watch the game and when I got involved as a player.

1) Jack Hobbs

Statistically he's one of the best batsmen the game has produced. Sir Jack played from 1905 to 1934, but through seeing film footage and talking to people, I was able to learn about his play. He scored 197 first-class centuries, the most by anyone in the history of the game, and many of his innings were played on uncovered pitches, so he therefore he had to adapt to all sorts of playing conditions.

2) Barry Richards

Barry was one of the most talented and gifted batsmen who could play every shot in the book, was a natural timer and had limited Test experience simply because of the South African isolation problem. His highlight was scoring a magnificent 356 for South Australia and that innings was described as 'Divine Inspiration'. He's one of the great batsmen of all time.

3) Donald Bradman

What can you say about this man that hasn't already been said? He averaged 99.94 and scored 29 Test centuries, which is phenomenal for the time he played in, and he was recognised with a knighthood for his outstanding contribution and services to the game. Analysts say that he saw the ball quicker than any other batsman. He had all the shots but the key statistic to show how good 'the Don' was, is that he scored a century every three innings.

4) Viv Richards

I looked at Graeme Pollock, who's probably the greatest left-hander the game has ever seen, but Sir Vivian got my vote because he was physically imposing with a build similar to a heavyweight boxer. He intimidated bowlers with his sheer presence: muscular, athletic, had that swagger when he walked out to bat and sometimes he'd hit his first ball for four, which would unsettle bowlers. He was the key wicket to take in the 1970s and 1980s and possibly the hardest hitter of the ball in the history of the game.

5) Sachin Tendulkar

Without doubt today's batting genius and in many ways likened to Bradman. You'd have to say Sachin is the maestro of batsmanship. He's a very powerful hitter, an attacking and often explosive batsman, but still very elegant in his execution of shots and a delight to watch. He's never afraid to hit the ball in the air, which is a sign of confidence that he can get to the pitch of the ball. He's likely to keep all batting records in Test and one-day cricket.

6) Garfield Sobers

Sir Garfield would have to be the best all-rounder in the history of the game and his left-handed batting would give the line up something different. He was a natural timer of the ball with all the shots: cuts, pulls, hooks and had the ability to be dynamic and explosive with sheer brilliance. He was a lively new ball swing bowler and if conditions suited, he could bowl left-arm orthodox spin. Add his athletic fielding and superb close-in catching, is there anyone better?

7) Ian Botham

I looked at Imran Khan, who was a wonderful all-rounder. Kapil Dev was another, so too was Australia's Keith Miller, but I've gone for Ian Botham, which may be a little controversial. However, Beefy was one of those players that made things happen either with the bat or with the ball. He dominated the 1980s with his all-round play, especially against the old enemy Australia, simply because he took on the challenges and he inspired his teammates to greater things and at times single-handedly won matches for his country. He was knighted for services to English cricket and supporting charities.

8) Alan Knott

He was athletic like a jack-in-the-box: quick, acrobatic and efficient behind the stumps, often brilliant. Half-chances were invariably dismissals. He was a perfectionist and performed a wonderful partnership with Derek Underwood. He could bat as well, with five Test centuries. Was effective against fast bowling and actually blunted Lillee and Thomson, which is no mean feat.

9) Fred Trueman

One of the great characters of the game. He was an aggressive bowler with a magnificent, fluent, side-on technique and he had the ability to bowl superb out-swingers at pace. He showed a lot of courage, got through a lot of work and he was the first man to capture 300 Test wickets and set the benchmark for others to follow.

10) Shane Warne

The most successful leg-spin bowler of all time and arguably the greatest spinner in the history of the game with over 700 test wickets. He flighted the ball, then spun it with the leggie, 'googly' and then he used the 'flipper' to deceive the batsman – he dismissed many of the world's greatest batsmen and helped win many games for Australia. He was always entertaining and it was a delight to watch him weave his magic and set batsmen up for the 'kill'.

11) Dennis Lillee

The greatest fast bowler of all time. Having played against him, I'm able to say how big, strong, aggressive and confident he was, with a magnificent approach to the wicket, gathering pace. He had a tremendous side-on action and bowled at about 90 mph. He had all the skills, pace and was a clever bowler who got wickets. His tally of 355 wickets was once the most by anyone in Tests.

SIR RICHARD HADLEE played 86 Tests for New Zealand between 1972–73 and 1990, taking 431 wickets at an average of 22.29 and scoring 3,124 runs at 27.16. Richard was one of four great Test all-rounders in his era along with Imran Khan, Kapil Dev and Ian Botham. He once held the record for most Test wickets until Kapil surpassed him. One of the best and most intelligent fast bowlers of his generation, he gleaned 1,490 wickets in first-class cricket at 18.11, through his ability to cut and swing the ball – he also captured five wickets in an innings on 102 occasions.

HANIF MOHAMMED'S XI

It's a matter of honour for me to be asked to contribute my World XI to a book encompassing so many great players.

1) Sunil Gavaskar

Truly a great batsman. His appetite for three figure scores was such that at one stage he had 20 centuries from 50 Tests. Nobody served India better; whenever India desperately needed runs, Gavaskar produced them. After retiring he joined the electronic media and I regard him as a shrewd expert in the game.

2) Leonard Hutton

One of the all time greats. Technically, Len Hutton was the most correct and sound batsman and a model of concentration. Despite a shoulder injury sustained in the war, which resulted in his left arm being two inches shorter, this batsman demonstrated his mastery over all types of bowling on all types of wickets.

3) Donald Bradman

Sir Don was undoubtedly the greatest ever batsman from any generation. No one played cricket as dominantly as him. His unparalleled record speaks for itself. Along with Sobers, he could walk in to any team of any era.

4) Viv Richards

A player who dominated cricket almost as much as Bradman. A master blaster of any attack, Richards had an uncanny ability to see the ball early and despatch it to any corner he desired. He was a man for the big occasion and the more formidable the opposition, the more formidable he became.

5) Garfield Sobers

The best player I ever played with or against. He was a four-in-one package of excellence. As a batsman he was sheer grace, as a new ball bowler he was very hostile in his first few overs, also a useful left-arm orthodox leg break, chinaman and googly bowler, and an excellent close-in fielder. There hasn't been another cricketer of comparable greatness to Garry Sobers.

6) Imran Khan

Imran was the most charismatic and charming personality of his generation. He was an all-round cricketer of the highest calibre: a very dependable batsman who could make it into a Test team on his batting alone. He was an exceptionally talented fast bowler whose devastating deliveries could destroy any batting line up. As a captain he was bold, daring and was always at the helm of team affairs. He was a source of inspiration on and off the field for so many people.

7) Godfrey Evans

The best wicketkeeper England has ever had. Despite being bulky he used to make diving stops and astonished spectators by snapping up catches on both sides of the wicket. Evans was also a more than useful batsman in the lower order. He was a jovial personality who always gave his team 100 per cent and his presence behind the wicket was an inspiration to his teammates.

8) Shane Warne

A leg-spin sensation. Shane Warne is the greatest leg-spinner of any era and a captain's dream. Shane is a very clever bowler who can mesmerise even the finest batsmen in the world. Batsmen find him difficult to cope with as his line of attack is usually outside the leg stump and his top spinners and flippers were almost unplayable. His googly made him an even greater challenge. Shane has been marvellous for cricket and has brought a new dimension to the art of spin bowling.

9) Fred Trueman

He was genuinely fast and certainly one of the finest bowlers of all time. His action and run-up to the wicket were beautiful and he always maintained a nagging line and length. A larger than life character, Trueman had an innate ability to bother a batsman with his aggressive attitude.

10) Dennis Lillee

One of the most complete and destructive fast bowlers, with a beautiful run-up and action. His hostility posed problems for the world's best batsmen – even the most technically correct. He and Jeff Thomson were the most fearsome bowling pair of any era.

11) Jim Laker

Cricket records are meant to be broken, but one that I think will remain unparalleled is Laker's 19 wickets against Australia at Old Trafford in 1956. He was a world-class spinner who had a lot of variation and, along with Tony Lock, formed a formidable spin partnership for Surrey and England. He was also a very decent gentleman and after retirement I felt that he was an excellent commentator.

HANIF MOHAMMED played 55 Tests for Pakistan between 1952–53 and 1969–70, scoring 3,915 runs at an average of 43.98. In first-class cricket he amassed 17,059 runs at 52.32. Hanif played in Pakistan's first Test match in 1952–53 against India, becoming one of the nation's earliest cricket legends. He was the first Pakistan batsman to register 1,000, 2,000 and 3,000 Test runs. In 1957–58, he scored 337 to save a Test against the West Indies in Barbados, which was the longest-ever Test innings. A year later, he made the then highest first-class score of 499.

NEIL HARVEY'S XI

I selected a side from players I have seen, either as spectator, player or selector. It wasn't easy and I must mention a few players who came close to selection: Peter May; Graeme Pollock; Viv Richards; Everton Weekes; Dennis Lillee – who was unlucky to be up against Lindwall; Andy Roberts; Alan Davidson and Hugh Tayfield – who I thought was better than Jim Laker on all types of wickets.

1) Leonard Hutton
He had the best technique for a batsman that I have ever seen. His record is tremendous and he achieved it while batting on uncovered wickets, which is why I haven't gone for too many of the modern guys because they've always played on covered pitches.

2) Arthur Morris
I think we had the best opening pair in 1948 that anybody could have had in the world, with Arthur and Sid Barnes. Arthur was a great opener who gave us a start on so many occasions.

3) Donald Bradman
The best cricketer the world has ever seen. He was a freak. His reflexes and his ability to pick up the line and length of the ball early were far superior to any other batsman I have known.

4) Denis Compton
For me, he was the pick of the three best English players I've seen – with Peter May and Hutton the others. Those two hundreds he scored against us in 1948 were two of the best knocks I've ever seen (184 at Nottingham and 145 not out at Manchester.) After his innings at Trent Bridge I thought he must have the broadest bat around.

5) Sachin Tendulkar
The best of the modern-day players. I went to Madras in 1998 to see Australia and the way Tendulkar tore in to a quality bowler like Warne during that match will stay in my mind for a long time. His record has held up all round the world as a top-class batsman, which is another significant reason for his selection here.

6) Garfield Sobers
The best all-rounder I have ever seen in my life. He could annihilate any bowler, was a good left-arm seamer, a great fielder and could also bowl his spinners.

7) Keith Miller
The second best all-rounder I have ever seen, almost the same as Sobers, but not quite. He is certainly Australia's best all-round cricketer ever. He never made as many runs as he should have – I think batting became a little too easy for him at times. While bowling wasn't something he enjoyed that much, he was still a magnificent bowler and could be as fast as anyone on his day.

8) Shane Warne

The best spin bowler I have ever seen. Bill O'Reilly must have been something special, but I never saw enough of him to pick him. Shane's record of over 700 wickets proves that he has been a tremendous bowler over the years and he has entertained a great deal.

9) Ray Lindwall

I rate him as the best fast bowler ever. He wasn't the quickest – that would be Wes Hall, Frank Tyson or Fred Trueman – but certainly the most skilful and most accurate. During his whole career he was brilliant. If he said he was going to bowl a yorker, it was a yorker; you'd never see a full toss or anything else. His stock ball was the out-swinger, but as he got older he developed a very good in-swinger.

10) Don Tallon

An absolute genius behind the stumps, probably the quickest keeper ever. I remember a catch he took at Lord's in 1948 to dismiss Cyril Washbrook from a full toss off Ernie Toshack – it was an unbelievable catch. His catch at the Oval though, to dismiss Len Hutton, was even better. Ray Lindwall bowled one down leg and I was moving round to field what I expected to be a leg glance. But when I looked up, Don had the ball in his left hand. Anybody that is capable of making a catch like that has to be pretty good in my mind.

11) Michael Holding

According to the blokes that played against him, he was the best of the great West Indian quickies, and there were a few of them. He looked a great bowler as well, but I'm going on what I heard from those who faced him. He would open the bowling with Lindwall.

NEIL HARVEY played 79 Test matches for Australia between 1947–48 and 1962–63 scoring 6,149 runs at an average of 48.41. In first-class matches he compiled 21,699 runs at 50.93. Neil is one of the greatest left-handed batsmen of all time, along with the likes of Sobers, Lara, Border, Lloyd and Graeme Pollock. His 834 runs against South Africa in the 1952–53 rubber was the fourth-best series aggregate in Tests.

* * * * *

VIJAY HAZARE'S XI

I've chosen Don Bradman as captain and Sunil Gavaskar as his vice-captain. If required, Jonty Rhodes would be 12th man for his incredible fielding displays.

1) Sunil Gavaskar, 2) Sachin Tendulkar, 3) Donald Bradman, 4) Brian Lara, 5) Javed Miandad, 6) Kapil Dev, 7) Richard Hadlee, 8) Ian Healy, 9) Shane Warne, 10) Allan Donald, 11) Erapalli Prasanna

VIJAY HAZARE played 30 Tests for India between 1946 and 1952–53 and scored 2,192 runs at an average of 47.65. In first-class cricket he scored 18,635 runs at 57.87 and took 592 wickets at 24.49. He's one of his country's greatest-ever batsmen and arguably *the* best Indian player of his era. His fourth-wicket partnership of 577 with Gul Mahomed in 1946–47 was the highest ever partnership in all first-class cricket.

[This team was received before Vijay passed away in 2004]

IAN HEALY'S XI

I attempted to give a spread between countries and eras from statistics (which are all rather good!) and player comments. For example, Sir Donald Bradman and the 1948 team rated Don Tallon as the best wicketkeeper they've ever seen. I don't know too much about Ken Barrington, but I wanted a gritty Englishman in the top order and he's spoken of very well. Trueman edges out Hadlee as the extra seamer in the squad if I wanted to play a four-man front-line seam attack. Fred's aggression would compliment Lillee's skill and Marshall and Miller's explosion of pace. I've had to leave out so many greats, especially Australian ones like Allan Border, Ian and Greg Chappell, Adam Gilchrist and Glenn McGrath, but what can you do?

1) **Sunil Gavaskar, 2) Sachin Tendulkar, 3) Donald Bradman, 4) Ken Barrington, 5) Viv Richards, 6) Garfield Sobers, 7) Keith Miller, 8) Shane Warne, 9) Don Tallon, 10) Malcolm Marshall, 11) Dennis Lillee**

IAN HEALY played 119 Tests for Australia between 1988–89 and 1998–99. He claimed a then world record 395 dismissals as wicketkeeper, with 366 catches and 29 stumpings. Healy's imposing haul exceeded the 355 dismissals by previous record holder and fellow countryman Rod Marsh. He scored 4,356 Test runs at an average of 27.39, including four hundreds. Healy formed an impressive partnership with leg-spinning great Shane Warne, as the two seemingly had a telepathic understanding.

* * * * *

MICHAEL HOLDING'S XI

I don't like to compare players from different eras so I just selected my team from people that I played against – the only way I could make such a selection. I omitted West Indies players because there are likely to be a lot of them and therefore people may accuse me of bias.

1) Sunil Gavaskar

He had an excellent technique. On bouncy wickets – because of his height – you had a better chance of getting him out, but if there wasn't any bounce you were pretty much helpless because sideways movement just didn't bother him at all.

2) Geoffrey Boycott

He would only play at balls that he thought he had a high percentage of getting runs from. If you bowled him one where the percentage was not in his favour, he didn't play at it.

3) Zaheer Abbas

I didn't play *Test* cricket against Zaheer, but every time I saw him he always looked very sound and got the ball away without too much trouble.

4) Greg Chappell

Again, very technically sound and he played in the 'V' for most of his innings. With him being a very tall and elegant batsman, he didn't have too many problems with bounce against our quicks.

5) David Gower

Gower was one of those guys who, you always felt, gave you an excellent chance of getting him out; but when you look back you realise he wasn't as easy to get out as you thought. He was elegant and had an excellent repertoire of strokes.

6) Allan Border

Very stubborn and gritty with a sound technique as well. He would play some shots when the percentages were not with him but at the same time nothing would ever faze him. When you beat him with a ball or when he played a bad stroke, you would still not feel that you were at an advantage. Although his game was to spend a lot of time at the crease like Geoffrey Boycott, it was never boring bowling to him like it could be when bowling to Boycott.

7) Alan Knott

Very sure-handed. I hardly ever saw him drop a catch. He was as good standing up to the spinners as he was standing back to the quicks. Just by watching him keep to people like Derek Underwood on a wet wicket, you could see what a great keeper he was. I saw him more towards the latter stage of his career but he was still great.

8) Imran Khan

He was a highly talented all-rounder. A great fast bowler and a top-class batsman who timed the ball very well, and also a great athlete when in the field. He could have made this team as either a batsman or a bowler.

9) Richard Hadlee

Had great control and moved the ball in both directions. Wasn't express in pace but quick enough to cause batsmen problems. Had a great strike rate and he didn't have to bowl too many overs to take wickets. Considering he never had another high-class bowler at the other end to keep the pressure on, it makes his achievements all the more impressive.

10) Dennis Lillee

He had everything a fast bowler could possibly want – pace, control, combative spirit, was always looking for whatever advantage he could gain over the batsman, great strike rate, great action and was a real strong character.

11) Abdul Qadir

A great leg-spinner who had very good control. One of the finest leg-spinners I saw who could put the ball where he wanted. He had good variety and could bowl big leg-breaks, small leg-breaks, googlies and top spinners. I don't like to compare but his variety was as good as Shane Warne's, maybe better. Control was his main asset, which is so important for leg-spinners. You can't set attacking fields if he's not putting the ball where he should be.

MICHAEL HOLDING played 60 Tests for the West Indies between 1975–76 and 1986–87, taking 249 wickets at an average of 23.68. He is widely regarded as one of the quickest bowlers that ever played, and with the most rhythmic, smooth action – hence his nickname 'Whispering Death'. Along with Roberts, Garner, Croft and Marshall, Michael contributed significantly to one of the most fearsome bowling attacks in Test history.

* * * * *

MERV HUGHES'S XI

With the exception of Bradman, I have selected my team from players I have seen myself. Making up the 12, and unlucky not to be in the team, is Richie Richardson: he was completely unflappable as a batsman and nothing you ever did would ever seem to worry him. My weapon was obviously the short ball but he loved that and would take you on and take you down. Richie scored at a good pace and when he got going he was just about impossible to put the brakes on.

1) Gordon Greenidge

I thought that he was a fantastic cricketer, who shared a terrific pairing with Desmond Haynes because of reasons such as running together and the ability to play off each other, as well as what he did himself as an opening batsman.

2) Sunil Gavaskar

Just for the sheer volume of runs that he scored in Test cricket.

3) Viv Richards

He was awesome. His power-hitting was intimidating and he is probably the hardest hitter that I ever bowled to. I was lucky, or unlucky enough, to come into Test cricket as he was starting to go out. In the Barbados Test in 1991, he was batting to set up a declaration and he flat-batted me down the ground and nearly killed me! It was going at a million miles an hour. I really did find him intimidating the first few times that I played against him because I just felt that he did not have a weakness at all. He was the master.

4) Don Bradman
Simply the greatest batsman of all time. There is very little that I can add, or need to add, to justify this selection.

5) Clive Lloyd
For his tremendous record as batsman and captain of that great West Indies team.

6) Allan Border
A great batsman who led by example. He was a real tough captain and we responded to him as a team.

7) Imran Khan
A tremendous fast bowler who was more than useful with the bat as well.

8) Adam Gilchrist
He changed the game. He came into the Australian team as a wicketkeeper but could eventually have played as a batsman alone because he had the ability to win games off his own bat. A quite amazing player. Pre-Gilchrist I would have gone for Rodney Marsh, as he *and* Ian Healy were superb glove-men, but Gilchrist has to be in.

9) Richard Hadlee
An excellent fast bowler who had a great variety of deliveries.

10) Shane Warne
The best spin bowler that I have ever seen.

11) Dennis Lillee
Another fantastic fast bowler who had tremendous determination and skill.

MERV HUGHES played 53 Test matches for Australia between 1985–86 and 1993–94 and took 212 wickets at an average of 28.38. He was a whole-hearted and immensely competitive fast bowler who always gave his captain, Allan Border, every ounce of energy he had. Merv was also a great character who entertained crowds all round the world.

✳ ✳ ✳ ✳ ✳

CONRAD HUNTE'S XI

Here is my Greatest XI. I have chosen mostly from cricketers that I have seen and those with the most impressive records.

1) Sunil Gavaskar
He was the highest run-scorer in Test cricket for so long and was the first to 10,000 runs and finished with a healthy average of 51.12. He scored a lot of his runs against the much-feared West Indies four-pronged pace attack.

2) Gordon Greenidge

Another great record and he scored 19 Test match centuries. He was one half of the most successful opening partnership in Test history (with Desmond Haynes).

3) Donald Bradman

The greatest batsman ever in my view with an average of 99.94. There cannot be any question about his place in the side. He scored 29 Test centuries in just 52 matches. He would be captain.

4) Viv Richards

The greatest batsman of recent times with a great record: he scored the most runs in Test cricket by a West Indian (before Brian Lara) with 8,540 at 50.23 with 24 centuries. That's some record.

5) Garfield Sobers

The greatest cricketer that has ever played the game with skills of excellence in every aspect of the game. With 8,032 Test runs at 57.78 and a highest score of 365, he is one of the greatest batsmen ever, never mind just all-rounders.

6) Richard Hadlee

With 431 Test match wickets, his record proves what a fantastic fast bowler he was and one who spearheaded his country's bowling attack almost single-handedly.

7) Alan Knott

The best wicketkeeper I ever saw and also a useful batsman who scored over 4,000 runs in Tests.

8) Wasim Akram

A great left-arm quick bowler with all the tricks that a fast bowler requires to succeed at the highest level, which he has done marvellously well.

9) Malcolm Marshall

The greatest of all the great West Indian quicks of recent times. A very intelligent cricketer who thought about his approach to bowling a great deal. His 376 Test wickets at 20.94 prove his class.

10) Shane Warne

The best spin bowler that I have ever seen, though my old colleague Lance Gibbs was close to selection. Warne gives the impression that he will take a wicket at any time.

11) Dennis Lillee

He came along just after I had retired, but I still saw enough of him to realise what a great quick bowler he was, with all the necessary qualities.

CONRAD HUNTE played 44 Test matches for the West Indies between 1957–58 and 1966–67, scoring 3,245 runs at an average of 45.06. He was an extremely dependable opening batsman and he played many important innings for the West Indies during his Test career. After starting out as a dashing stroke-player, Conrad later adjusted his game to selflessly become a player his team could rely on to see off the new ball and set the innings up for the stroke-makers down the order.

[This team was received before Conrad passed away in 1999]

✻ ✻ ✻ ✻ ✻

RAY ILLINGWORTH'S XI

I selected my 12 from different generations as I go back to the forties. It's unfortunate that I had to omit some great players and I would like to give a mention to players like Shane Warne, Fred Trueman, Barry Richards and Mike Procter. If my team had to play on a turning track then I would want Muttiah Muralitharan in the side at the expense of one of the quicks. I haven't seen an off-spinner turn the ball such distances as Murali. His action was questioned but if they say it's okay then he would definitely be in my XII, or XI given the right conditions.

1) Leonard Hutton
I played with him for four or five years before he retired. I felt he was really unlucky in that he injured his arm during the war, which resulted in one arm being longer than the other. Had he not sustained that injury I'm sure he would have broken all the records because he had the best batting technique I have ever seen, but he was not quite the same player after that injury.

2) Jack Hobbs
I have spoken with a fair number of people about Jack and most thought he was the best batsman before the war. His record is unbelievable; he scored many of his 197 centuries after the age of 40.

3) Donald Bradman
This man is out on his own. I never saw much of him but his record's outstanding. I played against him when we toured Australia in 1962–63 when he played for a Prime Minister's XI. Even though he was in his fifties you could still see the class of him. It was the same when Len Hutton played years after his retirement.

4) Viv Richards
There were a few who could have filled this position, but Viv was a destroyer who could win a match on his own. He was just sheer power and was as good as anyone.

5) Peter May
PBH is certainly the best batsman England has produced since the war. He scored a lot of runs on poor pitches, which he used to see quite often in the fifties. He was in a class of his own.

6) Garfield Sobers

Easily the best all-rounder the world has seen. He's as good a batsman as has ever been produced and would make this team in that role alone. He was also a fine left-arm bowler and a great fielder.

7) Keith Miller

There were a few to choose from with people like Botham, Imran and Procter, but Keith Miller was more explosive than any of them. I have spoken to people that played with Keith in the forties and fifties and they say that when he wanted to, he could really turn it on. He wasn't interested in averages. When the Australians piled on the runs against Essex in 1948 he gave his wicket away first ball – that wasn't his kind of cricket. With the ball, he was as quick as anybody and his bouncer was quicker than Ray Lindwall's.

8) Alan Knott

I played with Godfrey Evans and I played with Knotty, and Knotty was in a class of his own. As a batsman he was a genuine Test number six or seven who scored a lot of useful runs in difficult situations. As a keeper, though, he was something special: he used to catch bottom edges off spinners, thick inside edges off the quicks and other great catches that only he could have taken.

9) Richie Benaud

It's close between Richie and Shane Warne, but I just felt Richie's ability to get bounce *and* turn was the deciding factor. Warne may have had more variety, but later on he didn't use his googly that much as it was too hard on his shoulder. We faced Richie in 1962–63 and he was not only turning it but was also getting the ball to bounce chest-high at times! He was also a good batsman and a great fielder.

10) Michael Holding

Just for his sheer pace, his beautiful, rhythmic action and the ability to extract pace from flat wickets. He took a lot of his wickets by pitching the ball up and not always bouncing batsmen.

11) Curtly Ambrose

He was as quick as anybody in his prime. The amount of bounce he was able to get made life very difficult for batsmen. When I was in charge of the England team, most of the guys felt that if they could survive his first five or six overs, they would be okay. But if Curtly got a wicket in that time he could easily run through the side.

RAY ILLINGWORTH played 61 Tests for England between 1958 and 1973, scoring 1,836 runs at an average of 23.24, with 122 wickets at 31.20. In first-class cricket, in a long career from 1951 to 1983, he scored 24,134 runs at 28.06 with 22 centuries, and claimed 2,072 wickets at the economical average of 20.28. 'Illy' was an intelligent off-spinner and a useful middle to lower-order batsman. He skippered his country in 31 Tests and is considered one of England's finest leaders.

INZAMAM-UL-HAQ'S XI

This team was picked from players I have seen, so this obviously means there is no place for the likes of Bradman, Sobers, Hobbs, Hanif, Fazal, Wes Hall or any of these great players from history.

1) Sunil Gavaskar

I saw plenty of him on TV. He was a fantastic opener with a water-tight technique for Test cricket and that allowed him to play very long innings.

2) Matthew Hayden

Look at his record, it is amazing. He scored more than 8,000 runs with 30 centuries. He was a very intimidating opponent for bowlers.

3) Viv Richards

He has to be the best batsman ever produced anywhere in the world. I like positive cricketers and he was always positive and aggressive. He was the first man to adopt and succeed at front-foot cricket against the fast bowlers, hitting through the line.

4) Ricky Ponting

Another great player with a fine record against fast bowling or spin. I rate him very high because he always shows his quality in the big matches. The bigger the match the better he performs.

5) Brian Lara

Adds a left-hand style to this middle-order. He was special because he made big innings. He is the only man to score 400 and 500, as well as scores over 300 and 200 many times. That was his best quality, as well as being a very stylish batsman.

6) Garfield Sobers

The best all-rounder there has ever been anywhere in the world; a great batsman and a great bowler.

7) Adam Gilchrist

A fantastic player. He could get in this team as a batsman alone, but he just happens to be a great wicketkeeper as well. After Viv Richards he is the best stroke player I have ever seen.

8) Imran Khan

He was a big inspiration, not just to me but many people, because of the way he played his cricket. Every youngster who watched Imran Khan must have been impressed by the exciting way he played cricket, whether as a batsman or bowler.

9) Shane Warne

The best leg-spinner ever. Very few spinners, especially leggies, dominate games because, although they take wickets, they rarely contain the runs. But Warne was not only able to take wickets, he was also able to contain batsmen and keep the pressure on.

10) Wasim Akram

He was great in Test cricket and one-day cricket. He swung the new and old ball both ways and was always very difficult for batsmen to face. They were never comfortable against him on any pitch, in any conditions.

11) Malcolm Marshall

A quality bowler. He was not as tall as many fast bowlers, but he was better than most for his ability to bowl fast and to swing the ball from both sides of the wicket. I would recommend that any youngster taking up fast bowling should watch a DVD of Malcolm Marshall. His variation was excellent. I made my Test debut against him and scored 20 – before he bowled me. But I did manage to score 60 runs against him in the next match!

INZAMAM-UL HAQ played 120 Tests for Pakistan from 1992 to 2007–08, scoring 8,830 runs at an average of 49.60. He needed three more runs to leapfrog Javed Miandad as Pakistan's highest-scoring Test batsman. The graceful middle-order batsman had a Test best of 329 against New Zealand in Lahore in 2002, falling just short of Hanif Mohammed's Pakistani record 337.

✳ ✳ ✳ ✳ ✳

DEAN JONES'S XI

This team basically picked itself except for a couple of positions and I'm sure it would take some beating. It wasn't easy leaving out Sir Garfield Sobers for Ian Botham, but it's definitely a decision most selectors would relish. Other players unlucky to miss out include: Keith Miller – who was one of the first sex symbols in cricket along with Denis Compton – Geoff Boycott; Sunil Gavaskar; Javed Miandad; Kenny Barrington and Richard Hadlee. I would love to have made room for Sachin Tendulkar, but I've favoured players I saw more of in my day.

1) Gordon Greenidge

He was just a magnificent opener and technically one of the best batsmen I have ever seen.

2) Jack Hobbs

For the simple fact that he has scored more hundreds than anybody else and that he was over 40 when he scored a great deal of them. For perseverance at the crease, he'd have to be one of the best.

3) Donald Bradman
No need to explain the reasons for this choice. He is the greatest Australian that ever walked.

4) Viv Richards
He had everything: power, finesse, technique, he bowled and could catch well anywhere on the field, particularly at slip.

5) Allan Border
A street fighter; he was always there battling away when things got tough. AB would have to be one of the greatest players on all types of wickets and he absolutely hated losing.

6) Ian Botham
The greatest complete cricketer I have ever seen. Beefy was never out of the game and he was always trying to make something happen. He was an excitement machine. Sobers was unlucky not to get in as there is very little between the two.

7) Kapil Dev
To get 434 Test wickets, particularly on the lifeless tracks that he often bowled on in the sub-continent, was a magnificent tribute to what he achieved. If he were from Australia or the Caribbean he'd have taken a lot more wickets and been the record-holder out on his own.

8) Ian Healy
A very good wicketkeeper when standing back, but undoubtedly the best keeper ever when standing up to spin bowling, as we saw when he kept to Warney. He scored a few Test centuries and wasn't far behind Alan Knott for the most Test runs scored by a wicketkeeper, pre-Gilchrist, who is obviously better purely as a batsman.

9) Shane Warne
The greatest spin bowler that has ever lived. Warney has done a lot to pull the crowds back in to Test cricket, when they were declining. He's one of the best things to ever happen to the game.

10) Joel Garner
I faced many of the great quick bowlers of the past 30 years and I always had more trouble with Joel than anyone else, and I think that applies to a lot of Australians. He was an awesome bowler.

11) Dennis Lillee
Nearly all of the great quick bowlers consider Dennis to be the best by a street, which is the ultimate compliment.

DEAN JONES played 52 Test matches for Australia between 1983–84 and 1992, scoring 3,361 runs at an average of 46.55. He may not have played the number of Tests that his ability merited. However, he was a consistent and skilful attacking batsman for Australia and a key figure in Australia's resurgence in international cricket from the late 1980s under Allan Border's captaincy. In his third Test he scored 210 in Madras in what became the second tied Test match in history. He averaged 51.85 in first-class cricket with a highest score of 324 not out.

* * * * *

ALVIN KALLICHARRAN'S XI

For Rohan Kanhai not to be in this side just shows how good the others were. I rated him as a great player and he was one of my personal favourites. I agonised over Greenidge and Barry Richards, but I just thought that Gordon has been there and done it, and through no fault of his own, Barry didn't play that much Test cricket. With the bowling, I thought Michael Holding, Malcolm Marshall, Joel Garner and Jeff Thomson were all great bowlers, but I think Roberts and Lillee were a class above.

1) Sunil Gavaskar
He was born and brought up on slow wickets in India, yet a high volume of his runs were scored against quality fast-bowling attacks from West Indies and Australia against bowlers like Holding, Roberts, Garner, Marshall, Lillee and Thomson. So he must have been a high-class player. He played the spinners comfortably.

2) Gordon Greenidge
It was close between him and Barry Richards and I also rated Roy Fredericks a great deal. Gordon, though, was a very consistent opener who could hit the ball extremely hard and dominate bowling attacks and subsequently the innings itself. Not many openers do that.

3) Donald Bradman
I didn't see him but whatever team you're going to pick you cannot ignore this man's record. Whatever period you're playing in, Bradman's record is phenomenal.

4) Viv Richards
One of the greatest batsmen of all time. He dominated bowlers and it didn't matter where they bowled to him as he had a shot for every type of delivery. He was vicious as a batsman.

5) Graeme Pollock
He was so calculated in his own way and easy going and never had any nerves whatsoever. Batting was easy for him. Having batted with him for four years at Transvaal, he never showed any emotions. I remember Colin Cowdrey gave me the same impression as I was growing up. The coolness with which he dominated situations amazed me. A lot of

batsmen show anxiety and tension when they are batting – especially early on – but Graeme never did.

6) Garfield Sobers
He was like Pollock in that he played the game with a smile. When you put a team like this together you must look at Botham, Hadlee, Imran, Kapil and Procter and put Sobers aside and decide from the rest. Garry was in a class of his own.

7) Alan Knott
Without any doubt. I have played against Knotty in county cricket and Test cricket and he always did his own thing and just went about his job in his own peculiar way and that was what made him great, as a batsman and as a keeper.

8) Dennis Lillee
As a batsman playing for the West Indies, I always thought Dennis had something up his sleeve to surprise you with. When he walked back to his mark I wondered what he was thinking about and what he was planning, because there was always something he was working on in order to dismiss a batsman. Dennis was a strong fast bowler who never tired, like Roberts.

9) Andy Roberts
Andy was the greatest of all the great West Indies' fast bowlers. He is the Godfather of West Indies fast bowling. The others were also great but not like this man. I played a little against Wes Hall at the beginning of my career, but it's difficult to judge how good he was because he was at the end of his career. However, I couldn't imagine anyone being better than Roberts or Lillee.

10) Lance Gibbs
He was the Godfather of my career at Warwickshire and for the West Indies, with his strength and character, and his determination and professionalism. He was a great off-break bowler, as you'd expect from the first spinner to claim 300 Test wickets.

11) Bishan Bedi
I must include him as, in terms of spin bowlers, he was the same as Roberts and Lillee in that you were never sure what he was going to bowl you – he always kept you guessing. Bishan was the master of flight and guile and spin. He had the ball on a string.

ALVIN KALLICHARRAN played 66 Tests for the West Indies between 1971–72 and 1980–81, scoring 4,399 runs at an average of 44.43. He amassed 32,650 first-class runs at 43.64, including 87 centuries, and scored 100 not out and 101 in his first two Tests, both against New Zealand. Alvin was one of the best left-handed batsmen of his era. His sublime timing and ability to find the gaps were his hallmarks. 'Kalli' played for Warwickshire in county cricket for 19 years.

JACQUES KALLIS'S XI

I picked players that I've played with or against as opposed to players before my time. I know that excludes many great players and those who came close were Allan Donald, Imran Khan, Graeme Pollock, Gordon Greenidge, Desmond Haynes, Mark Taylor, Viv Richards, Ian Botham and Malcolm Marshall.

1) Matthew Hayden, 2) Rahul Dravid, 3) Ricky Ponting

4) Brian Lara
He was such a difficult guy to bowl to. You have to bowl a really good over just to get a maiden against him as there is so little room for error for bowlers.

5) Sachin Tendulkar
He's in for the same reasons as Brian Lara. Sachin has probably been the most outstanding and consistent batsman of his generation.

6) Steve Waugh
He was so difficult to get out. He knew his game plan and he stuck to it. It was very rare for bowlers to get him to hook or pull.

7) Adam Gilchrist
Gilly is just about the perfect wicketkeeper-batsman; an explosive batter but also pretty safe behind the stumps. He's scored some quite important runs against us over the years. Maybe Mark Boucher and Ian Healy would be slightly better keepers, but Gilly's batting adds a match-winning quality to this team.

8) Andrew Flintoff

9) Wasim Akram
What made him so special was his ability to swing the ball both ways and his change of pace; he's deceptively quick. His left arm gives the attack good variety.

10) Shane Warne
He has to be the best spinner ever. He never gave you much to score off. With leg-spinners you usually get a bad ball every now and again, but not with him. He's always on the spot and attacking you and he really makes you scrap for every run.

11) Glenn McGrath

JACQUES KALLIS has played 135 Tests for South Africa since 1995–96 and has scored 10,640 runs at an average of 54.56. He has also prospered as a medium-pace bowler with

260 wickets at 31.40. His early scores suggest Jacques found Test cricket a struggle initially, but the South African selectors were rewarded when he scored a resilient 101 in Melbourne in 1997–98 to save the game. Thereafter, he blossomed into one of the world's leading batsmen and South Africa's most prolific scorer.

* * * * *

KAPIL DEV'S XI

I've heard about players like Don Bradman, Barry Richards, Garry Sobers, Graeme Pollock, John Edrich and Len Hutton. No doubt they were great, but it is difficult for me to make a judgement on them so I selected players I have seen. I have still had to leave out great cricketers like: David Gower; Geoffrey Boycott – who was too much like Gavaskar for me to pick him; Javed Miandad – a great fighting batsman; Zaheer Abbas; Inzamam-ul-Haq; Bishan Bedi; Allan Border; Steve Waugh; Greg Chappell; Clive Lloyd – whose fielding impressed me in my early days; Rohan Kanhai – whom I didn't see a lot of; Gordon Greenidge – who could demolish an attack; Michael Holding, who narrowly misses out – he was the greatest athlete I ever saw on a cricket field; Rodney Marsh; Alan Knott – keeping can be made to look more difficult by those who dive everywhere, but Knotty always made keeping look easy, and as a batsman he wasn't very correct but effective and was a nightmare to bowl at as he would hit over cover or the slips; and Ian Botham, who could do wonders on a cricket field. I can honestly say I never played against anyone who enjoyed his cricket more than Botham, who had a wonderful sense of humour and was a good team man. I enjoyed playing against him. Muttiah Muralitharan would play if it was a turning track. Also in my 14-man squad, I would like Ricky Ponting and Rahul Dravid.

1) Sunil Gavaskar
He was so technically correct and had so much time to play his shots. Sunny liked to play himself in before playing extravagant shots as he used to assess the bowler's strengths and weaknesses. Once he was in he really knew how to construct an innings, and he would play each ball on its merits.

2) Virender Sehwag
Here we have a ruthless batsman who has a better strike rate than most, especially among the openers. I obviously didn't get to play with or against him, but it is clear that he has changed the face of cricket. Bowlers seek relief from his punishing stroke-play.

3) Viv Richards
I have to have a player of Viv's ability in my team. His greatest strength was that he never let a bowler dominate him. He could hit any ball for four off any bowler. Viv could play well on all types of wickets, whether quick or turning tracks.

4) Sachin Tendulkar
Sachin is the most talented batsman that I have ever seen, though it's close between him and Viv. Where Viv sometimes hit from outside leg to off or vice-versa, Sachin is more technically correct, but still with the same destructive results.

5) Brian Lara
When he got going he was capable of winning matches on his own, able to score big runs. I remember when India toured the West Indies in 1989 he scored a big hundred (182 while captain of West Indies Under-23s) against us in a side game. He was quick on his feet and his movement was excellent. He looked an interesting player for the future.

6) Imran Khan
He was a clever and crafty player, particularly with the ball. His ability to swing the old ball was better than any other bowler of recent times. I wouldn't say he was the most talented cricketer, but he would never try to cross the boundaries of his limitations – batting or bowling.

7) Richard Hadlee
After Lillee, I think Hadlee was the best fast bowler of my time; he was what I would call a computer bowler, so perfect. When he began to lose his pace, his use of the ball was the best I have seen. He would always make the batsman struggle and his line and length was awkward.

8) Adam Gilchrist
A totally ruthless batsman, which is how I would want my team to be. He tried to win matches rather than survive in them. He is the same as Sehwag, as someone who changed the way the game was played, especially for wicketkeepers.

9) Wasim Akram
He is the most difficult left-arm bowler I have ever seen, who was always capable of surprising the batsman at any time. Wasim was certainly one of the great bowlers of my time – he was so good. When you needed a breakthrough nobody could be better than him. He was genuinely quick and moved it around too.

10) Shane Warne
He is the best spin bowler I have ever seen; with great variety and the sharpness to turn the ball a long way. He never performed so well against India, but that is not too important, he is still a great bowler in my opinion.

11) Dennis Lillee
What can I say about Dennis – he would have to be the fast bowler's dream! Any fast bowler would want his run-up, his action, his pace, his aggression, the way he rattled batsmen – he was everything as far as quick bowling goes.

KAPIL DEV played 131 Tests for India between 1978–79 and 1993–94, taking a then-record 434 wickets at an average of 29.64. The all-rounder also scored 5,248 runs at 31.05, including eight centuries. Kapil is the best fast bowler in an Indian cricket history more familiar with great spin bowlers. Along with Imran Khan, Ian Botham and Richard Hadlee, he was not only one of the great all-rounders of his era, but of all time.

* * * * *

SYED KIRMANI'S XI

I have selected my team purely from the players that I witnessed first-hand, playing with and against. This would be my best and most balanced World XI to combat any opposition. As 12th man I would go for Jonty Rhodes for obvious reasons. I considered my old teammate Gundappa Viswanath, but he just misses out.

1) Sunil Gavaskar

A tremendous accumulator of his runs; and a bundle of concentration, determination, dedication personified. He could always be depended upon to go out and score runs on any wicket.

2) Gordon Greenidge

He had tremendous power to destroy any attack and was a very good player of both fast bowling and spin bowling.

3) Viv Richards

A magnificent batsman that could butcher any bowling attack at will and the best all-round batsman of my era.

4) David Gower

Probably the most elegant batsman to ever play Test cricket. Being a left-hander he would add variety to the top order.

5) Javed Miandad

The perfect batsman to come in if your side was in trouble. This great utility player brings stability under crisis, and was one of the few consistent batsmen, an electrifying fielder and a cheeky runner between the wickets.

6) Imran Khan

One of the best all-rounders the cricket world has seen. Great thinker of the game and had dictating leadership qualities. Fighter to the core, motivating and inspiring.

7) Kapil Dev

A great out-swinging seam bowler with gifted all-round ability and who could devastate any bowling on his day with the bat. Had terrific stamina and he swung the ball both ways.

8) Syed Kirmani

As it is my team I'll pick myself, though I feel my record justifies it. It was an immense challenge keeping to legendary spinners like B.S. Chandrasekhar and Bishan Singh Bedi and the art and ability of a wicketkeeper is judged only when he stands up to spinners. Yours sincerely was fortunate to have started keeping wickets to the likes of Chandra and E.A.S. Prasanna.

9) Michael Holding

The best athletic action that I have ever seen from a fast bowler and he extracted tremendous pace and bounce as well. An outstanding fielder on the outfield.

10) Bishan Bedi

An artist in left-arm off-spin bowling, with a beautiful rhythmic action. He had six different deliveries and possessed tantalising flight in the air. The world's best left-arm off-spinner ever.

11) Bhagwath Chandrasekhar

A freakish, fast leg-spin and googly bowler, one of the best in the world. There cannot be another Chandra born: a match-winning bowler with a great amount of consistency. His fastest delivery was considered as quick as Jeff Thomson's, according to Viv Richards.

SYED KIRMANI played 88 Tests for India between 1975–76 and 1985–86, achieving 198 dismissals as wicketkeeper. His agility and speed could be scintillating, but rarely at the expense of reliability. Syed was also a useful batsman down the order with a Test average of 27.04, with two centuries to his credit against Australia and England. England keeping legend Godfrey Evans elected him the best wicketkeeper in the 1983 World Cup, which India won.

* * * * *

ANIL KUMBLE'S XI

I have selected my team from first-hand experience with the exception of Bradman and Sobers. Each man is a potential match-winner in his own way. There are many more I haven't picked, but I have gone for variety. Those unlucky to miss out include: Ian Botham, Ian Healy, Imran Khan, Richard Hadlee, Viv Richards and Brian Lara. I almost went for Sunil Gavaskar too for his amazing record against the West Indies. He had so much patience, which is what you need for Test cricket.

1) Virender Sehwag

Tough to leave out Gavaskar, but having played with Viru I couldn't not have him in my side. He is such a destructive batsman that he can change a game in literally one session.

2) Gordon Greenidge

Another amazing opening batsman with a terrific record. He was a dominating player who could smash an opening bowler all over the park. These two would he a great opening partnership; destructive on one hand and patient on the other.

3) Donald Bradman

I obviously didn't see him but what I have read and heard is enough. His record speaks for itself. Anybody who has an average of 99.94 in Test cricket must have been an amazing player.

4) Sachin Tendulkar

Technically he's very sound and he dominates the bowler. He has got runs in all countries on different types of wickets. He can also bowl leg-spin and off-spin and would provide good support to Warne. I've known him a long time and he's a tremendous guy.

5) Steve Waugh

When Australia lost early wickets he showed there is no better man to come in in that situation. He's very solid and has got the runs to prove it. He has never let his side down, and in this team he would provide balance to the batting order.

6) Garfield Sobers

I never saw him but he must have been an amazing all-rounder. The runs he scored speak volumes about his ability as an attacking left-hander. He could bowl fast or spin, which would have its advantages in a match situation.

7) Kapil Dev

You can pick him on his batting alone. He was a tremendous batsman, plus he was a great bowler who took wickets on all types of pitches. I can't think of a better bowler who swung the ball both ways. His record is awesome; a great ambassador for Indian cricket.

8) Adam Gilchrist

I could have picked Ian Healy for his keeping to Warne, or Syed Kirmani for his keeping to Chandra, Bedi and Prasanna, but I've gone for Gilchrist. He also kept brilliantly to Warne, but his batting, like Sehwag, could change the direction of a game very quickly.

9) Wasim Akram

You couldn't find a better bowler to swing the ball and take wickets in all conditions. He's a left-armer, which provides variety, and he's the master of reverse swing. He gets in ahead of Lillee.

10) Malcolm Marshall

A genuine fast bowler who had an amazing range of deliveries. He was deceptive with the pace that he used to generate.

11) Shane Warne

The best leg-spinner I have ever seen. People say there were bowlers who could bowl similar to him, but I have not seen anyone who could bowl with so much control and turn the ball so much.

ANIL KUMBLE played 132 Tests for India between 1990 and 2008–09, taking an Indian record 619 wickets at an average of 29.65. In 1999, against Pakistan at Delhi, he matched Jim Laker's world record of 10 wickets in a Test innings. The leg-spinner was a key member of India's team throughout two decades, renowned for his accuracy, googlies and top-spinners – more than the stock leg-break. He managed 105 wickets in his first season of county cricket in 1995, with Northamptonshire.

* * * * *

CLIVE LLOYD'S XI

I have tried to include several of the greats from the different eras, but I'm particularly sorry not to have found a place for Everton Weekes, Frank Worrell, Clyde Walcott, Geoff Boycott and Brian Lara, who are all greats in their own right.

1) Leonard Hutton

I never saw him bat but I'm told that he was a real class player, very dependable and had great powers of concentration.

2) Sunil Gavaskar

The same as Hutton, though I saw a lot of Sunny. This guy had tremendous concentration and patience, which I suppose are qualities that all great opening batsmen have.

3) Donald Bradman

He has a Test match average of 99. He would have to be one of the best things to have ever happened to the game.

4) Viv Richards

Explosive as a batsman and totally professional in his approach to cricket. Viv had no respect for any bowler he faced; he wanted to dominate everyone no matter how good they were.

5) Allan Border

He was very dependable in the middle-order and was generally a tremendous cricketer for his country. AB is one of the finest that Australia has ever produced.

6) Garfield Sobers

The best thing on two legs; simply the greatest player that ever walked on to a cricket field.

7) Richie Benaud

A top-class leg-spinner and could do a fine job with the bat too. Also a great fielder and one of the best captains and astute thinkers the game has known.

8) Alan Knott

The finest wicketkeeper that I have had the privilege to play with or against, and also a more than useful batsman down the order.

9) Malcolm Marshall

One of the finest fast bowlers ever. He had it all as far as quicks go, but his best asset was his great cricket brain – Malcolm was always thinking. He gets in ahead of many of his teammates who could all have come into contention.

10) Jim Laker

It's very close between him and my cousin Lance Gibbs. Both were the best off-spinner of their time. Shane Warne is also unlucky not to make it, but picking these teams is not easy.

11) Dennis Lillee

He was totally professional and worked extremely hard at his game. It never mattered if the wicket was to his liking because he would always bowl his heart out. Dennis always made the batsman think and when you batted against him, you knew you were in a battle.

CLIVE LLOYD played 110 Tests for the West Indies between 1966–67 and 1984–85, scoring 7,515 runs at an average of 46.67. In first-class cricket (483 matches), he compiled 30,885 runs at 49.25. Clive was appointed West Indies captain in 1974–75 and for the next 10 years led a team that dominated world cricket. In the 18 series Lloyd captained, the West Indies lost just two. He is one of the finest left-handed batsmen of all time, and was an athletic fielder at cover point then slip.

✳ ✳ ✳ ✳ ✳

MAJID KHAN'S XI

I have attempted to give a fair reflection of talent from all generations. Don Bradman would be captain of this side.

1) Hanif Mohammed

When he started playing Test cricket he was in a very weak side that depended on him, yet he always seemed to score runs against the best teams in the world. If he folded, Pakistan folded, so for him to do so well in a weak side is better than a player scoring runs in a strong side. Like a good general saving his men, Hanif protected his teammates from more and heavier defeats by scoring big runs.

2) Sunil Gavaskar

He was a very difficult man to remove. I remember sitting next to Alan Davidson at the Lord's Bicentenary match in 1987 and he told me that he used to love bowling at top players like Garry Sobers, but he said he wouldn't have liked to bowl at Gavaskar because he never gives you a chance at all. He showed that he was a batsman who could score runs under all types of circumstances, whether facing pace or spin and in any conditions.

3) Donald Bradman

Well, you don't have to make too many comments about this man. I met him in Adelaide during Pakistan's tour in 1972–73. We invited him to lunch and he spoke to us. He was a very astute man who did his homework well. He also made a speech on our arrival in Adelaide and I was impressed by how he knew every player in our team and their records. He was well versed on our cricket. I can only imagine how organised and professional he must have been as a captain.

4) George Headley

His record is very impressive and he scored a lot of runs when West Indies cricket was not too strong, just after they began playing Test matches. He played well on all types of wickets.

5) Garfield Sobers

He would be in the team just as a wrist spinner, never mind his ferocious batting. He's a four-in-one cricketer and on every type of pitch. He would have to be the best all-rounder ever because of the versatility in his bowling.

6) Alan Knott

He took the art of wicketkeeping to such a height that no other keeper has yet matched him. He was the first keeper in world cricket to be so agile. He was also a very gritty batsman who would not throw his wicket away. He would force the other team to earn his wicket. His batting record is very impressive, with five centuries. But as a keeper Knotty was to his art as Mohammed Ali was to his: the best ever.

7) Michael Holding

He was the fastest bowler I ever faced, along with Jeff Thomson. With his sheer pace he would get any batsman in the world out on any type of pitch. The poetry to his bowling was amazing; you could not wish to see a more perfect bowler.

8) Dennis Lillee

There's no doubt that he was a very strong and fearless bowler. I saw him in a Test match in 1972–73 when he had a hairline fracture of the spine. He came onto the field and bowled for one and a half hours in that condition. He knew he had it as the doctor had told him. He was in a cast for six months afterwards. Also, on our 1976–77 tour he had a hamstring injury in one match but still got through 40 overs. A person with this much heart and dedication would be an asset to any team. But he was also a great bowler with his courage and I take a lot of pride out of the fact that I had some success against him.

9) Sydney Barnes

If ever there was an all-time great bowler it was him, because he hardly played serious cricket. He was never interested in playing county cricket; he only enjoyed playing league cricket. Given this background, he still took 189 wickets in his 16 Tests – astonishing.

10) Bishan Bedi

A bowler with wonderful flight and guile who was not afraid of getting hit; he was quite pleased to get hit for a six. He used to clap batsmen when they hit him for six as he enjoyed the fact they were taking a chance. He was happy to bowl against any batsman on any type of pitch. He regularly deceived batsmen with flight rather than huge turn. He didn't spin the ball that much, but his use of flight was so good. He had no equal in his generation as a slow, classic spinner.

11) Lance Gibbs

He was the first spinner to take 300 Test wickets. He had a tremendous heart and was a great fighter who was always determined to take wickets in any conditions at all costs. On a helpful wicket he could demolish any team in the world. He was also a fine close-in fielder. I played against him at the end of his career when he was with Warwickshire in the mid-seventies, but he still had that fire in his belly.

MAJID KHAN played 63 Tests for Pakistan between 1964–65 and 1982–83 and scored 3,931 runs at an average of 38.92. In first-class cricket, he scored 27,444 runs at 43.01 and took 224 wickets at 32.12. He was aged just 15 on his first-class debut in 1961–62, but still managed 111 not out and six for 67 for Lahore. Majid was a graceful batsman, though given his quality he probably did not realise his full potential.

＊ ＊ ＊ ＊ ＊

MALCOLM MARSHALL'S XI

This is my 12 based on players that I have played with and against. If I had to pick a side based purely on cricketers that I played against in Test cricket, I would add: Graham Gooch – an outstanding opener who could take you apart if he got in; Martin Crowe – technically, one of the best middle-order players in the world, who was the backbone of New Zealand's batting for a long time; David Gower – he played more like a West Indian than an Englishman. He was a very elegant middle-order batsman; and Richard Hadlee – a tremendous bowler with a great variety of deliveries. Desmond Haynes and Shane Warne are also unlucky not to be included, but they would certainly be in the squad. If the match was to be played on a turning wicket, I would play Abdul Qadir and leave out one of the quicks. Qadir would provide leg-spin, flippers and googlies and is preferred just ahead of Shane Warne. Otherwise, I would go in with four quicks.

1) Sunil Gavaskar

He was the best opening batsman that I ever bowled to in my career. I thought I conquered him when I bowled to him in India and had some success as he reverted to the middle order from his usual opening position, but then he scored an unbeaten 236!

2) Gordon Greenidge

Technically, he was one of the best batsmen in the world, who didn't get the recognition he deserved. He is selected ahead of Haynes who was also a great batsman in Test cricket, and particularly one-day cricket.

3) Viv Richards

Viv speaks for himself; the world's best batsman who could murder spin bowling and pace bowling.

4) Allan Border

A very gritty player with a phenomenal record who was the backbone of the Australian middle-order in the eighties. He had great fighting qualities.

5) Javed Miandad

He was a terrific student of the game and a great fighter. Miandad was always a challenging opponent.

6) Clive Lloyd

He'd be captain of this team. Clive was an outstanding captain and a dangerous number six to follow that top five. He was also a very good fielder, particularly at slip.

7) Imran Khan

A very talented all-rounder who gets in just ahead of Richard Hadlee because of his extra pace and ability to bat.

8) Ian Healy

The best wicketkeeper-batsman in the world. Jeff Dujon was great for the West Indies team I played in, but Healy had more chance to impress with his outstanding keeping to Shane Warne.

9) Wasim Akram

The left-arm quick in the team with the ability to swing the ball both ways, and at good pace.

10) Michael Holding

Known to us all as the Rolls-Royce of world cricket and for his genuine pace.

11) Dennis Lillee

Phenomenal record at Test level, with a great out-swinger. He would definitely partner Michael Holding with the new ball.

MALCOLM MARSHALL played 81 Tests for the West Indies between 1978–79 and 1991, taking 376 wickets at an average of 20.94. Throughout his Test career he spearheaded possibly the most daunting pace attack in Test history and was widely credited as the best of that pack in the 1980s. He also served county cricket loyally with Hampshire from 1979 to 1993.

[This team was received before Malcolm passed away in 1999]

* * * * *

GRAHAM MCKENZIE'S XI

I considered players from many generations rather than just my own era. Had I picked more from my own day then Graeme Pollock would have been in as one of the best batsmen I ever bowled at, but in this team I'm afraid he'll have to settle for 12th man. Others I would like to have picked include Neil Harvey, Alan Knott, John Snow, Mike Procter, Wes Hall and many more. My team has unbelievable batting strength with Sobers coming in at seven, while Lillee, Larwood, Sobers and Hammond make for an excellent pace attack. Warne and Viv Richards provide the spin and Sobers also bowled slow left-arm.

1) Jack Hobbs

I remember meeting him at a dinner as a youngster on Australia's 1961 Ashes tour of England. Although I never saw him play, it was great just to meet him and have a conversation with him. He was the greatest batsman of the first quarter of the 20th century.

2) Barry Richards

Of all the batsmen I ever played with or against, Barry was the most gifted. Unfortunately he didn't play a lot of Test cricket, but if he had he would have had a fantastic record. He was able to play all the shots and with so much time. He had to have a challenge, because batting was so easy for him. I bowled against him when he scored over 300 in a day for South Australia – that was some innings.

3) Donald Bradman

His selection is undisputed as his record stands out. I never saw him play; I'm just going on opinion. Throughout most of my career he was chairman of selectors, so I chatted with him many times. He was always very incisive and talked in a constructive manner. Every player used to hang on to every word he said, so I could only imagine how players looked up to him when he was captain of Australia.

4) Viv Richards

I didn't play Test cricket against him, just county cricket. He dominated bowlers and he could do anything on his day. He was so belligerent at the wicket that it intimidated opponents. He could also bowl useful off-spin and was a very athletic fielder.

5) Victor Trumper

He's a true great from the early part of the 20th century, who played so many good innings and most of them on bad wickets. Even if he'd played in another era, he'd still have been quite outstanding. Until Bradman, he was the main man.

6) Walter Hammond

In the late 1920s and 1930s he had a fantastic record. He was a great slip fieldsman, was a good pace bowler and was one of the best batsmen of his time. If it hadn't been for Bradman, Hammond would have received much more adulation for his brilliance.

7) Garfield Sobers

I played a lot of cricket against him and it's hard to imagine that you could find a better all-rounder than Sobers. I would rank him in the top three batsmen that I ever bowled to. As a swing bowler, when he put his mind to it, he could be as sharp as anyone. He also bowled useful wrist spin when the conditions suited.

8) Don Tallon

The best keeper I ever played against was Alan Knott, but Don Tallon was just regarded so highly, particularly by Don Bradman. He was Australia's keeper when I was a youngster, but he was at the end of his career then. In his early days he scored quite a few centuries and, although he never scored many runs in Tests, he batted well for Queensland and was actually one of their main batsmen.

9) Shane Warne

I don't think anyone could bowl better leg-spin than him. He spun the ball a long way in his early days and though he lost some turn and his flipper after his shoulder injury, he adapted and was still effective and sustained his wicket-taking capabilities. He was a revelation for leg-spin bowling and for cricket generally. For over 15 years before he came along the West Indies dominated world cricket with four fast bowlers, which became tedious. They were certainly effective and great fast bowlers, but it didn't make interesting viewing. Warne changed that and added a new dimension to world cricket.

10) Harold Larwood

Having been a fast bowler myself, I always looked up to Harold Larwood. I never saw him play but I loved meeting and talking with him, as he lived for many years in Australia. We didn't talk about Bodyline or about his career — we just discussed genialities — but it was good to be around such a personality. He must have been some bowler to cause the Bodyline furore almost single-handedly. Without him there wouldn't have been a Bodyline controversy.

11) Dennis Lillee

I haven't seen a greater fast bowler than Lillee. He had all the qualities that great fast bowlers need: pace, aggression, attitude, endurance to keep going and intelligence. Although I played a few Shield matches with him, it was a shame I never played Test cricket with him, as I never did have a partner of his class. Dennis was fortunate enough to have Jeff Thomson as a strike partner in his career.

GRAHAM McKENZIE played 60 Tests for Australia between 1961 and 1970–71 and took 246 wickets at an average of 29.78. In first-class cricket he claimed 1,219 wickets at 26.96. 'Garth' McKenzie was the youngest to take 100, 150 and 200 Test wickets. He retired two wickets short of Richie Benaud's Australian record tally. He may have taken more with better support – his time came after Lindwall and Miller, and Davidson, and he was succeeded by Lillee and Thomson.

✳ ✳ ✳ ✳ ✳

MOHAMMED YOUSUF'S XI

I wanted to also include the names of Ricky Ponting, Javed Miandad, Inzamam-ul-Haq and Clive Lloyd, but there are only 11 positions available and therefore I could not fit them in. I am obviously more familiar with players of recent times, but there was no way I could leave out Bradman and Sobers. In my opinion a bowling attack could not possibly get any better than the one in this team.

1) Sunil Gavaskar

One of the most consistent openers of all time, who always gave his team a solid start to an innings.

2) Sachin Tendulkar

I could not leave this man out of any team in any format; his record is incredible.

3) Viv Richards

The greatest batsman of his generation.

4) Donald Bradman

Like Viv Richards, he was the greatest batsman of his time by far.

5) Brian Lara

Along with Tendulkar he has to be the best batsman of my generation; good to watch even when scoring runs against you.

6) Garfield Sobers

The greatest all-rounder of all time.

7) Adam Gilchrist
A great wicketkeeper and an even better batsman who can dominate any bowling attack in any conditions.

8) Imran Khan
Imran is my captain. He was an inspirational leader for Pakistan, as shown by the World Cup win; also a great all-rounder.

9) Wasim Akram
He was the type of bowler who could bowl so many different deliveries that batsmen were always guessing when facing him.

10) Shane Warne
The greatest spin bowler of all time. I always enjoyed my battles against him.

11) Malcolm Marshall
He retired before my time but he looked to be the best fast bowler in that great West Indies team.

MOHAMMED YOUSUF has played 88 Test matches for Pakistan between 1997–98 and 2009–10, scoring 7,431 runs at an average of 53.07 – the highest average for any established Pakistan player. He also made 24 Test centuries. The middle-order batsman was a prolific contributor to Pakistan for a decade and in 2006 he broke Viv Richards' record to become the highest-scoring Test batsman in a calendar year (1,788 runs).

* * * * *

MUDASSAR NAZAR'S XI

This team wouldn't lose too many matches. I'm just glad that I never had to face a bowling attack of this quality. It's very difficult to leave out players like Botham, Hutton, Border and Kapil Dev, but I'm happy with this side. With regard to modern players like Tendulkar, Lara, Inzamam and Mark Waugh, they just miss out, narrowly.

1) Sunil Gavaskar
In my playing career, I never played against a better batsman than him. Against the West Indies particularly, his record is unbelievable. He was such a complete player who played spin as good as quick bowling. He should walk into any team in any era.

2) Jack Hobbs
The man scored 197 hundreds, which is a phenomenal record; he must have been a great player. He gets in ahead of Leonard Hutton and Geoffrey Boycott.

3) Viv Richards

He was outstanding in our part of the world, like everywhere else. He was one of few players that got the better of Lillee.

4) Donald Bradman

If you were to pick a World XI in another 20 years, he would still be in it. There is no doubt whatsoever about his selection.

5) Javed Miandad

Having grown up with him and played most of my career with him I could not leave him out. He was superb and a great team man. When he first played for Pakistan he smashed everybody around the ground, but when the team suddenly had too many stroke-makers he became a lot more dogged and defensive. He gets in just ahead of Allan Border, who was a similar player.

6) Garfield Sobers

An absolutely brilliant all-rounder who played with a smile but with aggression at the same time. At number six you need somebody who is consistent but who can score runs quickly as well. He shades it over Ian Botham.

7) Alan Knott

Without a doubt he's the greatest keeper I've ever seen, and I played against Bob Taylor, Rodney Marsh, Syed Kirmani, Farokh Engineer and with Wasim Bari. Marsh and Ian Healy have been more successful, but Knotty was simply the best in my opinion.

8) Imran Khan

It is a close call between Imran, Ian Botham. Richard Hadlee and Kapil Dev, but I feel Imran was a better bowler who could bowl well on any pitch in the world and also quicker than the others. He was genuinely fast, and I have played alongside him and seen a lot of him.

9) Shane Warne

At one time I would probably have selected Abdul Qadir instead, but now Warne is clearly the greatest spinner ever. Qadir had more variety, but he never spun his leggie as much as Warne. Along with Bradman and Sobers, Warne is now a player that would get into any team from any era.

10) Malcolm Marshall

An outstanding bowler who was always thinking people out and was very quick at his peak. I saw him bowl on some really flat tracks but he still took wickets and never gave up.

11) Dennis Lillee

The most outstanding fast bowler to ever play Test cricket. He was a captain's dream because you could throw him the ball at any time and he would give everything for you. Dennis is one of few bowlers with whom you could put all nine fielders on the off-side with any confidence.

MUDASSAR NAZAR played 76 Test matches for Pakistan between 1976–77 and 1988–89 and scored 4,114 runs at an average of 38.09. The greatest highlight of his Test career was scoring 761 runs at 126.83 in the home series against India in 1982–83. He was once Pakistan's most prolific opening batsman, who could also bowl medium-pace; sometimes with great success, as in the Lord's Test of 1982, when his six for 32 guided Pakistan to their first Test win at cricket's headquarters.

✳ ✳ ✳ ✳ ✳

DERYCK MURRAY'S XI

I don't how and/or why I allowed myself to be talked into this selection. It is difficult enough to select any national team from among current players, far more so a World XI. And here across eras! At the outset let me say that I can find no justification for leaving out some really great players, especially those whom I had the great privilege of playing with and against. Can you imagine not including players such as Hobbs, Cowdrey, Dexter, May, Trueman, Statham, Knott, Bedser (all of England); Miller, Lindwall, Davidson, Benaud, Ian and Greg Chappell, Marsh, Gilchrist, Ponting, McGrath (Australia); Bedi, Chandrasekhar, Tendulkar (India); Imran Khan, Majid Khan, Fazal Mahmood, Wasim Akram, Hanif and Mushtaq Mohammed (Pakistan); Hadlee, Vettori (New Zealand); Graeme Pollock (South Africa); Muralitharan (Sri Lanka); and the West Indians: Kanhai, Richards, Lara, Weekes, Greenidge, Haynes, Kallicharan, Hall, Griffith, Holding, Marshall; and the list goes on. Anyway, here is my team, and Frank Worrell would be my captain.

1) Sunil Gavaskar

Technically sound in defence with a full array of attacking strokes.

2) Conrad Hunte

Could curb his attacking instincts to suit the team's needs.

3) Donald Bradman

His record speaks for itself.

4) George Headley

Known as the 'Black Bradman', although West Indians referred to Bradman as the 'White Headley'.

115

5) Garfield Sobers
The greatest cricketer ever.

6) Frank Worrell
The greatest captain of all time and not a bad player either.

7) Wally Grout
The best wicketkeeper that I have ever seen.

8) Andy Roberts
Together with Dennis Lillee he transformed fast bowling to include the subtlety and guile previously only associated with spin bowling.

9) Shane Warne
Took bowling to another level.

10) Dennis Lillee
(See Roberts.)

11) Lance Gibbs
A spinner with the aggression of a fast bowler.

DERYCK MURRAY played 62 Tests for the West Indies between 1963 and 1980, achieving 189 dismissals as wicketkeeper. In the 1963 series in England he made 24 dismissals (a world record at the time) and 849 in the whole of his first-class career – both still West Indies records. After playing in England for Cambridge University, he spent eight seasons in county cricket with Nottinghamshire and then Warwickshire. He was vice-captain of the West Indies teams which won the first two cricket World Cups in 1975 and 1979.

* * * * *

MUSHTAQ AHMED'S XI

My team was selected from players I've seen. Waqar Younis, Richard Hadlee, Kapil Dev, Curtly Ambrose, Malcolm Marshall, Saqlain Mushtaq, Steve Waugh, Javed Miandad, Desmond Haynes, Jeff Dujon and Inzamam-ul Haq were all considered, but I couldn't fit them in, unfortunately.

1) Sunil Gavaskar
A lovely player to watch, with great concentration and technique. One of the best batsmen the world has seen.

2) Sachin Tendulkar

He has broken so many records, he is a true champion. If I opted for a conventional opener I would have gone for Desmond Haynes, as he was a very quick reader of bowlers and he didn't take much time to adjust to different conditions.

3) Viv Richards

The King of Cricket. He could change the game with his batting and was capable of destroying bowlers. Most of the games I played against him he smashed me. I gave him a hard time when Somerset played Glamorgan, but he was then at the end of his career.

4) Ricky Ponting

Ponting, one of the modern greats, gets in just ahead of Javed Miandad, who was a very gutsy player for Pakistan.

5) Brian Lara

A match-winning player who could turn a game on its head with the attacking way in which he batted. When the opposition believed they had won, Lara was able to change things around in no time. He gets in ahead of Sachin Tendulkar, who is another great.

6) Imran Khan

I admired him very much. I noticed when I started my career what a great competitor he was – he never gave up on a situation. He wanted to win all the time and never minded when he was beaten because he had the self-belief to know he would come back.

7) Ian Botham

A genuine all-rounder who was great for England. He was aggressive with bat and ball and was a brilliant slip fielder.

8) Adam Gilchrist

My old favourite was Jeffrey Dujon; I saw him take some great catches and make some important runs for the West Indies but Adam Gilchrist has raised the bar for wicketkeepers.

9) Wasim Akram

I played a lot of cricket with this guy and was able to see the talent he had close up. He could bowl so many different deliveries; he had great variation. He was useful with the bat too.

10) Shane Warne

Probably the best leg-spinner the world has seen. When his rhythm was good he was capable of destroying any batting side anywhere in the world.

11) Courtney Walsh

He was the first to 500 Test wickets and rightly so. You could throw the ball to this guy, ask him to bowl all day and he wouldn't complain. I admired the way he played all year round for the West Indies and Gloucestershire and hardly suffered from injury.

MUSHTAQ AHMED played 52 Tests for Pakistan from 1989–90 to 2003 and snared 185 wickets at an average of 32.97. He was one of the best spinners of his generation and the diminutive leg-spinner often proved a challenging opponent in all conditions, possessing great variety, including a deadly googly that turned prodigiously.

* * * * *

MUSHTAQ MOHAMMED'S XI

I selected my team from players I have seen with the exception of Donald Bradman. I'm sorry not to find a place for Javed Miandad as he was my boy; I took him under my wing when I was captain and gave him his opportunity. His aggression on the field and his knowledge of the game were second to none. Javed was a great fighter in any situation. But you can only select 11 after all. I also rated Andy Roberts and John Snow as the best fast bowlers I faced along with Dennis Lillee, who was the pick of them all. Imran's all-round skills just get him in ahead of both Roberts and Snow.

1) Sunil Gavaskar

His record alone is so impressive. He was always hungry for his runs and I admired his will to bat on and on.

2) Hanif Mohammed

Maybe I'm biased, as his younger brother, but I saw more of him than most and he was outstanding. He had a great technique and was phenomenal against both spin and pace. On a bad wicket he had the quality to adjust himself according to the surface he was playing on. His determination and concentration was masterly.

3) Donald Bradman

I didn't see him but he must have been a spectacular player to average 99.

4) Sachin Tendulkar

A fantastic player, there's nothing not to like about him. He is a down to earth man, and having achieved so much in the world of cricket he is still full of humility and modesty. I admire him as a player and human being. He is a great ambassador for cricket.

5) Greg Chappell

A very upright and correct player. He was a great accumulator of runs, though he also had the ability to destroy the opposition.

6) Garfield Sobers
He is the greatest human being that ever walked on a cricket field in all departments of the game. Batting, bowling, fielding – he was superlative.

7) Alan Knott
He is the best glove-man I have ever seen. His ability keeping to the fast bowlers and to the spinners was tremendous, while scoring runs in sticky situations was his trademark.

8) Imran Khan
A great self-believer who had the ability to swing the ball both ways and bowl at 90mph. Also a very gritty batsman.

9) Dennis Lillee
He was a lion-hearted bowler and had a fast out-swinger that made life very difficult for batsmen, as I found out to my cost in Australia. He was another that believed in himself a great deal.

10) Lance Gibbs
This man caused me a few problems in the early part of my Test career. He kept setting me up to be caught at midwicket, hitting against the turn. He had a lovely upright action and not only made the ball turn, but also bounce. Gibbsy bowled well on all types of wickets because he had so much variation.

11) Bishan Bedi
He was an artist at work and is the best left-arm spinner that I have ever seen. There was a flow in his rhythm and approach to the game. He would always back himself when bowling against the best batsmen and he always bowled to get them out.

MUSHTAQ MOHAMMED played 57 Test matches for Pakistan between 1958–59 and 1978–79, scoring 3,643 runs at an average of 39.17, and he took 79 wickets with his leg-spin at 29.24. In first-class cricket, the tenacious all-rounder scored 31,091 runs at 42.07 and took 936 wickets at 24.34. In county cricket, Mushtaq led Northamptonshire to their first trophy in 1976 when they claimed the Gillette Cup.

* * * * *

MAKHAYA NTINI'S XI

I have selected my team from players I have known from playing with or against them. Malcolm Marshall was my favourite bowler, but I have gone mainly for players I spent more time with in the game. I also considered Chris Gayle, who scored a triple century (317) against us in the Caribbean and who always seems to score runs against us, and Virender Sehwag, a similar player.

1) Gary Kirsten
He was a very strong and durable left-hander who never threw his wicket away and stayed at the wicket for his team. He made a lot of fast bowlers struggle for his wicket.

2) Sachin Tendulkar

One of the top players of all time. I've always regarded him as a great timer of the ball. He doesn't go after every ball; he has the patience to wait for the bad ball so as a bowler you don't get too many chances from him. Sachin also impressed me with the way he detects slower balls – it is hard to deceive him.

3) Jacques Kallis

Jacques is like a wall, very similar to Tendulkar in the way he doesn't give many chances. He can be slow-scoring, but you need that balance in a team. Bowlers know he will be hard work.

4) Ricky Ponting

He is the kind of batsman who likes to increase the scoring rate very quickly. He likes to see the ball hitting the boundary rope. It is good to have these players in your team, who are capable of scoring a century in 80 or 90 balls.

5) Brian Lara

One of the best of all time. He was an entertainer. You could tell what kind of form and mood he was in when he walked into bat from his body language. If he was in the mood he could easily score a double century. He would make big runs and dominate you.

6) Steve Waugh

He was the anchor who let others play around him; he didn't take too many risks. Sometimes he appeared so untroubled that you felt the only way he was going to get out was run out! When I bowled to him I tried not to give him any balls to score off and play on his patience. You could bounce him all day, but it never bothered him.

7) Adam Gilchrist

He is an all-rounder, with his keeping and batting. He would usually come in when the ball was old and dictate matters from ball one. When he came in he would just climb into you, whatever the state of the Test match or whether you were a spinner or fast bowler. He was capable of scoring at four or five runs per over.

8) Shane Warne

Warney is the best spinner I have ever seen. He's incredible. He would pitch the ball outside leg stump and hit off. Even if batsmen tried to cover their leg stump with their pads, he could turn it so much that he could bowl batsmen around their legs.

9) Glenn McGrath

McGrath was a line and length bowler who never tried to do anything extraordinary, he was just so consistent. Number nine may be high for him, but look at the two batsmen behind him! Hopefully he wouldn't be required to bat anyway with this top eight.

10) Muttiah Muralitharan

He is everybody's favourite, with his bag of tricks. He has got his doosra – his wrong ball, and those huge off-breaks. Murali could turn the ball on concrete. With Warney bowling from one end and Murali from the other it would make great viewing and there would be no place to hide for batsmen. I have enjoyed playing with him in the Indian Premier League; he's a lovely bloke.

11) Courtney Walsh

We respected him a great deal, with his pace and his slower balls and he could swing the new ball from both sides of the wicket. Courtney had variety and you never knew what he would bowl next. He always wanted to bowl and never knew when to stop; every time his captain needed him he would be ready.

MAKHAYA NTINI has played 90 Tests for South Africa from 1997–98 and taken 390 wickets at an average of 28.82. He is the second-highest Test wicket-taker for his country (trailing Shaun Pollock). The fast bowler spearheaded South Africa's attack for a decade, first with Allan Donald, then Shaun Pollock, and latterly Dale Steyn. Apart from wicket-taking ability, endurance is his main asset; he has a capacity to keep bowling, unlike many fast bowlers. He claimed a national record match haul of 13–132 against the West Indies at Trinidad in 2005.

* * * * *

GRAEME POLLOCK'S XI

My team is from players I played with or against. I've gone for a very positive line up: players who always looked to take wickets or to score runs. I feel that batting is about attacking as opposed to just staying there. I had to leave out some very fine players and some of those include: Richard Hadlee, Graham Gooch, Eddie Barlow, Colin Cowdrey, Rohan Kanhai and Kenny Barrington. Don Bradman's omission is due to the fact that I never saw him. His average is 40 runs higher than most good players of his era, which illustrates how good he must have been, though I am sticking to my selection policy of only picking those I saw during my era.

1) Barry Richards

As an all-round player, he was technically as good as anyone that has ever played the game. He was supremely strong in each and every department.

2) Geoffrey Boycott

Boycs was technically very sound, which is important for an opening batsman. He is not anywhere near as attacking as my other batsmen, but somebody needs to put runs on the board before the stroke players can blossom and dominate.

3) Ted Dexter

A great player of quick bowling, which is essential when batting at number three. Ted was a real attacking batsman who loved to take control of a situation.

4) Greg Chappell

He was a tall, classy player who wasn't normally attacking straight away, but once he was in he liked to dominate.

5) Garfield Sobers

A genius all-round cricketer. As far as I am concerned there has never been a better all-rounder than him in first-class cricket. He was explosive with both bat and ball and a marvellous fielder too.

6) Clive Lloyd

Another tremendous player who really gives this side depth batting at six. By the time he comes to the crease, the bowlers should be quite weary and there is no better man to come in this position to maintain the initiative. He would be my captain.

7) Mike Procter

Procky was certainly a great all-rounder and very close to the Sobers level. He batted superbly as his runs in county cricket showed, and as a bowler he took 41 wickets in just seven Tests. He would open the bowling for me with Dennis Lillee.

8) Alan Knott

He was an excellent all-round keeper who kept to the quicks as well as he did to the spinners. Also, Derek Underwood is my spinner and he and Knotty were a great team for both Kent and England and that's an added bonus to my side.

9) Graham McKenzie

I played against him in three series and he bowled superbly in all of them. He was not in the super-quick bracket, but he moved the ball away from the bat, which is important when bowling to the classy players.

10) Derek Underwood

Generally, he was an all-wicket bowler and didn't need specific conditions to be effective. Certainly, he was the best spinner that I ever faced.

11) Dennis Lillee

As far as I'm concerned, he's the greatest fast bowler of all time. He was aggressive, very quick and had great control. He had it all, no doubt about it. I find it difficult to believe there has been a better quick bowler than him.

GRAEME POLLOCK played just 23 Tests for South Africa between 1963–64 and 1969–70, due to isolation. He still compiled 2,256 runs at an average of 60.97 for the second best Test average to Sir Donald Bradman out of the Test cricketers that played in this many matches. He is regarded as one of the finest batsmen of all time and arguably the finest left-hander, along with the likes of Sobers, Lara, Border and Harvey.

✳ ✳ ✳ ✳ ✳

SHAUN POLLOCK'S XI

I have chosen my team from modern-day players whom I have seen. The main criterion, apart from skill, is the ability to entertain. Test cricket should be entertaining and the batsmen I have selected would certainly be that. To watch them in the same team would be awesome. With the bowling, there are left and right-arm bowlers who can swing the ball, and an out-and-out quick in Donald. I never saw a lot of the great players from older generations, though I have selected my uncle for sentimental reasons and from what I heard about his batting.

1) Virender Sehwag
It was close between Sehwag and Desmond Haynes, whom I watched play for Western Province. My old Natal teammate Malcolm Marshall used to tell me so much about him. But I played a lot against Sehwag and he is certainly an entertaining opener of note.

2) Brian Lara
He holds two world records so, on those stats alone, he gets in. He is a great batsman to watch. Even when his team struggled in South Africa he was still a good performer.

3) Sachin Tendulkar
He is a class act and will almost certainly end up breaking all of the batting records in both forms of cricket.

4) Graeme Pollock
A sentimental choice. Having grown up in South Africa, where there was no international cricket, he was the best player that we were exposed to during the years of isolation.

5) Viv Richards
I would make him captain because of all the feats he achieved with the West Indies and because he was the great, intimidating cricketer that he was. A great slip catcher and a useful off-spinner.

6) Ian Botham
Probably the best all-rounder the game has seen in modern-day cricket. I am looking for an entertaining team and Botham was certainly entertaining.

7) Adam Gilchrist

This guy is a great attacking batsman. I'm pleased to say I missed the match when he scored his 204 not out in Johannesburg! Nobody likes to miss a Test match but that was a good one to miss. Ian Healy would be close, but Gilchrist's batting gets him in.

8) Wasim Akram

A great left-arm bowler who enjoyed an illustrious career. He swung the ball both ways at good pace, and he was not the worst batsman either.

9) Malcolm Marshall

Just awesome; he was my mentor. I was lucky enough to spend four seasons with him at Natal. To see how good he was then made me think he must have been some bowler in his youth. Malcolm was the man who told me to 'get nasty' and bowl more bouncers.

10) Shane Warne

He has a great Test record and having played against him and seen what he has done in world cricket, he is a certainty for this team. He has had the biggest impact on cricket in the modern era.

11) Allan Donald

AD has to be in, he's a remarkable guy. To have played with him and experienced what he has achieved and bowled with him out in the middle, is a great honour for me. There was no doubt that I would pick him in my team. Not only was he a fantastic bowler with a great record to prove it, he was also a tremendous athlete.

SHAUN POLLOCK played 108 Tests for South Africa between 1995–96 and 2007–08 and took 421 wickets at an average of 23.11. He was also a useful middle-order batsman and his 3,781 Test runs at 32.31 prove his versatility. The pace bowler mastered the art of swing and seam at an early stage of his career. Accuracy was a further strength as he would often probe away patiently on off stump or just outside.

✳ ✳ ✳ ✳ ✳

ERAPALLI PRASANNA'S XI

This is a very strong team that I have selected mainly from my own era. With Dennis Lillee, Wes Hall and Kapil Dev providing the seam attack, I would use Sobers as a spin bowler. I have also picked four back-up players, who have just failed to make the full XI: Colin Bland, myself, Derek Underwood and Michael Holding.

1) Sunil Gavaskar

I couldn't leave out Sunny after I saw from close quarters what he did for Indian cricket. He gave us a start on so many occasions.

2) Barry Richards

I never played Test cricket against him, unfortunately, but you only have to see his stats and listen to people who played with and against him to know what a great player he was.

3) Tom Graveney

He was a good player of spin and never an easy batsman to work out.

4) Viv Richards

He scored a big century (192 not out) in only his second Test, against us at Delhi in 1974. It was an early indication that he had a great deal of talent and would enjoy a good career.

5) Garfield Sobers

In only my second Test, when on tour in the Caribbean, I realised what a great player he was, when he scored 153 and took a few wickets as well. There cannot have been a better all-rounder.

6) Sachin Tendulkar

You only have to look at all the runs he has scored and the records he has broken to know he is one of the best ever.

7) Alan Knott

Knotty was simply wonderful behind the stumps; entertaining but also a faultless performer with the gloves.

8) Kapil Dev

India should be proud of what Kapil Dev did for the country, as we do not have too many great fast bowlers in our history.

9) Subhash Gupte

I know I could pick Shane Warne and (Muttiah) Muralitharan from the modern era, but my personal favourite would be Subhash Gupte, a magician of a leg-spinner. The sad part is that I only started playing for India in 1962, as he was ending his career.

10) Dennis Lillee

There cannot have been too many better fast bowlers than Lillee, if one exists at all. He was very strong and very good.

11) Wes Hall

Full of commitment and raw pace. He was a great competitor and batsmen knew they were in a contest against Wes.

ERAPALLI PRASANNA played 49 Test matches for India between 1961–62 and 1978–79 and took 189 wickets at an average of 30.38. In all first-class cricket he claimed 957 wickets at 23.45. He was an off-spinner that turned the ball prodigiously, imparting a tremendous rip on the ball. His best figures in Test cricket were eight for 76 against New Zealand at Auckland in 1975–76. 'Pras', as he was known, combined with Bishan Bedi and Bhagwat Chandrasekhar in a feared spin attack for India.

✳ ✳ ✳ ✳ ✳

MIKE PROCTER'S XI

With the obvious exception of Bradman I preferred to select a side from players that I have seen.

1) Sunil Gavaskar – I saw a lot of Sunny and he was a fantastic player of quick bowling. His balance was *so* good. He had great footwork.

2) Barry Richards
Technically the best batsman that I have ever seen. He was one of those guys who saw the ball very early. The better the bowler, the better he performed. He loved a challenge.

3) Viv Richards
The best batsman that I have ever seen. He could destroy any attack with devastating results.

4) Donald Bradman
I never saw him but he is recognised worldwide as the best ever, so who am I to argue with so many?

5) Graeme Pollock
An absolutely fantastic player. His Test average is second only to Bradman, and it's a shame he never had more of a chance to play at that level.

6) Garfield Sobers
The greatest all-rounder the world has seen and is likely to see. He was great whether batting, bowling or fielding. He could bowl spin or seam, and when he came off his long run he could be really quick.

7) Ian Botham
A match-winner. He was a guy who was always likely to score runs or take wickets, and at the right time too. Always stood up to be counted in tight situations; a fabulous all-rounder.

8) Alan Knott

The best wicketkeeper I've ever seen. His glove work was outstanding. He played a lot of very useful innings too. Adam Gilchrist would be the better batsman, but Knott gets in for pure glove work.

9) Shane Warne

He's a freakish, amazing bowler. He spun the ball so consistently so often with great control, variation and he also got that dip which made him such a tough proposition. I would have gone for Richie Benaud for his all-round skills and shrewd cricket knowledge as a captain, but since Warne emerged I can only go one way.

10) Michael Holding

He was called 'Whispering Death' and that sums him up: Very fast and a truly great all-round bowler.

11) Dennis Lillee

He really is one of the great fast bowlers, along with Michael Holding. A great effort-bowler who would still be as committed even when his figures were two for 120.

MIKE PROCTER played only seven Tests for South Africa, between 1966–67 and 1969–70, due to isolation, but still managed to claim 41 wickets at an average of just 15.02. He was one of the great all-rounders of his era and in first-class cricket scored 21,904 runs at 36.15 and took 1,407 wickets at 19.37. He became the first player to take a hat-trick and score a century in one match on two occasions, for Gloucestershire.

* * * * *

SONNY RAMADHIN'S XI

There are so many great cricketers to pick from and selecting this side was not easy at all. I have based my team on players that I played with or against.

1) Leonard Hutton

The best batsman against all types of bowling and on all types of wickets.

2) Bobby Simpson

A fine attacking or defensive opening batsman and a brilliant slip fielder.

3) Garfield Sobers

The best all-rounder that I have ever seen. He could bat anywhere in the top seven and adapt to any situation.

4) Everton Weekes

A fine attacking batsman and comfortably one of the best of his generation. He could be difficult for bowlers to tie down.

5) Frank Worrell

Another fine all-rounder, but a far greater batsman. He played the game in the right spirit and was a true gentleman.

6) Rohan Kanhai

He is my keeper, as he started as a wicketkeeper-batsman before he became a tremendous front-line batsman. He was good against all types of bowling.

7) Ray Lindwall

Simply one of the greatest fast bowlers of all time and was useful enough with the bat to come in this high in the order.

8) Fred Trueman

Same as Lindwall. Fred was a real character and a captain always knew what he would get from this man: commitment.

9) Wes Hall

A wonderful fast bowler whom I played a lot of cricket with. Wes was full of heart and commitment. He had great pace and stamina.

10) Lance Gibbs

I believe he is the best off-spinner of his type and could turn the ball on any kind of wicket.

11) Subhash Gupte

A very fine leg-break googly bowler who was so good to watch. Shane Warne has dominated the modern era, but Gupte was as good in his day, I believe.

SONNY RAMADHIN played 43 Tests for the West Indies between 1950 and 1960–61, taking 158 wickets at an average of 28.98. 'Ram' bowled off-breaks and leg-breaks that were spun by the finger, not the wrist. Along with Alf Valentine he formed a prolific spin duo. In 1950 at Lord's, when the West Indies won for the first time in England, Sonny's contribution was 11 for 152. He achieved 758 first-class wickets at 20.24.

Ken Kelly

Gordon Greenidge
'The power of some of his shots was frightening' – Sir Ian Botham

Michael Holding
'Had such grace and elegance; we'll never see one of his kind again' – Andy Roberts

Viv Richards and Ian Botham
'He is one of the most gifted cricketers I've seen' – Sir Garfield Sobers on Ian Botham

Viv Richards
'There was no such thing as a good ball to him' – Sunil Gavaskar on Viv Richards

Kapil Dev
'His record is awesome; a great ambassador for Indian cricket' – Anil Kumble

Desmond Haynes
'A player who preferred to dominate (the bowling)' – Gordon Greenidge

Wasim Akram
'What made him so special was his ability to swing
the ball both ways and his change of pace' –
Jacques Kallis

Allan Border
'It physically hurt him to lose… AB was the ultimate pro' – Sir Ian Botham

Jacques Kallis
'The best modern day all-rounder' – Alec Stewart

Curtly Ambrose
'He's a fast bowler whom I would go to war with and be confident of winning' – Richie
Richardson

Allan Donald
'If you didn't know where your off stump was he would find you out' – Herschelle Gibbs

Sachin Tendulkar
'Will almost certainly end up breaking all of the batting records in both forms of cricket' –
Shaun Pollock

Brian Lara

'If he was in the mood he could easily score a double century' – Makhaya Ntini

Muttiah Muralitharan
'Even if he played on Tarmac, he would still turn it' – Arjuna Ranatunga

Glenn McGrath

'He gets in over Dennis Lillee because he had better success in the sub-continent'
– Wasim Akram

Shane Warne
'The best leg-spin bowler ever to play the game' – Richie Benaud

Adam Gilchrist
'He tried to win matches rather than survive in them' – Kapil Dev

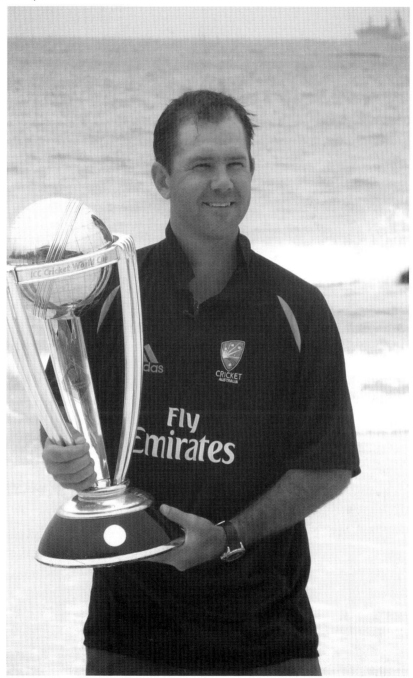

Ricky Ponting
'He always shows his quality in the big matches. The bigger the match the better he performs' – Inzamam-ul-Haq

Virender Sehwag
'He is such a destructive batsman that he can change a game in literally one session' – Anil Kumble

ARJUNA RANATUNGA'S XI

I have selected my side from cricketers that I have played with or against in Test cricket. I would include Abdul Qadir in a squad of 12 and would play him instead of Ambrose if the conditions and opposition were suitable for playing two spin bowlers.

1) Sunil Gavaskar
Sunny is the best opening batsman that I ever played with or against. He had a lot of patience and, consequently, he was able to compile big scores.

2) Sachin Tendulkar
Although he plays in the middle-order in Test cricket, Sachin would still be as good if he opened. He is one of the best cricketers I've seen and among the top three batsmen in the world today.

3) Greg Chappell
I saw him in the latter stage of his career, but even then he was brilliant. I rated him as a top-class captain and he would lead this side.

4) Aravinda De Silva
He is the best cricketer that Sri Lanka has ever produced, maybe along with Murali and Jayasuriya. His results speak for themselves. He's a genuine great Test match batsman.

5) Javed Miandad
A super player whom I was to learn a lot from. He is a person who could change a game at any time and play to the situation of the game perfectly. He was undoubtedly one of the greatest batsmen of all time.

6) Allan Border
Getting 10,000 runs is not a joke in whatever cricket you play. I learned a lot from his captaincy and his batting: I think there are similarities between how we both played.

7) Rodney Marsh
I played one game against Marshy and he was unbelievable; the best keeper I've ever seen. His keeping impressed me most, but with the bat he could get a hundred for you at any time.

8) Wasim Akram
I rate him as comfortably the most dangerous bowler I ever faced, both to the body and to my wicket. If you have somebody like him in your team, you are lucky.

9) Richard Hadlee

Unfortunately, when I played against him it was near to the end of his career, but he still seemed to get five wickets against us every time. Any young cricketer could learn a lot from the way he bowled; he was so great and with a simple action.

10) Curtly Ambrose

I have rated him very high because he's someone who could always take wickets at vital times, which is a crucial factor in Test cricket. I nearly picked Joel Garner, but I never quite saw enough of him in Test cricket.

11) Muttiah Muralitharan

Wherever he plays, even if he played on tarmac, he would still turn it, which is a significant advantage to have in your side. He has a strong character, which he has shown in the face of all the criticism about his action, yet he has still produced the goods.

ARJUNA RANATUNGA played 93 Tests for Sri Lanka from 1981–82 to 2000 and scored 5,105 runs. A left-hand middle-order batsman, he was able to adapt his batting to the situation of a match expertly, which helped make him an effective limited overs player. A great player of spin and a very astute, uncompromising captain, he was key in building Sri Lanka's reputation in world cricket, culminating in a 1996 World Cup win.

* * * * *

BARRY RICHARDS'S XI

Without doubt the most difficult thing to do is not to pick the team, but to decide who to leave out. My feeling is that I could pick another 11 and, on a given day, they could beat this team. That's how great some of the following players are who I've had to leave out. I'm disappointed at not being able to include: the Chappell brothers, the Waugh brothers, Border, Healy and Marsh (Australia); Haynes, Lara, Lloyd and that great quartet of quicks – Marshall, Garner, Ambrose, Holding and the under-rated Courtney Walsh (West Indies); Underwood, Edrich, Gower, Gooch, Snow and Knott – who went about his business with the minimum amount of fuss, which is what good keepers should be like, but able to bring out the spectacular when you need it (England); Akram, Imran, Zaheer, Hanif and Miandad (Pakistan); Kapil Dev, Prasanna and especially Bedi (India): Procter, Donald, Adcock, Barlow, Bland, Waite and Lindsay (South Africa); Hadlee, Martin Crowe and Turner (New Zealand). Finally, I would like to apologise to anybody who I have left out of this list. My 12th man would be Jonty Rhodes for his fielding.

1) Sunil Gavaskar

Sunny was very well organised and compact with a good technique and a very good, typically calm, Indian temperament.

2) Gordon Greenidge

My old Hampshire opening partner; he was a very flamboyant opener. He had a good technique and was a guy who could bat well on all types of wickets. Gordon was also a fine slip fielder.

3) Donald Bradman

Enough said, I think. No doubt this selection has been more than adequately covered by everybody else in the book.

4) Viv Richards

He and Graeme Pollock were the two most destructive players I have seen. Viv was totally dominating and awesome.

5) Graeme Pollock

Same as Viv but a left-handed version. Graeme put games into a winning situation because of the rate at which he scored.

6) Garfield Sobers

He could make a Test side as a batsman, bowler or a fielder, which is an amazing feat; the complete cricketer.

7) Ian Botham

Boys' Own stuff. He had an aura and a presence and everything you would want from a cricketer purely for the enjoyment of the game. He put bums on seats, which is what the game's all about.

8) Adam Gilchrist

Five or 10 years ago I would have gone for Alan Knott, but Gilchrist has changed the landscape for keepers. He is a very good glove-man and a destructive batsman, capable of changing games.

9) Shane Warne

He burst on to the scene in style: everybody remembers 'the Gatting ball'. Since Grimmett there hasn't been such an exciting prospect. You always have the feeling of expectancy when he bowls his array of deliveries, which has added an exciting dimension to cricket.

10) Dennis Lillee

Always aggressive and was as quick in his second spell as his first; subsequently, Dennis was the captain's dream.

11) Andy Roberts

Andy, whom I knew at Hampshire, was not a naturally aggressive bowler, but never backed off from a situation. If he smelt fear in a batsman he was one of the quickest I've seen to go for the jugular.

BARRY RICHARDS played just four Test matches for South Africa, due to isolation, but still scored 508 runs at a superior average of 72.57. In first-class cricket he amassed 28,358 runs at 54.75, including 80 centuries. He is one of the greatest opening batsmen of all time, who always looked to bat positively to secure a victory for his team. In county cricket, he served Hampshire loyally from 1968 to 1978.

* * * * *

RICHIE RICHARDSON'S XI

I found it too difficult to select my team from previous generations as I never saw them. Players like Peter May and Len Hutton must have been great, but I'm a better judge of those from more recent years – Bradman is an obvious exception. There are quite a few who came very close to finding a place in this team. I won't mention them all, but they include players like Allan Border, Abdul Qadir – who was better than Warne initially – Alan Knott, Clive Lloyd, Brian Lara, Sachin Tendulkar, Javed Miandad, Desmond Haynes and Richard Hadlee – whom I'd love to have found a place for, but he just misses out.

1) Gordon Greenidge
Technically, he's the most accomplished batsman I've ever seen. Gordon had tremendous application and concentration and could always be relied upon to get the team off to a flying start, usually with Desmond Haynes, another great opener.

2) Sunil Gavaskar
For his sheer ability to bat. Sunny was always composed and could go out and score runs in any conditions. The fact he was the first player to score 10,000 Test runs proves what a great accumulator he was. I wouldn't say I used to worry about how we would ever dismiss him; instead, I used to enjoy watching him bat. Sachin Tendulkar's style reminds me of Gavaskar.

3) Viv Richards
He's definitely the best batsman I've ever seen. He's probably the only batsman I've seen intimidate bowlers just by his very presence. His talent was special as he went about his game in his own unique way, backing himself against any bowler.

4) Donald Bradman
Even though I never saw him bat, he has to be the first one down on this team sheet. Everyone that saw him says that he was very special. I have to have him in my side.

5) Greg Chappell
There were a few others, like Lara and Tendulkar, that I nearly picked for this place, but Greg Chappell was a personal favourite of mine. He was one of the most mentally strong players I've ever seen. When he was at the wicket he always looked as though he was in

control. I recall him once having a run of low scores against us – which didn't happen very often – and his approach never changed despite his form. His expression and confident, graceful style remained the same and that impressed me tremendously. He also has a fine record, with over 7,000 runs at an average of over 50.

6) Garfield Sobers
No doubts here. I only saw a little of Sobers's play, but he's clearly the best all-rounder of all time. From what I've heard he was an explosive batsman, could bowl fast or bowl chinamen and googlies and was also one of the best-ever fielders close to the bat.

7) Rodney Marsh
It's very close between Marsh, Knott and Gilchrist, but I saw more of Marsh up close. One of the key reasons why I opted for Marsh was that he was a prominent part of the Lillee and Thomson partnership – Marsh was an integral member of that Australia team. Particularly, there was a real connection between Lillee and Marsh, who are both Western Australians. Marshy was a like a hub – everything was centred around him. Lillee wasn't complete without Marsh behind the stumps.

8) Malcolm Marshall
The greatest artist in fast bowling terms that I've ever seen. He seemed to know everything about every batsman he bowled to. He would tell us in the dressing room and on the field how he would dismiss a certain player, and usually he made it happen. I was impressed by his knowledge and the way he analysed batsmen more than his express pace and all-round bowling talent.

9) Shane Warne
I rated Abdul Qadir above Shane Warne at one point, but when selecting a team of all time you have to consider a player throughout his career. Qadir was probably more magical than Warne when he started, but over time Warne proved he was the best. It was a great challenge playing against Warne because of his variety and the distances he turned the ball. More impressive though was that no matter how much you attacked him he never lost confidence.

10) Curtly Ambrose
He was a fast bowler whom I would go to war with and be confident of winning. He never let me down once when I was captain and I never saw him bowl a bad spell. If he couldn't get you out, you still wouldn't get control of him or score freely off him. I've seen batsmen get on top of Malcolm Marshall, but never Curtly.

11) Dennis Lillee
The classical fast bowler and one of the greatest of all time. He was almost the perfect fast bowler in terms of his action, approach to the wicket, his pace and aggression and ability.

RICHIE RICHARDSON played 86 Tests for the West Indies between 1983–84 and 1995. He scored 5,949 runs at an average of 44.39. In first-class cricket he amassed 14,618 runs at 40.71. Richardson was a protégé of fellow Antiguan Viv Richards, possessing the same natural ability to destroy bowling attacks with similar flamboyance and power. Richardson, who took over the West Indies captaincy from Richards, was also a safe catcher at slip.

* * * * *

ANDY ROBERTS' XI

With the exceptions of Bradman and Headley, I selected my side from players I have played with or against in Test cricket. This was not an easy task and I would like to mention a few names I was not able to include: Clive Lloyd – who was as good as anybody towards the end of his career; Lance Gibbs; Imran Khan; Joel Garner; Ian Chappell – probably the most determined batsman Australia has produced; Barry Richards – whom I would rate as the second-best batsman I have seen behind Viv Richards, though I left him out due to his lack of Test cricket, through no fault of his own of course. Likewise, Graeme Pollock and Mike Procter fall into the same category. There is no spinner in the team but Sobers and Richards can fill that role.

1) Sunil Gavaskar
To me, he is one of the best openers ever to play the game. He had his limitations, mainly because of his height, but on the right pitch he was almost impossible to bowl at.

2) Gordon Greenidge
A fantastic player even though he had his problems in Australia, which is something I have never been able to understand, given that his main strengths were pulling and cutting – shots you need to be good at on the hard Australian pitches. These problems aside, he was a great player of both spin bowling and fast bowling, and consequently he has an excellent record to prove it.

3) Viv Richards
His footwork was a lot quicker than most and his reflexes and ability to see the ball early were his greatest strengths. He could be either the best attacking batsman or the best defensive batsman and I have seen him play both roles. In my view he was in a class of his own and is easily the best batsman I have ever seen.

4) Donald Bradman
His record speaks for itself. I've also read and heard a lot of great things about him.

5) George Headley
The same reasons as Bradman. He was an excellent ambassador for West Indies cricket in our early days of Test cricket.

6) Greg Chappell

A great Australian batsman capable of destroying any attack. He was an elegant batsman who played superbly off the front and back foot. Towards the end of his career we worked out a formula against him, which was to attack his body when he came in. We had reasonable success from that plan, though we knew that if we didn't get him early he would be very difficult to remove.

7) Garfield Sobers

His record says it all. He is the greatest cricketer that ever lived. It's pretty obvious that he is the best all-rounder of all time, but he is also not far from being the best batsman as well.

8) Alan Knott

I played with him during the World Series Cup. He was a wicketkeeper supreme both to spin bowling and fast bowling, and his batting was just as good in the middle-order. His approach to batting was very unorthodox but successful. Rodney Marsh would not be far behind.

9) Malcolm Marshall

One of the greatest fast bowlers that ever lived. Not a bowler of great height, but one of tremendous strength and will to succeed. Malcolm could do a lot more with the ball than most fast bowlers, but it took him about 20 Test matches before he really learnt his trade. He was fortunate that the West Indies have always given new players a lengthy run in the side initially, unlike certain other countries. Eventually, his strike rate was probably better than anyone's.

10) Michael Holding

My good friend Mikey had such grace and elegance; we'll never see one of his kind again. He had pace, movement and learned in the early stages of his career to conserve his energy, as he cut his run-up down by half and was still as quick. Along with Jeff Thomson, he was the quickest bowler of his generation.

11) Dennis Lillee

The best fast bowler that I ever saw. He had everything that you could ever ask of a quick bowler: a good run-up, aggression, pace, will to win and the ability to move the ball at speeds of 90mph and above.

ANDY ROBERTS played 47 Tests for the West Indies between 1973–74 and 1983–84, taking 202 wickets at an average of 25.61. In first-class cricket he claimed 889 wickets at just 21.01. He was one of the greatest quick bowlers of his era and was a founder member of the West Indian pace quartet in the mid-seventies that enjoyed so much success under Clive Lloyd's captaincy. He was a great exponent of changing his pace.

LAWRENCE ROWE'S XI

I had a hard time picking players before my time, but the records of Bradman and Headley are just superb and cannot be ignored. It does mean, though, that I have had to leave out Viv Richards, which wasn't easy. I wanted positive cricketers in my team who entertain. Although I admired players like Geoff Boycott and Ken Barrington, they would never bring too many people through the turnstiles with the way they batted. Others I considered but finally left out were Richie Benaud, Greg Chappell, Abdul Qadir, Andy Roberts and Len Hutton. I would like to think that I might have made one of these teams if I had not suffered from so many injuries. My hundreds per Test match ratio is as good as most. However, I'm very pleased with this line up and feel it only needs five batsmen given the quality of the top five.

1) Sunil Gavaskar
He was probably the greatest opener of my time. He made a lot of runs against a very strong West Indies team and went on to score more Test centuries than anyone.

2) Barry Richards
He was a super bat. His Test career was only short but he proved his class in the limited time he had in Tests before South Africa was kicked out of world cricket. Even just before he retired, when I went to South Africa in the eighties, he was still scoring lots of runs.

3) Donald Bradman
I don't know much about him, but his record speaks for itself. The Don must have been a real great player.

4) George Headley
His record is awesome: 10 centuries in 22 Test matches at an average of over 60 – that says it all.

5) Garfield Sobers
I think this man is the greatest of all time. He was my first captain in the West Indies team and he was a very attacking one too. Garry didn't like drawn games so he would always be trying desperately to win. I always found Garry to be a super guy.

6) Alan Knott
I had the privilege of playing with him in the World Series and I remember him stumping me for 76 – it was a remarkable piece of keeping. I was playing well and it was the first ball I had missed all day. Suddenly Derek Underwood got one to turn

sharply, which beat me, and as I tried to get back in my ground Knotty was already congratulating Underwood – he was that quick. Good with the bat as well.

7) Michael Holding

He was the quickest of all time. He's a superb guy and a great bowler who could get the ball to swing, bounce and move off the seam. He was the master of the front foot rule as he hardly bowled a no-ball.

8) Dennis Lillee

The greatest fast bowler of all time. He was a real hard worker who was always probing away against batsmen. Regardless of how good the batsman was, Lillee always punished a poor stroke.

9) Wes Hall

I remember the days when Wes – along with Charlie Griffith – carried the West Indies fast bowling attack. Wes was a hard-working bowler who could bowl long spells, but not at the expense of pace. He took 191 Test wickets and he and Fred Trueman would have to be the two greatest quick bowlers of the 1960s.

10) Lance Gibbs

Simply the best off-spinner that has ever played the game, in my opinion. I have never seen a better off-spinner than him in my time or after. He made the ball bounce and turn dangerously.

11) Subhash Gupte

For his wrong ones especially. I didn't see this great leg-spinner in action, but through talking to so many respected people in the game who did see him or play with him, Gupte has to be in my team.

LAWRENCE ROWE played 30 Tests for the West Indies between 1971–72 and 1979–80, scoring 2,047 runs at an average of 43.55. This stylish right-hander, who could open or bat in the middle-order, is regarded as one of the most naturally gifted players ever to grace a cricket arena, but sadly a number of injuries curtailed a Test career that would certainly have been much longer and probably much more prolific. His finest moment was his innings of 302 against England at Barbados in 1973–74.

SAEED ANWAR'S XI

It's a strong batting side and Allan Border and Sachin Tendulkar just miss out. With the opening pair, there's one who can stay there and one who will play his shots in Greenidge. In the bowling department, Dennis Lillee and Malcolm Marshall just fail to get in because I feel the two all-rounders add more depth to the side.

1) Sunil Gavaskar
He is the best opener of all time because he was consistent and scored runs not only in India, but everywhere. He batted particularly well against a strong West Indies side, which was a key factor in why he was such a great player.

2) Gordon Greenidge
He was entirely different to Gavaskar; he took charge from the outset and played attractive shots – my type of opener.

3) Viv Richards
Since I have been watching cricket I have not seen anybody as good as Viv. He played all types of bowlers with ease because he had unbelievable talent, great eyesight and good reflexes.

4) Brian Lara
There are a few players good enough to fill this slot, but I just think that Brian Lara is the best batsman of the modern era. He's scored 500, 400 and 300 and several double hundreds and that's the reason why I have not selected Sachin Tendulkar instead.

5) Garfield Sobers
Without a doubt, he's the best all-rounder ever. He was a wonderful batsman and could bowl fast or left-arm chinamen. Sobers gave his team tremendous depth.

6) Steve Waugh
For a decade he was the mainstay of the Australian batting. If they lost three or four quick wickets he came in and regularly scored hundreds. He was always so determined.

7) Ian Botham
One of the best all-rounders the world has seen. He could bat, bowl well in any conditions and field brilliantly at slip.

8) Imran Khan
He was a great fast bowler and had a sound technique as a batsman as well. The most impressive aspect of him was his ability to swing the old ball and the new ball. He was a good competitor and an excellent captain. People wanted to go into battle alongside him.

9) Alan Knott

I saw a fair bit of him and he was a great keeper. There have been many great keepers, like Rodney Marsh, Ian Healy and Wasim Bari. But I feel Knott is the best. He could bat well and keep to pace and spin superbly. Adam Gilchrist misses out as he was nowhere near the same class as Knott as a keeper, even if he could bat better.

10) Wasim Akram

I am a great fan of both Lillee and Marshall, but I consider Wasim to be the best all-round fast bowler I have ever seen. He could bowl any kind of delivery that you can possibly think of and at great pace too. He was also a pretty handy batsman.

11) Shane Warne

He is the best leg-spinner that I have ever seen. I know he didn't perform so well against India, but he had problems with his shoulder so I don't think we always saw a fair reflection of his ability.

SAEED ANWAR has played 55 Test matches for Pakistan since 1990–91 and has scored 4,052 runs at an average of 45.52. He is a dynamic left-handed opening batsman capable of dashing stroke-play. Saeed began his Test career with a pair against a West Indies side that hadn't lost a Test series for 10 years, but subsequently proved himself one of the best opening batsmen of his era and certainly one of the most graceful.

* * * * *

SAQLAIN MUSHTAQ'S XI

I selected my team from players I've seen. It was a hard job and I have to mention some who were unlucky not to make the team: Don Bradman – obviously one of the true greats, Garry Sobers, Gordon Greenidge, Desmond Haynes, Waqar Younis, Brian Lara, Sachin Tendulkar, Ian Botham, Glenn McGrath, Shane Warne, Abdul Qadir and Mushtaq Ahmed – an underrated leg-spinner. If the game were to be played on a turning wicket, I would play two spinners and omit one of the seamers.

1) Sunil Gavaskar

One of the greatest players ever. Tremendous powers of concentration, very stylish and had great balance. I never saw that much of him, but the senior members of the Pakistan team used to tell me just what a brilliant player he was.

2) Saeed Anwar

He is a man who always performed in a difficult position; when the team needed him to score well he usually did. Very stylish, aggressive and was a very intelligent player as well.

3) Viv Richards
An all-time great. When you saw Viv standing there at the wicket, it always looked like he was playing against kids – his presence was that imposing.

4) Javed Miandad
He was a great batsman to watch as I was growing up in Pakistan. He wore his heart on his sleeve, was always patriotic and never gave his wicket away.

5) Steve Waugh
Although I think he was a great batsman, whenever I bowled to him I never thought along those lines; he was just another batsman. I tried to dictate where I wanted him to be playing, whether leg stump, off stump, or wherever. It's important to gain the initiative over the batsman, especially against someone like Waugh who will look to bat for a long time otherwise.

6) Imran Khan
Another great all-rounder. He was my idol along with Wasim and Waqar. Imran was a strong, intelligent captain with great fighting qualities who never knew when he was beat.

7) Adam Gilchrist
I could have picked Ian Healy, but Gilchrist is a good keeper and an amazing attacking batsman anywhere in the order. He always seemed to make runs in crucial situations, when the team needed them most. He's proved himself a good wicketkeeper standing up to Warne and back to the likes of McGrath.

8) Richard Hadlee
A brilliant all-rounder. The thing that impressed me most about Richard Hadlee was that if he had a catch dropped off his bowling he never seemed to mind because he knew that he could do the same again next time. He carried the New Zealand bowling attack for many years and his attitude was excellent throughout.

9) Wasim Akram
The best left-arm pace bowler ever, and a great captain with a clever mind. He's the kind of bowler who was dangerous on any type of wicket, because he had such a wide variety of deliveries. He was also a very good batsman.

10) Malcolm Marshall
The best fast bowler ever. He had a wonderful action, a lovely run-up and was very quick.

11) Muttiah Muralitharan
His record is so great, in any format of the game. He turns it big and on any wicket. It doesn't matter if he plays in Sri Lanka, Australia or England, he always performs.

SAQLAIN MUSHTAQ played 49 Test matches for Pakistan from 1995–96 to 2003–04, taking 208 wickets at an average of 29.83. The off-spinner soon elevated himself to among the elite of modern spinners. He was not a conventional off-spinner, instead possessing great variety, and was renowned particularly for the drift he created and especially his signature, well-disguised delivery that spun the other way – the so-called 'doosra'.

* * * * *

RAVI SHASTRI'S XI

There are a lot more good players unable to make the side, but I am particularly disappointed to have to leave out Greg Chappell, Wasim Akram, Kapil Dev and Ian 'Beefy' Botham. I also think if I did this in another three years Virender Sehwag would have pushed out Hayden. I was very tempted to pick Barry Richards along with Sunny but he just didn't play enough Test cricket, which is obviously no fault of his own.

1) Sunil Gavaskar

The best defensive technique I have ever seen from an opening batsman, who also had the ability to play all the shots. The great things about Sunny were his concentration and balance, when playing the quicks or the spinners.

2) Matthew Hayden

He's a modern-day giant, very imposing and stamps his authority on the opposition from the outset. Hayden is also the right guy to balance the opening combination with Sunny, and he adds the left-hand element to the top order.

3) Viv Richards

The best batsman of my era and that I ever saw. Viv was tremendous, with justified arrogance and a brilliant eye.

4) Donald Bradman

His average of 99.94 speaks for itself. The Don would have to be an automatic choice whether I saw him or not.

5) Sachin Tendulkar

He has shown he is the world's best player in the modern era, and on all surfaces. He's a very attacking player in the Viv Richards mould, and although Sachin isn't a tall man he's still very strong. What's amazing about him is his balance, like Sunil Gavaskar. But the one thing he has shown that Sunny did not have to worry about is an ability to handle the huge pressure from the public and increased media coverage. He handles it amazingly well.

6) Garfield Sobers

Arguably the greatest cricketer of the 20th century. Because he was such a versatile cricketer he could lend balance to any team. He could bowl as sharp as anyone, bat superbly, and was a great fielder; a tremendous player to have at five or six.

7) Imran Khan

He was the best all-rounder of his era. He was quick and was one of the first guys who started reverse swing. Technically, he was the best batsman of the great all-rounders in the 1980s.

8) Alan Knott

It's close between him, Rodney Marsh and Ian Healy, but Knott is a better all-round wicketkeeper. He was also an unorthodox but effective batsman. Adam Gilchrist would get the vote for batting alone, but I've gone for the best keeper.

9) Malcolm Marshall

He was the quickest bowler I ever faced and he could bowl well on any surface. He once came to India and picked up over 30 wickets in the series on slow wickets because Marshall had great ability to bowl with an old ball.

10) Shane Warne

When this man bowled well, he got wickets very quickly. He didn't need to bowl 40 overs to pick up five wickets; if the ball turned he got his wickets in no time. He may not have been the same after his shoulder injury, but he was truly a great bowler before.

11) Dennis Lillee

He was a great fast bowler and had tremendous aggression, a superb run-up and a lovely out-swinger. Dennis had a very big heart, and recovered from a couple of back operations and still came out and bowled well.

RAVI SHASTRI played 80 Tests for India between 1980–81 and 1992–93, scoring 3,830 runs at an average of 35.79, and claimed 151 wickets as well. He was the first to emulate Garfield Sobers's feat of six sixes in an over. Ravi was versatile in all departments, capable of explosive innings or defiant stays at the crease, while being a useful left-arm spinner.

✳ ✳ ✳ ✳ ✳

MICHAEL SLATER'S XI

There are so many great cricketers to pick from that I found it almost impossible to do, but in the end I mainly went for players that I have seen as it was too difficult to compare eras. How do you compare Lindwall and Larwood with Marshall and Holding? It's tough. I'm disappointed not to have found a place for several players but particularly Ian Botham, who was a consistent match-winner for England. He's in the 12 but just misses out on a place in the team.

1) Sunil Gavaskar
I never saw that much of him, but his record is awesome. He was a brilliant opener with a tremendous technique.

2) Gordon Greenidge
This second opening position caused me a few problems, but I eventually went for one of my personal favourites. I relate very well to the way Greenidge played; we approached batting in a very similar way. Desmond Haynes was not far behind; I just felt that Greenidge had a bit more style.

3) Donald Bradman
The greatest ever! Not much doubt about this choice.

4) Viv Richards
An all time legend. 'The Master Blaster' was a player I used to love watching as a kid. He always played the game in a positive way.

5) Allan Border
AB's record is just amazing. He was not as exciting to watch as someone like Richards, but you need Border's type in your side. He was full of grit and determination, always leading by example. He gets in ahead of Steve Waugh.

6) Garfield Sobers
Like Bradman I never saw him play, but his record is superb and his reputation as the world's greatest all-rounder is justified.

7) Adam Gilchrist
I would have said Ian Healy until 'Gilly' made such an impact on world cricket. He's just a phenomenon. He rarely missed behind the stumps and could turn a match in a session with the bat.

8) Shane Warne
Without doubt the best spin bowler of all time, arguably the best cricketer of all time. The impact he has had on the game is incredible.

9) Wasim Akram
I just think this man is one of the greatest bowlers of all time. He is left-arm, which gives variety to the bowling attack, and he can do it all – in-swingers, out-swingers, bouncers, slower balls, you name it. He could also handle a bat.

10) Malcolm Marshall
I never faced him in Test cricket unfortunately – or should I say fortunately – but I did play against him when the West Indies played New South Wales in a warm-up game. He was pure pace and probably the pick of the great West Indian quicks.

11) Dennis Lillee

It was close between him and Richard Hadlee, but as I'm Australian I've gone for Lillee! His record is fantastic and he would have to be one of the greatest fast bowlers of all time.

MICHAEL SLATER played 74 Tests for Australia between 1993 and 2001 and scored 5,312 runs at an average of 42.83. The offensive technique of this free-scoring opener exhilarated crowds in the same way that his boyhood idols Viv Richards and Gordon Greenidge had entertained years before him. He began his Test career emphatically, scoring a 50 on his debut in an Ashes Test, and followed that with 152 at Lord's in his second match.

* * * * *

ROBIN SMITH'S XI

I selected my team from players I've seen. I must mention Michael Holding, Graham Gooch, Gordon Greenidge, Anil Kumble, Curtly Ambrose and Ricky Ponting – who were all unlucky not to be in.

1) Barry Richards

He was a sheer genius, but unfortunately he was not able to perform as a Test cricketer for as long as he should have done. He had so much time to play his shots and also had a wonderful technique whether playing on the front or back foot.

2) Sachin Tendulkar

Has a great record; he proved himself against all the class bowlers of the 1990s. In my opinion he is the best batsman of the modern generation.

3) Viv Richards

The most naturally talented batsman I have seen and he was so entertaining to watch; he could destroy any bowling attack at will. Viv was one of the most determined cricketers I have ever come across. Everyone that played the game respected him.

4) Brian Lara

A classical left-hander. I played against him when he scored his 375 and the innings was absolutely faultless; he never looked like getting out. He is a genuine match-winner and on his day he can destroy the best bowling attack in the world. I admire the fact that when he scores a century, it's usually a big one; he is very run-hungry.

5) Graeme Pollock

He was very much a front-foot player and a fantastic driver of the ball. When he got in, he never gave his wicket away. He was one of the most complete batsmen that you could ever wish to see – which is evident in his Test average of over 60.

6) Garfield Sobers

A great all-rounder, whose left-arm bowling offers the attack variety, either as a quick bowler or as a spin bowling partner to Shane Warne. With the bat he was a genius who was capable of putting together some really big scores, like his 365.

7) Ian Botham

Another great all-rounder. With over 5,000 runs, 383 wickets and 120 catches in Tests, he was a genuine world-class all-rounder. Beefy was a great influence in the dressing room and a wonderful inspiration to everybody that played with him.

8) Alan Knott

I didn't see a great amount of him, but what I did see and what I have heard is very impressive. He had a safe pair of hands, was very consistent and with the bat he was a good, aggressive player.

9) Malcolm Marshall

Malcolm had a fantastic strike rate in international cricket – better than anybody else who has played the game, I think. He had the ability to swing the ball both ways and at pace, but equally impressive was his intelligence, as he could think batsmen out. On his day he was as quick as anyone in the world.

10) Shane Warne

He was voted one of the top five cricketers of the century and was the only bowler in the list, so that must make him the best bowler of all time. He has taken spin bowling to new heights; a prodigious turner of the ball and well worth his place in this team.

11) Dennis Lillee

His record is fantastic. He was everybody's favourite bowler because of his classic action. He had sheer pace and could swing the ball without losing any of his speed. His spirit in the dressing room meant that he was popular in every team that he played with.

ROBIN SMITH played 62 Test matches for England between 1988 and 1995–96 and scored 4,236 runs at an average of 43.67. He was famous for his hard hitting, particularly square of the wicket. Few batsmen played the square cut better than this man. He excelled particularly against fast bowling. His Test career may have ceased prematurely, given his impressive Test match figures.

JOHN SNOW'S XI

The only player that I haven't seen in my team is Bradman, but I think with his average of 99.94, he must be an automatic choice for anybody's side. He might not have been able to achieve that kind of average in today's game, but I'm certain he would still be one of the very best if not the best. All of these players would be able to excel in any era. Knotty is in ahead of Adam Gilchrist – the better keeper-batsman – on his keeping alone, as we bowlers don't like to see catches dropped and I wanted the best possible wicketkeeper. There were quite a few others who I considered and some of those include: Allan Border, Jeff Thomson, those great West Indian quicks, Greg Chappell, Ian Botham, Brian Lara and many more. If the match were to be played on a turning track then I would bring in Bishan Bedi and leave out Richard Hadlee.

1) Barry Richards, 2) Sunil Gavaskar, 3) Donald Bradman, 4) Viv Richards, 5) Graeme Pollock, 6) Garfield Sobers, 7) Richard Hadlee, 8) Alan Knott, 9) Shane Warne, 10) Dennis Lillee, 11) Glenn McGrath.

JOHN SNOW played 49 Tests for England and took 202 wickets at an average of 26.66. In first-class cricket he claimed 1,174 wickets at 22.72. Snow is widely considered the best English fast bowler of his time – excelling particularly in the early 1970s. His greatest success came in 1970–71 against Australia, when he snared 31 wickets in the series, including his Test best figures of seven for 40 at Sydney.

* * * * *

ALEC STEWART'S XI

My greatest XI is based on the players I have played against as opposed to players that I have only read about or seen TV footage of (for example Bradman and Sobers). Leaving out Murali, Thorpe, Steve Waugh, Andy Flower, Ambrose, Walsh, Pollock, Waqar, Crowe, Donald, Kumble, Hayden, Dravid and others was not easy. Viv Richards and Ian Botham had both just about finished their careers when I started, otherwise they would have been in.

1) Gordon Greenidge
One of the cricketers I have always looked up to and I loved the way he dominated the bowlers.

2) Desmond Haynes
I think the older he got the better he got. He destroyed all types of bowlers.

3) Brian Lara

Simple fact: the very best player that I played against.

4) Sachin Tendulkar

Maybe I'm splitting hairs, but Sachin is second to Lara in my opinion.

5) Ricky Ponting

I first played against him when he was 16 and it was obvious he had lots of class even then.

6) Jacques Kallis

The best modern-day all-rounder. He warrants a place in the team as both a batsman and bowler.

7) Adam Gilchrist

The best-ever batsman-wicketkeeper. He could change a game with the bat in the space of an hour.

8) Wasim Akram

He was the best left-arm quick bowler of the modern era with both the new and old ball.

9) Shane Warne

Warney is simply the best bowler the game has ever seen.

10) Malcolm Marshall

He was quick and clever on any surface.

11) Glenn McGrath

He didn't know how to bowl a bad ball.

ALEC STEWART played a record 133 Tests for England from 1989–90 to 2003, scoring 8,463 runs at an average of 39.54, with 15 centuries. Stewart also claimed 241 dismissals as a wicketkeeper – the second most by an Englishman after Alan Knott and seventh highest in the all-time list. He was an aggressive batsman who was at his best when opening the batting, as when he scored centuries in both innings against the West Indies in Barbados in 1994.

BERT SUTCLIFFE'S XI

Comments: My team only includes players against whom I played Test cricket. Please bear in mind that I never played an official Test match versus Australia (during 18 years of Test cricket). Furthermore, the West Indies had no quick bowlers, unlike after my retirement in 1965, and neither did India or Pakistan.

1) Leonard Hutton, 2) Hanif Mohammed, 3) Colin Cowdrey, 4) Everton Weekes, 5) Denis Compton, 6) Garfield Sobers, 7) Godfrey Evans, 8) Jim Laker, 9) Alec Bedser, 10) Brian Statham, 11) Fred Trueman.

BERT SUTCLIFFE played 42 Tests for New Zealand between 1946–47 and 1965 and scored 2,727 runs at an average of 40.10. His 385 for Otago against Canterbury in 1952–53 was the highest first-class score by a New Zealander and his 355 for Otago against Auckland in 1949–50 became the second-highest New Zealand first-class score, behind his own record. Bert was a fluent left-handed stroke-player and the mainstay of New Zealand's batting throughout his Test career.

[This team was received before Bert passed away in 2001]

* * * * *

BOB TAYLOR'S XI

I have chosen my team almost from my era – except for the obvious. There are and have been so many great players: Compton, May, Trueman, Statham, Evans, Knott, G. Pollock, Donald and so on. My selection, though, is based on entertainment, class, and to beat any team in any country in any conditions.

1) Sunil Gavaskar
The most consistent and most prolific batsman I have ever seen. I spent too long watching him from behind the stumps!

2) Barry Richards
The most stylish batsman I've ever seen, yet he was still a big innings man.

3) Donald Bradman
His Test average speaks for itself and makes him an obvious choice in this team.

4) Sachin Tendulkar
He is comfortably the best batsman of today's crop as his wonderful stats demonstrate.

5) Viv Richards
A quick scorer who was very difficult to bowl at, most of the time.

6) Garfield Sobers
Quite simply he was the best all-rounder of all time.

7) Ian Botham
The next best to Sobers and such a great entertainer.

8) Ian Healy
I admired his skills as a wicketkeeper. An excellent cricketer, especially when keeping wicket to Shane Warne.

9) Shane Warne
He would have to be the best spin bowler of all time, at least in my opinion.

10) Richard Hadlee
A tremendous fast bowler on all types of wickets; a useful bat too.

11) Dennis Lillee
A truly great competitor and a real match-winner. Dennis always gave everything for the cause.

BOB TAYLOR played 57 Tests for England between 1970–71 and 1983–84 and achieved 174 dismissals as wicketkeeper. He holds the world record for the most dismissals in first-class cricket with 1,649, and shares the Test record for the most dismissals in an innings (seven) with Wasim Bari and Ian Smith. He would surely have played many more Tests had he not played at the same time as the great Alan Knott.

* * * * *

JEFF THOMSON'S XI

It's impossible for me to select players that I didn't see, apart from Bradman of course, so I picked my team from those that I played with and against – with the other exception of Warne. I almost opted for Joel Garner – because of his height, Joel was unorthodox and that made him a difficult proposition for batsmen. He was as quick as anybody when he wanted to be and probably the hardest guy to score off. But I went for Marshall instead.

1) Barry Richards
He was one of the best batsmen around in my time. He was technically correct and was capable of taking any bowler apart.

2) Sunil Gavaskar

Generally, he was pretty steady and was one of those consistent performers who scored runs regularly. It's close between him and Desmond Haynes, but Gavaskar was less chancy and he really knew where his off stump was.

3) Donald Bradman

He gets in easily for what he did, even though I never saw him play. I bowled to him when he was 67 and he was still good enough for this side even then!

4) Viv Richards

He was easily the most destructive player of my time. On his day he was like dynamite – an absolutely sensational bat. He could bowl useful off-spinners as well.

5) Greg Chappell

Comfortably the best batsman of my time. His Test record is nearly half as good as Bradman's, and Greg was so good that I find it difficult to believe that to be true. He was a batsman who you would back every time to get a hundred.

6) Garfield Sobers

He gets in for being the best all-round cricketer of all time. I never played against him, but his ability was unbelievable in that he could bat well and bowl spin or pace.

7) Ian Botham

He gets in for his record and for his general all-round natural ability. He took a heap of wickets, scored a load of runs and took great catches at slip too.

8) Rodney Marsh

It's close between Marshy and Knotty, but Marshy shades it with his batting, and for being Australian. He was a great competitor who never backed away from a challenge.

9) Shane Warne

He is the best spinner that I have ever seen; he has tremendous wicket-taking ability. Warney's also not a bad fielder and quite useful with the bat.

10) Malcolm Marshall

Marshall is in just ahead of Joel Garner. He had it all for a fast bowler and would make a pretty fearsome new-ball partnership along with Dennis.

11) Dennis Lillee

He was the best fast bowler of my time. He could win any sort of match on his own – he was that good. Dennis was a great guy to have in your team and would often bowl through the pain barrier for the cause. I was lucky to have him bowling at the other end.

JEFF THOMSON played 51 Tests for Australia between 1972–73 and 1985 and claimed exactly 200 wickets at an average of 28.00. He was famed for unofficially clocking the quickest delivery ever recorded at 99mph. An injury to his right shoulder sustained in a fielding collision in 1976–77 had an adverse affect on his ability to bowl as fast as he had done previously. However, Thomson and new-ball partner Dennis Lillee remain one of the most respected quick bowling duos in cricket history.

∗ ∗ ∗ ∗ ∗

GRAHAM THORPE'S XI

This is mainly a team of players I have seen first-hand and know of through talking to players of that era. There are lots of players bordering on greatness, but I can only pick 11. Those who narrowly missed out were: Javed Miandad, Desmond Haynes, David Gower, Graham Gooch, Curtly Ambrose, Courtney Walsh, Richard Hadlee, Abdul Qadir, Steve Waugh, Allan Donald, Imran Khan and Kapil Dev. I feel I have the perfect attack with Botham swinging the ball, Marshall and Akram both able to swing the old ball and new ball at pace and with the left-arm variety of Akram and Sobers as well. I felt the ability to swing the old ball as well as the new ball was the main aspect that separated these guys from Walsh and Ambrose. Although they were both great bowlers they tended only to swing the new ball. Obviously Warney is there as the spin option and there cannot be anyone better to fill that role.

1) Sunil Gavaskar
For the sheer weight of runs he scored in his era, and he scored a lot of them against a fearsome West Indies attack.

2) Gordon Greenidge
He looked sheer class every time I saw him play. He scored a lot of runs against England, which is why I rated him so highly. Greenidge was also a top fielder, usually at slip.

3) Viv Richards
The best modern-day batsman. He was my boyhood hero, along with Botham. It was Viv who inspired me to pursue the game that bit further.

4) Sachin Tendulkar
Probably the best batsman of the current era. He has scored runs in most parts of the world and in great volumes. Over a period of time Sachin has become one of the greatest players ever.

5) Brian Lara
I think England has seen the best of him. His exploits against Australia in 1999 put him back on the mantle of genius. He only had to concentrate to score runs.

6) Garfield Sobers

I did not see him play, but many people of his era say he was one of the very best. Not only was he a great batsman, but he was also a more than useful seam and spin bowler. When you have someone like that in your side, you're very lucky.

7) Adam Gilchrist

His record as a keeper is equal to Ian Healy, who was my other consideration for this position. But as a batsman Gilchrist is in a different league. He was very destructive coming in down the order and was able to take the game away from a team purely because he could score at a run a ball more often than not.

8) Ian Botham

Probably the most influential player that England has ever produced. I loved his cavalier approach. He never gave in, he was always willing to try different things with the ball and he was willing to throw caution to the wind for success. Also a great slip fielder.

9) Malcolm Marshall

He was a master of fast bowling – he had a great cricketing brain on him. He knew how to bowl on different pitches and at good pace too. His bouncer used to skid on to you, but he was then intelligent enough to pitch the ball up once he had you on the back foot.

10) Wasim Akram

His left-arm action gives a bit of variety to the attack. He just ambles up to the crease and bump, it all happens. He is decidedly quick off the pitch and he's the master of cleaning up the tail.

11) Shane Warne

Although I probably didn't struggle with him as much as some of the right-handers, I still regard him as not only the best spinner I played against, but the best spinner I have ever seen. What made Warney special was that after six balls he could see what mood you were in and how confident your stroke-play was likely to be that day. That was the main thing that separated him from (Muttiah) Muralitharan. His game-plans were just brilliant.

GRAHAM THORPE played 100 Test matches for England from 1993 to 2005, scoring 6,744 runs at an average of 44.66. He was a gritty left-handed middle-order batsman who always kept the scoreboard ticking over; a clever batsman able to manoeuvre the ball with ease. On his Test debut against Australia in 1993, he scored 114 not out at Nottingham, a typically pugnacious Thorpe innings.

MARCUS TRESCOTHICK'S XI

I have chosen players from my own generation. I would play Courtney Walsh for Murali if I needed to play an extra fast bowler.

1) **Matthew Hayden**, 2) **Virender Sehwag**, 3) **Ricky Ponting**, 4) **Sachin Tendulkar**, 5) **Brian Lara**, 6) **Jacques Kallis**, 7) **Adam Gilchrist**, 8) **Shane Warne**, 9) **Wasim Akram**, 10) **Muttiah Muralitharan**, 11) **Glenn McGrath**

MARCUS TRESCOTHICK played 76 Tests for England from 2000 until 2006, scoring 5,825 runs at an average of 43.79, as one of England's premier openers of modern times. Trescothick was renowned for the way in which he counter-attacked bowlers from the outset. His game was all about aggression and intent to score runs rather than occupation of the crease. An unfortunate stress-related illness prevented him going on to further success and playing 100-plus Tests.

✳ ✳ ✳ ✳ ✳

FRED TRUEMAN'S XI

It was very difficult picking this side and I must apologise to the likes of Peter May; Colin Cowdrey; Tom Graveney; Herbert Sutcliffe; Jack Hobbs; Keith Miller; Hedley Verity; George Headley – whom Len Hutton, Bill Edrich and Denis Compton rated as a superb bat; Kenny Barrington; Brian Statham; Johnny Wardle; Bill O'Reilly; Shane Warne; Bob Appleyard; Trevor Bailey; Tony Lock; Jim Laker; Hanif Mohammed and especially Everton Weekes, who was a very unorthodox player – people just didn't know where to bowl to him. But this team I picked would never lose a game. I haven't got an off-spinner but I don't need one with Barnes playing.

1) Leonard Hutton

He was the greatest player on all types of wickets by far. He was a masterful technician, and what a lot of people don't realise is that he missed his best years due to the war. If he had played during that time he would have easily scored over 200 centuries (he scored 129) and beat Jack Hobbs's record. Furthermore, Len didn't play on those flat wickets that Hobbs was used to at the Oval.

2) Sunil Gavaskar

I got the impression that due to his lack of height, bowlers didn't know what length to bowl to him. He always had plenty of time to play his shots. He scored his runs against very good bowling attacks as his own side wasn't strong in that area. Gavaskar is a modern great who could play in any era.

3) Walter Hammond

The true measure of just how good this player was came when Hutton and Compton rated Wally the best batsman they saw before the war – not Don Bradman as you would expect them to have said. A lot of batsmen abroad were always playing on good wickets, not like here, which is another reason why Hammond was so good.

4) Donald Bradman

Although I only ever saw him once in 1948 at Sheffield, when he didn't score any runs, I just think his record is unbelievable. His Test average is over 30 runs better than anybody, which is quite phenomenal.

5) Denis Compton

He was unbelievable in every way. Denis was an entertainer as well as a great batsman. People didn't know where to bowl to him. I actually saw him come down the wicket to bowlers like Ray Lindwall and Keith Miller. He was a very fine player.

6) Garfield Sobers

As far as I'm concerned he was the greatest all-round cricketer of the 20th century by far. He was so talented in every department.

7) Wilfred Rhodes

I never saw him play, but his record stands out. With over 4,000 first-class wickets and nearly 40,000 first-class runs he had to be in this team. His left-arm spin was as dangerous as any other bowler that has played the game, but when I spoke to Wilfred he rated Colin Blythe of Kent as a better bowler than himself.

8) Alan Knott

There's not a lot between him and Godfrey Evans as a wicketkeeper, but Knotty scored over 4,000 runs in Test cricket and at a good average so that's enough to guarantee his place in my side.

9) Ray Lindwall

The greatest quick bowler I ever saw. The best way that I could describe him is as a quick bowler of the highest class with the accuracy of a medium pacer. He swung the ball in the air too and at good pace. I used to phone Ray Lindwall up and ask him for advice. I first met him in 1952 at Headingley when he was playing Lancashire League cricket. We were introduced and we chatted for one-and-a-half hours. We were firm friends until he died.

10) Alec Bedser

He swung the ball and moved the ball off the seam better than anyone I have ever known. He was a master of the leg-cutter; in fact I would say that he was the greatest exponent of the leg-cutter ever. Alec could be unplayable.

11) Sydney Barnes

I never saw him play but his record is absolutely unbelievable (189 wickets at 16.43 in 27 Tests). I find it hard to imagine there could have been a better bowler than him.

FRED TRUEMAN played 67 Test matches for England between 1952 and 1965, claiming 307 wickets at an average of 21.58. In first-class cricket he took 2,304 wickets at 18.30. Fred became the first bowler to take 300 Test wickets when playing against Australia at the Oval in 1964. His best bowling analysis was eight for 28 for Yorkshire against Kent in 1954 – with all those wickets falling before lunch on the first day!

[This team was received before Fred passed away in 2006]

✳ ✳ ✳ ✳ ✳

FRANK TYSON'S XI

I have assembled my World XI as best I can, taking into consideration such matters as pitches – covered or otherwise – and opposition. Notable omissions which I regret are: Frank Worrell – one of the most elegant and graceful of batsmen; Colin Cowdrey – the best timer of the ball I have ever seen; Sid Barnes – the Australian opener, and one of the most tenacious of opponents; Everton Weekes – an explosive batsman capable of devastating the best opposition in the world; Dennis Lillee – a fast bowler of great variety and hostility with an unparalleled ability to take wickets; Fred Trueman – the master of the parabolic swing and an astute cricketing brain; and Graeme Pollock – second in the Test averages to Bradman and a wonderfully powerful dispatcher. It's a pity we did not see more of him due to the South African tragedy; Jack Hobbs and Herbert Sutcliffe – surely two of the most polished and correct openers the world has ever seen, and men able to play on the most difficult pitches; the elegant Barry Richards – correct and deft, another South African tragedy; Harold Larwood – my favourite fast bowler who must surely have been the fastest and a bowler with the perfect run-up and action; Shane Warne – the man who has spun the cricket ball further than anyone else; obviously there are many more I do not have the space to enumerate: May, Greg Chappell, Thomson, Benaud, Statham and the rest. In the final analysis, a lot of what you choose is based on subjective and emotional choice. My opening pair poses the problem of left and right-hand batsmen for bowlers. My team is as follows:

1) Arthur Morris

I regard Morris as one of the most solid percentage players I have seen who was absolutely unflappable – even when up against the best bowlers around.

2) Leonard Hutton

Hutton was one of the greatest technicians the game has seen. He was able to adapt his stroke-play to every sort of condition, from an Australian sticky dog to an English green-top.

3) Donald Bradman

Bradman is the *sine qua non*: a person who played his strokes according to his own capabilities rather than the challenge of the bowler and the position of the stumps.

4) Neil Harvey

Harvey was the greatest player of spin bowling I have seen – he never let the ball pitch. He gave the quick bowlers a chance through gully, but if a side did not get him out early he would score 200 in a day. He is another left-hander in the side to upset the opposing bowlers further.

5) Denis Compton

Compton was a genius and an improviser who did not play according to Hoyle, and could tear an attack apart with an array of totally original strokes.

6) Garfield Sobers

He was a three-in-one bowler and a genius with the bat. Could win matches with the ball, was a tremendous catcher close to the wicket and with the bat at number six he was not a very pleasant prospect for a tiring attack.

7) Keith Miller

Not as versatile as Sobers, but he could still score a century, bowl fast or slow and was a dynamic cricketer. More than any other player I ever met, Keith could swing the destiny of a match in the space of a few overs. He refused to be subdued or dictated to by boring, negative tactics or players.

8) Bill O'Reilly

I have chosen Bill O'Reilly ahead of Shane Warne largely on the recommendation of Don Bradman, who rated him as the best bowler he had ever faced. His assets were his aggression, his speed through the air and bounce off the wicket and his complete arrogance towards batsmen.

9) Ray Lindwall

Ray Lindwall gets my nod ahead of Dennis Lillee and Harold Larwood, largely because of his accuracy and his supreme ability to swing the ball. He was a fast bowler with the mentality and subtlety of a spin bowler.

10) Don Tallon

Tallon gains the wicket-keeping spot on the vouchsafe of Len Hutton, who rated him as the best wicketkeeper he ever encountered. Tremendously mobile, especially down the leg side, his hands were almost infallible and he was a more than useful batsman.

11) Sydney Barnes

S.F. Barnes must be one of the greatest bowlers who ever lived in any century. He controlled the ball in enormously long fingers and could swing or spin the ball on the most unresponsive of wickets and in the most unhelpful climatic conditions. When Lancashire Second XI played Staffordshire (and Barnes) in the 1920s, according to George Duckworth – the former Lancashire and England wicketkeeper – it was not unusual to see the whole side padded up and waiting to go in and face Barnes!

FRANK TYSON played 17 Tests for England between 1954 and 1958–59 and took 76 wickets at an average of 18.57. In his first-class career, which encompassed 244 matches, Frank claimed 767 wickets at 20.89. He was nicknamed 'Typhoon Tyson' for the immense speed with which he propelled a cricket ball. He is regarded as one of the quickest fast bowlers of all time, who enjoyed his most successful period on the 1954–55 tour of Australia when he took 28 wickets in the series that England won 3–1.

* * * * *

'POLLY' UMRIGAR'S XI

I selected my team from players I played with or against.

1) Leonard Hutton, 2) Hanif Mohammed, 3) Neil Harvey, 4) Colin Cowdrey, 5) Garfield Sobers, 6) Vinoo Mankad, 7) Godfrey Evans, 8) Lance Gibbs 9) Alec Bedser, 10) Wes Hall, 11) Subhash Gupte

'POLLY' UMRIGAR played 59 Test matches for India between 1948–49 and 1961–62 and scored 3,631 runs at an average of 42.22. In first-class cricket, he compiled 16,154 runs at 52.28 and took 325 wickets with his medium pace at a respectable 25.69. The middle-order batsman captained India in eight Tests. On India's 1959 tour of England he scored 1,826 runs at 55.33.

[This team was received before Polly passed away in 2006]

* * * * *

DEREK UNDERWOOD'S XI

The only way I can select my greatest team is from players I have seen. They're all great players with marvellous records. It's unfortunate that I had to leave out Greg Chappell, Clive Lloyd and the Indian spinners of my era, but I could only pick 11.

1) Gordon Greenidge

A very forceful square cutter of the ball and was able to play attacking or defensive innings without really changing tempo. He learned a lot of his cricket in England and that may be the reason why he was more orthodox than his West Indies teammates.

2) Barry Richards

Barry was the most perfectly balanced batsman I have ever seen. He was able to play forward or back with just a sway. He was also the first player to bat inside out in one-day cricket, or hitting from outside leg to off.

3) Viv Richards

There has never been a greater destroyer than Viv, as he showed on so many occasions. I played against him in 1976 when he hit two double hundreds and we bowlers were pretty much helpless to stop him. In one match in county cricket, he hit me over the pavilion roof off my first ball and that just about sums up what type of player he was.

4) Graeme Pollock

I didn't see much of him but he seemed to be a wonderful timer of the ball. He used a heavy bat and the ball seemed to travel fairly quickly when he middled it. He scored a hundred against Kent in 1965 for South Africa and I was immediately impressed. I played with him for a Rest of the World XI against Australia and against him for various teams; he always impressed me.

5) Zaheer Abbas

Zed was a very wristy batsman and a great player of spin. On wickets that did a little bit he was one of the better players I came across; when other batsmen struggled to hit the ball off the square, Zed always seemed at ease.

6) Garfield Sobers

Garry is the greatest of them all. I was young and impressionable when I first played against him and it could be intimidating with him standing there. He was frustrating to bowl to: after one delivery he would say 'well bowled', and then, when I bowled an identical ball, he would hit it for four. That's what geniuses are able to do.

7) Ian Botham

'Both' was a dangerous batter but I would never categorise him as a great batsman, although I would categorise him as a great bowler. He could swing the ball, seam it, bowl with terrific aggression and would dismiss top five batsmen as well as being the most clinical bowler to finish off a tail. A great team man and always in the game.

8) Alan Knott

Simply an out and out genius. I consider myself very fortunate in my life that I was able to play in the same Kent and England teams as this man. His wicketkeeping is unsurpassed and with the bat I lost count of the times he contributed when the chips were down: if the score was 370 for 6 it wasn't his scene, but if it was 120 for 6, he thrived.

9) Malcolm Marshall

A terrific bowler: he swung the ball and at express pace. Of all the overseas cricketers in the county game down the years I would say that none tried harder for their team than Malcolm; he was a 110 per center all the time. He was always there, bowling his heart out for Hampshire and the West Indies. He got my vote for being a top cricketer, a top man and a top ambassador for his country.

10) Shane Warne

I've always admired him from afar. He's the best spin bowler the game has ever seen by a mile because of his skill and variation. Wrist spinners usually get better with age, so it's all the more astonishing when you think how good he was in his early days, though he's been lucky with the pace attacks he's usually bowled with and the runs on the board. I would have liked to see him bowl more on spitting turners where he's expected to take six for 20 and be under pressure more that way, but I'm sure he would still have succeeded.

11) Dennis Lillee

I chose DK mainly for his attitude. He is the greatest trier I have ever seen on a cricket field. He would be as keen to bowl at six in the evening as at 11 in the morning. I was full of admiration for him when he came back from massive back problems and still performed as well as ever. I'm proud to call him a mate in the cricket world.

DEREK UNDERWOOD played 86 Tests for England between 1966 and 1981–82 and claimed 297 wickets at an average of 25.83. In first-class cricket he took 2,465 wickets at 20.28, which makes him the 14th most successful bowler in first-class history. Nicknamed 'Deadly' for his unwavering accuracy, he remains one of the greatest left-arm spinners of all time after a distinguished career with Kent and England.

* * * * *

ALF VALENTINE'S XI

It wasn't easy selecting this team, but I'm very pleased with it. There are great batsmen, great bowlers and it's a good fielding side too. I would have liked to have seen this team play together, that's for sure.

1) Sunil Gavaskar

This guy scored more runs as an opening batsman than anybody else. He played a lot of Test cricket against a fearsome West Indies bowling attack and scored more hundreds against them than anybody.

2) Jack Hobbs

When I think of this guy, I think of him as the father of openers. I never saw him play, but he must have been something special to get 197 first-class hundreds.

3) Frank Worrell

I believe he was one of the greatest West Indies batsmen in all types of conditions. He could also bowl good medium-pace. He was a great team man.

4) George Headley

He scored 10 centuries in 22 Test matches and had a Test batting average of over 60. What more can I say? I'm very proud that he was a native of Jamaica like me!

5) Donald Bradman

The greatest batsman this world has ever seen. He was superb on all kinds of wickets, whether slow, fast, wet or dry.

6) Garfield Sobers

I believe that he blossomed into the best all-rounder this world has ever seen: a great batsman, superb fielder and he could bowl spin or fast-medium pace.

7) Keith Miller

This man could do it all. He bowled the fastest delivery that I ever saw, in Australia. Keith could be really quick when he was in the mood. He was also a good, attacking batsman and a great slip fielder.

8) Godfrey Evans

He was the best wicketkeeper ever. Most keepers specialise and are best keeping to either spin *or* pace, but Godfrey was as good keeping to both. He was a good batsman down the order, too. I remember him getting 104 against us at Old Trafford and it was a typical, exciting Godfrey innings.

9) Harold Larwood

The Bodyline King. Harold must have been a wonderful, whole-hearted fast bowler who would do any captain proud with his effort and commitment.

10) Jim Laker

He imparted a lot of spin on the ball, as well as being a master of line and length. I admired him a great deal.

11) Hedley Verity

He was left-arm, which gives variety to the attack. I never saw him play, but I heard a lot about him from other players or ex-players; he sounded like a great bowler.

ALF VALENTINE played 36 Tests for the West Indies between 1950 and 1961–62, taking 139 wickets at an average of 30.32. In first-class cricket, he took 475 wickets at 26.22. He linked up in a famous spin twin duo with Sonny Ramadhin for the West Indies, with Alf bowling slow left-arm. He enjoyed his finest performance in 1950 at Old

Trafford when he took eight for 104. On that tour on the same ground he claimed eight for 26 against Lancashire, for 123 wickets on the tour at an incredible 17.94.

[This team was received before Alf passed away in 2004]

* * * * *

DILIP VENGSARKAR'S XI

I selected my team from players I know about. There were greats before my time, but I never saw them. I'm sorry to have to leave out Allan Border, Richard Hadlee and Michael Holding. I would also have selected Javed Miandad had it not been for the emergence of Tendulkar. Miandad was very gutsy and had a good temperament for cricket, shown by the vast number of runs he scored in the Test match arena.

1) Sunil Gavaskar
He was a great accumulator of runs, very skilful and had an excellent temperament for an opening batsman.

2) Gordon Greenidge
He had a sound defence, but could also be a tremendous attacking batsman when he wanted to be.

3) Viv Richards
The best batsman I have ever seen; was great against spin and pace. He was capable of winning a match on his own.

4) Greg Chappell
A beautiful player to watch, very elegant and played very straight. He always had time to play his shots.

5) Sachin Tendulkar
I have watched him from the time he was a boy as I was his captain at Mumbai in his debut season. What he has achieved is incredible: his consistency to stay at the top for so long, his level of commitment, his passion for the game, his focus, and for succeeding on all kinds of wickets against all types of opponents.

6) Ian Botham
One of the greatest all-rounders ever, capable of changing a match on his own, with a catch, or with bat or ball.

7) Imran Khan
Another terrific all-rounder, with great ability to swing the ball and a sound batting technique.

8) Kapil Dev

I saw a lot of this man and his ability to take wickets on all kinds of pitches was excellent, particularly the slower wickets of India. A useful attacking batsman as well.

9) Alan Knott

The best wicketkeeper I have ever seen. He was excellent technically, but he could also be flexible when the match situation suited, either as keeper or as a batsman.

10) Malcolm Marshall

The most lethal fast bowler I played with or against. He was capable of ripping out several batsmen in no time at all.

11) Erapalli Prasanna

The best spinner I have ever seen. He turned the ball a long way and had great control as well. There are so many alternatives, like Anil Kumble, Shane Warne, Muralitharan and those from years earlier, like Bishan Bedi, but Prasanna is my personal choice.

DILIP VENGSARKAR played 116 Tests for India between 1975–76 and 1991–92 and scored 6,868 runs at an average of 42.13. He began his Test career with little success as an opener, but eventually found his niche as an elegant middle-order player. Dilip's finest moment was at Lord's in 1986 when he scored 126 not out to become the first overseas batsman to complete three Test hundreds on the famous ground.

* * * * *

JOHN WAITE'S XI

I selected my team from those I played with or against in Test cricket, which is the best way to judge a player. That means there is no place for the likes of Garry Sobers or Viv Richards, who were obviously terrific cricketers, but I never played against them. I would add that if the pitch was a green-top, then Keith Miller would play instead of Tayfield or Benaud.

1) Leonard Hutton

He was just about the most perfect batsman I ever played against. His technique was faultless.

2) Trevor Goddard

This is probably a controversial choice given other names I could have gone for, but I felt that he could have played for South Africa as a batsman alone or as a bowler alone – he was that good in both departments. Batting-wise, he was particularly strong against the quicks, while as a bowler, if he wasn't taking wickets he would still be extremely tough to get away.

3) Peter May
I thought he was the complete batsman, strong in all areas. England had a very good batting line-up in those days and I rated May as the best of them.

4) Neil Harvey
He scored so many runs against us that it was impossible to leave him out. He's a left-hander and that gives this team some balance.

5) Denis Compton
He's certainly one of the best batsmen I've seen. At his best Denis was a terrific player who could take a game away from you. He was also a wonderful batsman to watch when in full flow.

6) Graeme Pollock
A fantastic batsman who dominated opposing bowlers. With him coming in at number six, it's one hell of a batting side.

7) Richie Benaud
A very astute captain – there couldn't be anybody else who knows more about the game of cricket. He was a fine leg-spinner, a useful attacking batsman and a good fielder.

8) Alan Davidson
Probably the best new ball bowler I ever came across. He bowled a dangerous in-swinger, which was difficult to keep out. He was an underrated batsman capable of scoring Test centuries.

9) Ray Lindwall
With Alan Davidson bowling in-swingers to the right-hander and Ray bowling his out-swingers, they would be quite a handful for batsmen. At Test match level, quick bowlers really need to be able to bowl the ball that goes away from batsmen and that delivery was Ray Lindwall's strength, which is why he was such a great bowler.

10) Godfrey Evans
I feel he was far superior to his challengers Bob Taylor and Alan Knott. The interesting thing about Godfrey was that he was at his best in a Test match as opposed to playing for Kent. It wasn't unusual to walk away from a day's Test cricket when England were playing and single out Godfrey as the day's most excellent performer. He was an entertainer either with his gloves on or with the bat.

11) Hugh Tayfield
This may surprise some people, as I could have gone for Jim Laker, but I felt he needed the right pitch to take wickets on. But Tayfield could bowl on any surface. Nearly everybody he bowled to tried to collar him, but I don't remember any getting the better of him.

JOHN WAITE played 50 Test matches for South Africa between 1951 and 1964–65, and he claimed 141 dismissals as wicketkeeper. He scored 2,405 runs at an average of 30.44, including four centuries. In first-class cricket John scored 9,812 runs at 35.04 with a highest score of 219 for Eastern Province in 1950–51. Against New Zealand in 1961–62 he made 26 dismissals, setting a record for a five-match series.

* * * * *

SIR CLYDE WALCOTT'S XI

I selected my side from players that I played with or against. I had great difficulty in doing this and in the end some great players were left out. I was particularly disappointed to leave out Jim Laker, Brian Statham, Fred Trueman, Richie Benaud and especially Subhash Gupte.

1) Leonard Hutton

He was technically the best opening player on all types of wickets. He had great powers of concentration.

2) Frank Worrell

He was another technically correct player, and certainly too good a player for me to leave him out of my side, so I chose him to open, which he did on occasions.

3) Neil Harvey

One of the best left-handers ever, who could get on top of any bowling attack and destroy them.

4) Peter May

One of my favourite batsmen. I liked his orthodox style in defence and attack.

5) Everton Weekes

The best middle-order batsman of my time. He could rip any bowling attack apart and, although he was a hard hitter of the ball, he only hit one six in his Test career, which indicates just how risk-free his game actually was.

6) Garfield Sobers

The best all-round cricketer I have ever seen and a natural ball player. As a batsman he had the ability to pick up the ball early and get in to the perfect position to play his shots. As a bowler he could bowl seam or orthodox spin and either role would have got him in to a Test team. When bowling seam, he wasn't as quick as guys like Lindwall and Miller, but he swung the ball a lot.

7) Keith Miller

Another great all-round cricketer. His batting skills were extremely good, while as a bowler he was an excellent new-ball partner for Ray Lindwall. Keith was quite explosive in both capacities.

8) Godfrey Evans

He was an attacking keeper; even against medium fast bowlers that swung the ball, Godfrey would stand up to the stumps – and get a few stumpings as well. He was a useful batsman down the order.

9) Ray Lindwall

Ray had the ability to move the ball late, and at very quick pace. He was easily the best fast bowler of my time.

10) Wes Hall

He was fast and hostile and could bowl a very good away swinger, which, at his pace, caused most batsmen an awful lot of problems.

11) Lance Gibbs

Lance was a great spinner of the ball and he had a high arm action, and therefore got good bounce off the pitch, which put pressure on batsmen with fielders around the bat.

CLYDE WALCOTT played 44 Test matches for the West Indies between 1947–48 and 1959–60 and scored 3,798 runs at an average of 56.69. In first-class cricket he made 11,820 runs at 56.56. He set a world record in 1954–55 when he scored five centuries in a Test series against Australia (827 runs in the series). Along with Frank Worrell and Everton Weekes, Clyde formed the infamous and successful batting trio, 'The Three Ws'.

[This team was received before Clyde passed away in 2006]

✳ ✳ ✳ ✳ ✳

DOUG WALTERS'S XI

I haven't seen all of these players, but through speaking to people that did see them, I've no worries selecting them. I would have liked Graeme Pollock and Sachin Tendulkar, but I can't fit them all in.

1) Arthur Morris

He had a great record and Bradman rated him the best left-hand opener ever, so that is good enough for me.

2) Brian Lara

One of my favourites of the modern era. He holds a few records so he deserves to be in this team. I would have liked (Bill) Ponsford even though I never saw him as his figures were awesome. But Lara is the only other batsman to score over 400 twice, so he's qualified!

3) Donald Bradman

The greatest of them all. No doubts whatsoever.

4) Neil Harvey

I didn't see a great deal of Harvey, but what he achieved in his career (over 6,000 Test runs at an average of 48) and the way he scored his runs in different conditions make him an automatic choice.

5) Viv Richards

Viv was just an absolute destroyer of great bowlers. It didn't matter who the bowler was, he could dominate anyone.

6) Garfield Sobers

The best cricketer that I ever played with or against, certainly the best all-rounder, possibly the greatest batsman too.

7) Keith Miller

I didn't see Keith but what I've heard about him is enough for me. He sounded like an exciting player to watch.

8) Adam Gilchrist

He plays cricket the way cricket should be played; if the ball is there to be hit, he hits it, and it stays hit! Pre-Gilchrist I would have opted for Don Tallon as all the great Australians of his era rated him the greatest keeper they ever saw.

9) Shane Warne

The best of his sort that I have ever seen and am probably ever likely to see.

10) Clarrie Grimmett

Just for the number of wickets (216 in Tests) he took in an era where the others failed to emulate him.

11) Dennis Lillee

He never knew when to give in or whether there was a wicket suitable for him; he would always give everything on whatever surface he played on. He just kept plugging away.

DOUG WALTERS played 74 Tests for Australia between 1965–66 and 1980–81, scoring 5,357 runs at an average of 48.26. In first-class cricket he made 16,180 runs at 43.85, and scored 155 on his Test debut against England and 115 in his second Test. Doug became the first batsman to score a century and a double-century in the same Test when he made 242 and 103 against the West Indies at Sydney in 1968–69.

✳ ✳ ✳ ✳ ✳

WAQAR YOUNIS'S XI

My team is from players who I have played with or against, which is the most accurate way to judge a player, I think. I found it hard to pick this team, but could not leave out any from this 11. However, there are some great players that I haven't picked, like Garry Sobers, Don Bradman and Jack Hobbs, but I never saw them play. I am also sorry to leave out Saeed Anwar, Ian Healy, Ian Botham, Kapil Dev, Richard Hadlee and Dennis Lillee.

1) Gordon Greenidge
This guy had a solid defence but could also play his shots. He was an expert puller and hooker of the ball, which is important for a top-order batsman and it shows the guts and bravery of a great player.

2) Sachin Tendulkar
The same as Gordon Greenidge. For a small guy he can still strike the ball as hard as anybody and with his height he probably finds it easier to duck out of the way when facing the quicks.

3) Brian Lara
I don't have to say too much about him because his record says it all – the record holder for the highest scores in Test and first-class cricket. When he gets going it's hard to bowl at him and it doesn't matter what sort of bowler you are or how good you are because Lara will smash anybody when he is switched on. The fact he scored a lot of runs against Australia – the best team in the world – proves what a great batsman he was.

4) Viv Richards
He's a legend in cricket. He used to make good bowlers look like nothing when he was batting because he was so talented and also a very attractive batsman to watch. The way Viv batted, if the ball was swinging, seaming, bouncing, whatever, it rarely mattered to him because he just played the same way. He can also bowl off-spin and, as his record shows, he wasn't too bad at that either.

5) Steve Waugh
The most determined cricketer I have seen. People say that he can't play short deliveries, but I just feel that he narrowed his game down so that he only played the shots he wanted

to. He has often gone to the crease when his team has been in trouble and continued to play a long and vital innings. Personally, it seemed like it was easy to get him out because he is not the most naturally talented player around, but he was so strong-minded that it was in fact very difficult to dismiss him.

6) Imran Khan

A legend in Pakistan cricket. He was a very focused player who just never gave up. I remember on several occasions when we had just come back to the dressing room after bowling, Imran would start to put his pads on even when he was batting at six – that's how focused he was. His record is excellent and I would pick him in any team in the world.

7) Jeffrey Dujon

The best wicketkeeper that I have ever seen. I feel that he could have played another couple of years in Test cricket. It's not easy keeping to four or five fast bowlers like Marshall, Ambrose and Garner when the ball is seaming, swinging and bouncing, but he coped with it perfectly. He also scored a lot of runs and made some very important contributions with the bat. I feel sorry there's no place for Ian Healy, who was another great wicketkeeper, and Adam Gilchrist, probably the best batsman-keeper, but Dujon is my personal choice.

8) Wasim Akram

He took over 400 wickets in both one-day cricket and Test cricket, which speaks a great deal for his ability as a fast bowler. He played his cricket hard and was a great competitor. Wasim was quite deceptive and could be a lot quicker than he looked. The fact he's left-arm and can swing the ball both ways is very important and I have no doubt about picking him in my team.

9) Malcolm Marshall

The reason I selected Marshall over other great fast bowlers like Lillee, Hadlee and Botham was because he could bowl on any kind of surface in the world and still take wickets. Whether the pitch was fast or slow didn't matter, he just wanted to get on with the game and bowl. He could also move the ball around. That's why he was so successful in India. Fast bowlers don't come any more intelligent than Malcolm Marshall – he could think batsmen out.

10) Shane Warne

No doubt whatsoever here. He is not only the best leg-spinner that I've ever seen, but has to be the best the world has ever produced. No other bowler can match the things he could do with a cricket ball. He's taken wickets on hard and fast tracks, on slow tracks and he has performed in all conditions, which made him a quality bowler.

11) Curtly Ambrose

A very fine bowler. I could have gone for Courtney Walsh or Kapil Dev, but I just think Ambrose was better than both of them. He could bowl really long spells and make the batsman play at everything. He was a very intelligent bowler and easily one of the best I've seen.

WAQAR YOUNIS played 87 Tests for Pakistan from 1989–90 to 2002–03, taking 373 wickets at an average of 23.56, with an incredibly low strike rate of 43.40. The fast bowler made a sensational impact early on because he possessed a lethal in-swinging yorker (to right-handers) that was bowled at express pace. Waqar went on to become one of the leading bowlers of his era and infamously partnered Wasim Akram in a formidable new-ball attack throughout the 1990s.

* * * * *

SHANE WARNE'S XI

I have left out some fantastic names, like Brian Lara, Curtly Ambrose and Wasim Akram, but it's very tough to compare different eras. I idolised some of these guys, like Dennis Lillee and Allan Border, and my brother Jason and I would often pretend we were them when playing backyard cricket growing up as kids. The game has changed so much, but generally my feeling is that a great player in one era should be able to adapt to any other era. Keith Miller would be 12th man for his all-round abilities.

1) Barry Richards, 2) Sachin Tendulkar, 3) Donald Bradman, 4) Viv Richards, 5) Allan Border, 6) Garfield Sobers, 7) Ian Botham, 8) Rodney Marsh, 9) Bill O'Reilly, 10) Dennis Lillee, 11) Glenn McGrath

SHANE WARNE played 145 Tests for Australia between 1991–92 and 2006–07, taking 708 wickets at an average of 25.41 – he was first to 700. Warne retired as the world record holder and still trails only Muttiah Muralitharan. The leg-spinner was voted one of the five greatest cricketers of the 20th century and is widely regarded as the best-ever spinner. Also a useful batsman, he made the most Test runs (3,154) without scoring a century (top score was 99). Warne was a key factor in Australia's dominance in world cricket throughout his time in the arena.

* * * * *

WASIM AKRAM'S XI

I feel it is best that I base my team on players whom I have seen. Obviously I have heard about Bradman and other greats, but I haven't seen them. This is the best team that I have actually seen. They are all very aggressive players who play their cricket positively.

1) Desmond Haynes
In my opinion he was a very difficult batsman to bowl at. He gets in just ahead of Graham Gooch.

2) Sunil Gavaskar
He was always there mentally and physically. I never bowled at him much but I always found that he knew where his off stump was and he would leave balls that were only missing by an inch.

3) Viv Richards

His aggressive and forthright approach to cricket meant that his influence made a difference to whatever team he played for.

4) Javed Miandad

He is in for the positive way in which he played and also for his fighting spirit. He never gave up on a situation.

5) Brian Lara

It was very difficult to leave out Sachin (Tendulkar), but in my opinion Lara was the best batsman in the world when I played.

6) Garfield Sobers

I saw bits and pieces of him and I have seen his record, which is clearly better than all the other great all-rounders.

7) Adam Gilchrist

Apart from the fact he's a top keeper, he's one of the best batsmen I ever bowled against. He's one of the only batsmen who I wouldn't say scared me, but made me wary when bowling against him. He was as good a keeper as Ian Healy and a match-winner with the bat.

8) Imran Khan

A good bowler who bowled with great pace. He could also bat well and had a very good technique. He played the game aggressively. He just squeezes out Ian Botham, who was another positive cricketer that I admired a great deal.

9) Malcolm Marshall

He is the most intelligent bowler that I have ever seen in Test cricket. He could work out the weaknesses of any batsman, which is why he is one of my favourite bowlers of all time.

10) Muttiah Muralitharan

There are a lot of controversies involved with his action, but in my book he's the best spinner I've ever seen in the history of the game because of the variety he bowls, his fitness and his enthusiasm for the game, even after taking over 700 wickets.

11) Glenn McGrath

He was an outstanding bowler, always at the batsman with good pace and a very good bouncer. He gets in over Dennis Lillee because he had better success in the sub-continent. Lillee used to opt out in that part of the world.

WASIM AKRAM played 104 Tests for Pakistan and took 414 wickets at an average of 23.62, scoring 2,898 runs at 22.64. He is the most successful Pakistan bowler ever and widely regarded as the best left-arm pace bowler in the history of cricket ahead of Sobers and Davidson (at least that was the belief of the great Sir Donald Bradman). Not only quick, but with great variety, he was also a destructive lower-order batsman.

✳ ✳ ✳ ✳ ✳

BOB WILLIS'S XI

Here is my Greatest XI selected from all different eras.

1) Herbert Sutcliffe
Underrated partner of Jack Hobbs and other more fêted openers; never let England down.

2) Sachin Tendulkar
The fact he has 50 Test centuries on the way suggests he must be able to play a bit.

3) Donald Bradman
This man would score runs in any era – he has an extraordinary record.

4) Viv Richards
The best batsman I ever bowled at by far.

5) Brian Lara
400 and 375 speaks for itself.

6) Garfield Sobers
Great entertainer; always played the game in the right spirit.

7) Adam Gilchrist
He took Test match batting strike rates to a new level.

8) Imran Khan
He had a phenomenal bowling record considering he was mostly operating on flat pitches.

9) Richard Hadlee
His number of 10-wicket hauls in Test matches playing for a poor team underlines his greatness.

10) Glenn McGrath

He proved that raw pace wasn't everything in dismissing top orders all round the world.

11) Sydney Barnes

An unbelievable record proves he was possibly the best bowler of all time.

BOB WILLIS played 90 Tests for England between 1970–71 and 1984 claiming 325 wickets at an average of 25.20. The fast bowler, renowned for his courage overcoming injury and his long run-up to the crease, also took 899 first-class wickets at 24.99. His stats are impressively economical for an express fast bowler, especially his List A (one-day) career average of 20.18 after 293 games. Bob's finest moment came at Headingley in 1981 when he achieved second innings figures of eight for 43 to bowl Australia out in what is now remembered as one of the most dramatic Test matches ever.

* * * * *

JOHN WRIGHT'S XI

The dilemma between Bradman and Tendulkar was the toughest part of this team as I wanted to pick Bradman, but because I played against Sachin and saw him up close as India coach, I could not leave him out. I only picked players I have seen a lot of with Sobers the only exception. It was too difficult to bring into the equation players from other eras like Lindwall, Compton, Weekes and so on, so I have kept my team largely to players I have seen a fair bit of. It was still hard to leave out the likes of Greg Chappell, Steve Waugh and Michael Holding.

1) Sunil Gavaskar

A great opener and the best leaver of the ball I have ever seen.

2) Barry Richards

I used to love watching Barry play; a beautiful, elegant and correct batsman and it's a great shame that he didn't play more Test cricket because he would have treated a lot of cricket fans with his stroke-play.

3) Viv Richards

He was such an exciting player to watch who took up the challenge with bowlers and was so aggressive at the crease. Greg Chappell was unlucky not to make this spot, but I couldn't leave out Viv.

4) Sachin Tendulkar

I was tempted to select Don Bradman, for obvious reasons, but I didn't see him so have instead opted for a player I saw a lot of, having worked with Sachin with the India team. A genuine great.

5) Allan Border

AB was a guy who I just think you need in a Test team. He was very gritty, determined and a dedicated professional player. Steve Waugh's not far behind for this role.

6) Garfield Sobers

I lived out in the country in New Zealand, so unfortunately I didn't see much live Test cricket, though I did see Sobers bowl when I went to Christchurch for a day. He was a great, great player.

7) Alan Knott

He had everything. His keeping was awesome and he averaged well with the bat in Test cricket (32.75). Knotty was one of the most competitive and professional cricketers I encountered.

8) Richard Hadlee

I saw what he gave to our side and I don't think enough people realise what he did for New Zealand cricket. He led the bowling attack on his own, without a great bowler at the other end to keep the pressure on; not like the great West Indian quick bowlers who all gave vital support to one another.

9) Malcolm Marshall

He was a different type of quick; very skiddy and awkward. I faced him a lot and it was always a great challenge against him. There's not much to choose from between him and Michael Holding.

10) Shane Warne

Who's to say whether Shane Warne is any better than Clarrie Grimmett? However, I've seen enough of Warne for myself to know just how great a bowler he is and what an exciting one as well.

11) Dennis Lillee

A great strike rate and was always a tough competitor. He had all the qualities that a great fast bowler requires.

JOHN WRIGHT played 82 Test matches for New Zealand between 1977–78 and 1992–93, scoring 5,334 runs at an average of 37.82. This left-handed batsman was one of the grittiest competitors of his era. His resilience at the crease was a significant factor in him becoming New Zealand's most prolific opening batsman in Tests. He enjoyed a fruitful county career with Derbyshire from 1977 to 1988.

ZAHEER ABBAS'S XI

This is a team based on players I have seen. Jonty Rhodes would be 12th man for his great fielding. I have selected two players who don't usually open in Test cricket, but I'm confident they would do a good job for the team as they had success opening in one-day cricket. I also considered Saqlain Mushtaq as the off-spinner, but Murali has to be in given his record, which is incredible.

1) Brian Lara

His performances were off and on and he's not as consistent as other batsmen, but he's won Test matches on his own. I can't ignore a guy who holds the two main batting records in world cricket. A World XI is not complete without him.

2) Sachin Tendulkar

He's been the most consistent batsman in the world for a number of years. His strength is his reliability.

3) Viv Richards

He was probably the best player in the world during my time. Viv scored so heavily in Test cricket, one-day cricket, county cricket, whatever. He could hit balls to anywhere he felt like because his eyes were so sharp and footwork so quick.

4) Garfield Sobers

I didn't play that much against him, but he was the complete cricketer. We played together for a World XI team in Australia in 1971–72 when he was my captain. He wasn't just a good captain, he was a good batsman, spinner, paceman, fielder, everything. His name would still be prominent in a World XI in many years to come.

5) Allan Border

He was one of the best batsmen of his time. He was a consistent player, a tough opponent and a captain that led by example. Although a fiery competitor, he was also a gentleman.

6) Richard Hadlee

I faced so many fast bowlers in the world, but the reason why I think Hadlee was better than most was because he was quick off a short run-up, which surprised batsmen. He could get the ball to fly off a good length.

7) Wasim Akram

His excellent performances in Test and one-day cricket showed what a top-class player he was. I've not seen a better left-arm fast bowler. Garry Sobers could be quick in his first six or seven overs but slowed down afterwards, but Akram could be quick all the time. He was another who got the ball to explode off a good length.

8) Alan Knott

He wasn't just a great wicketkeeper, he was also a good batsman. Knotty was a good keeper to spinners and pace bowlers.

9) Shane Warne

He's the best leg-spinner I've ever seen and I played with another great leggie in Abdul Qadir, but didn't play against Richie Benaud. Qadir was good on spinning wickets, but Warne has taken wickets on pitches that don't encourage spin.

10) Dennis Lillee

I've never seen a more accurate fast bowler in my life. He used to make everyone play his every ball. Like the other quicks in my time, his strength was to make the ball rise from a good length. He had problems with his back and was never as fast afterwards, but he still took a lot of wickets. He struggled hard for his wickets, but because of his line and length he was successful.

11) Muttiah Muralitharan

He gets in just ahead of Saqlain Mushtaq. He's taken wickets prolifically on spinning and seaming wickets with many coming against India and Pakistan, whose batsmen usually play spin well. He turns the ball so far, his flipper is good and you can ask him to bowl 60 overs in an innings and he won't complain.

ZAHEER ABBAS played 78 Test matches for Pakistan between 1969–70 and 1985–86 and scored 5,062 runs at an average of 44.79. In first-class cricket he amassed 34,289 runs at 52.11, including 107 centuries. Zaheer, renowned for his graceful batting, played over 200 first-class games for Gloucestershire in the 1970s and 80s.

✳ ✳ ✳ ✳ ✳

PLAYER POLL RESULTS

Voting Players: Abdul Qadir, Neil Adcock, Bob Appleyard, Asif Iqbal, Mohammad Azharuddin, Trevor Bailey, Bishan Bedi, Sir Alec Bedser, Richie Benaud, Colin Bland, David Boon, Sir Ian Botham, Geoffrey Boycott, Sir Donald Bradman, Bill Brown, Bhagwath Chandrasekhar, Greg Chappell, Colin Croft, Martin Crowe, Danish Kaneria, Alan Davidson, Aravinda De Silva, Allan Donald, Rahul Dravid, Jeffrey Dujon, John Edrich, Joel Garner, Sunil Gavaskar, Herschelle Gibbs, Lance Gibbs, Trevor Goddard, Graham Gooch, Darren Gough, Tom Graveney, Gordon Greenidge, Charlie Griffith, Subhash Gupte, Sir Richard Hadlee, Hanif Mohammed, Neil Harvey, Vijay Hazare, Ian Healy, Michael Holding, Merv Hughes, Conrad Hunte, Ray Illingworth, Inzamam-ul-Haq, Dean Jones, Alvin Kallicharran, Jacques Kallis, Kapil Dev, Syed Kirmani, Anil Kumble, Clive Lloyd, Majid Khan, Malcolm Marshall, Graham McKenzie, Mohammed Yousuf, Mudassar Nazar, Deryck Murray, Mushtaq Ahmed, Mushtaq Mohammed, Makhaya Ntini, Graeme Pollock, Shaun Pollock, Erapalli Prasanna, Mike Procter, Sonny Ramadhin, Arjuna Ranatunga, Barry Richards, Richie Richardson, Andy Roberts, Lawrence Rowe, Saeed Anwar, Saqlain Mushtaq, Ravi Shastri, Michael Slater, Robin Smith, John Snow, Alec Stewart, Bert Sutcliffe, Bob Taylor, Jeff Thomson, Graham Thorpe, Marcus Trescothick, Fred Trueman, Frank Tyson, 'Polly' Umrigar, Derek Underwood, Alf Valentine, Dilip Vengsarkar, John Waite, Sir Clyde Walcott, Doug Walters, Waqar Younis, Shane Warne, Wasim Akram, Bob Willis, John Wright, Zaheer Abbas.

Nationalities: Australian: 15, English: 20, Indian: 14, New Zealand: 4, Pakistani: 15, South African: 12, Sri Lankan: 2, West Indian: 18

Results: *(in order of popularity / number of votes / 100)*

Garfield Sobers – West Indies (73)

Viv Richards – West Indies (64)

Shane Warne – Australia (61)

Sunil Gavaskar – India (58)

Donald Bradman – Australia (53)

Dennis Lillee – Australia (53)

Sachin Tendulkar – India (42)

Malcolm Marshall – West Indies (35)

Alan Knott – England (34)

Wasim Akram – Pakistan (27)

Gordon Greenidge – West Indies (26)

Adam Gilchrist – Australia (26)

Brian Lara – West Indies (25)

Len Hutton – England (21)

Imran Khan – Pakistan (21)

Richard Hadlee – New Zealand (19)

Ian Botham – England (18)

Barry Richards – South Africa (17)

Allan Border – Australia (16)

Jack Hobbs – England (14)

Ray Lindwall – Australia (14)

Keith Miller – Australia (13)

Greg Chappell – Australia (12)

Javed Miandad – Pakistan (12)

Jim Laker – England (12)

Lance Gibbs – West Indies (11)

Sydney Barnes – England (10)

Denis Compton – England (10)

Godfrey Evans – England (10)

Michael Holding – West Indies (10)

Graeme Pollock – South Africa (10)

Neil Harvey – Australia (9)

Fred Trueman – England (9)

Everton Weekes – West Indies (9)

Kapil Dev – India (8)

Glenn McGrath – Australia (8)

Don Tallon – Australia (8)

Alec Bedser – England (7)

Wes Hall – West Indies (7)

George Headley – West Indies (7)

Ian Healy – Australia (7)

Peter May – England (7)

Arthur Morris – Australia (7)

Muttiah Muralitharan – Sri Lanka (7)

Ricky Ponting – Australia (7)

Colin Cowdrey – England (6)

Walter Hammond – England (6)

Clive Lloyd – West Indies (6)

Rodney Marsh – Australia (6)
Steve Waugh – Australia (6)
Frank Worrell – West Indies (6)
Bishan Bedi – India (5)
Hanif Mohammed – Pakistan (5)
Matthew Hayden – Australia (5)
Andy Roberts – West Indies (5)
Curtly Ambrose – West Indies (4)
Desmond Haynes – West Indies (4)
Richie Benaud – Australia (4)
Joel Garner – West Indies (4)
Subhash Gupte – India (4)
Jacques Kallis – South Africa (4)
Bill O'Reilly – Australia (4)
Virender Sehwag – India (4)
Geoffrey Boycott – England (3)
Alan Davidson – Australia (3)
Allan Donald – South Africa (3)
Clarrie Grimmett – Australia (3)
Conrad Hunte – West Indies (3)
Syed Kirmani – India (3)
Harold Larwood – England (3)
Graham McKenzie – Australia (3)
Hugh Tayfield – South Africa (3)
Abdul Qadir – Pakistan (2)
Ken Barrington – England (2)
Bhagwath Chandrasekhar – India (2)
Jeffrey Dujon – West Indies (2)
David Gower – England (2)
Tom Graveney – England (2)

Wally Grout – Australia (2)
Rohan Kanhai – West Indies (2)
Erapalli Prasanna – India (2)
Wilfred Rhodes – England (2)
Herbert Sutcliffe – England (2)
Derek Underwood – England (2)
Hedley Verity – England (2)
Courtney Walsh – West Indies (2)
Zaheer Abbas – Pakistan (2)
Neil Adcock – South Africa (1)
Ian Chappell – Australia (1)
Aravinda De Silva – Sri Lanka (1)
Ted Dexter – England (1)
Bruce Dooland – Australia (1)
Rahul Dravid – India (1)
Andrew Flintoff – England (1)
Trevor Goddard – South Africa (1)
Gary Kirsten – South Africa (1)
Bill Lawry – Australia (1)
Stan McCabe – Australia (1)
Jackie McGlew – South Africa (1)
Vinoo Mankad – India (1)
Shaun Pollock – South Africa (1)
Mike Procter – South Africa (1)
Saeed Anwar – Pakistan (1)
Bobby Simpson – Australia (1)
Brian Statham – England (1)
Mark Taylor – Australia (1)
Victor Trumper – Australia (1)
John Waite – South Africa (1)

Players selected in the 100 XIs and those who voted for them:

Abdul Qadir (2) Abdul Qadir, Holding

Adcock (1) Adcock

Ambrose (4) Illingworth, Ranatunga, Richardson, Waqar Younis

S.F. Barnes (10) Appleyard, Bailey, Benaud, Boycott, M. Crowe, Goddard, Majid Khan, Trueman, Tyson, Willis

Barrington (2) Griffith, Healy

Bedi (5) Gavaskar, Kallicharran, Kirmani, Majid Khan, Mushtaq Mohammed

Bedser (7) Bedi, Bradman, Brown, Davidson, Sutcliffe, Trueman, Umrigar

Benaud (4) Adcock, Illingworth, Lloyd, Waite

Border (16) Abdul Qadir, Boon, Botham, Garner, Gooch, Greenidge, Holding, Hughes, Jones, Lloyd, Marshall, Ranatunga, Slater, Warne, Wright, Zaheer Abbas

Botham (18) Abdul Qadir, Donald, Gooch, Gough, Hadlee, Jones, Mushtaq Ahmed, B. Richards, Procter, S. Pollock, Saeed Anwar, Smith, Taylor, Thomson, Thorpe, Underwood, Vengsarkar, Warne

Boycott (3) G. Pollock, Gough, Holding

Bradman (53) Bailey, Bedi, Bedser, Benaud, Appleyard, Bland, Boon, Boycott, Bradman, Brown, G. Chappell, M. Crowe, Danish Kaneria, Dravid, Dujon, Gavaskar, L. Gibbs, Goddard, Gough, Hadlee, Hanif Mohammed, Harvey, Hazare, Healy, Hughes, Hunte, Illingworth, Jones, Kallicharran, Kumble, Lloyd, Majid Khan, McKenzie, Mohammed Yousuf, Mudassar, Murray, Mushtaq Mohammed, Procter, B. Richards, Richardson, Roberts, Rowe, Shastri, Slater,

Snow, Taylor, Thomson, Trueman, Tyson, Valentine, Walters, Warne, Willis

Chandrasekhar (2) Griffith, Kirmani

G. Chappell (12) Azharuddin, Botham, Donald, G. Pollock, Garner, Holding, Mushtaq Mohammed, Ranatunga, Richardson, Roberts, Thomson, Vengsarkar

I. Chappell (1) Griffith

Compton (10) Adcock, Bedser, Edrich, Graveney, Harvey, Goddard, Sutcliffe, Trueman, Tyson, Waite

Cowdrey (6) Adcock, Appleyard, Bland, Chandrasekhar, Sutcliffe, Umrigar

Davidson (3) Adcock, Bland, Waite

De Silva (1) Ranatunga

Dexter (1) G. Pollock

Donald (3) H. Gibbs, Hazare, S. Pollock

Dooland (1) Bedser

Dravid (1) Kallis

Dujon (2) Donald, Waqar Younis

Evans (10) Bedser, Appleyard, Goddard, Graveney, Hanif Mohammed, Sutcliffe, Umrigar, Valentine, Waite, Walcott

Flintoff (1) Kallis

Garner (4) Botham, Croft, Dujon, Jones

Gavaskar (58) Abdul Qadir, Asif Iqbal, Azharuddin, Benaud, Bland, Boon, Botham, Chandrasekhar, G. Chappell, Croft, Danish Kaneria, De Silva, Dravid, Dujon, Edrich, Garner, L. Gibbs, Gooch, Greenidge, Gupte, Hanif Mohammed, Hazare, Healy, Holding, Hughes, Hunte, Inzamam, Kallicharran, Kapil Dev, Kirmani, Lloyd, Majid Khan, Marshall, Mohammed Yousuf, Mudassar, Murray, Mushtaq Ahmed, Mushtaq Mohammed, Prasanna, Procter, Ranatunga, B. Richards, Richardson, Roberts, Rowe, Saeed Anwar, Saqlain Mushtaq, Shastri, Slater, Snow, Taylor, Thomson, Thorpe, Trueman, Valentine, Vengsarkar, Wasim Akram, Wright

L. Gibbs (11) Chandrasekhar, L. Gibbs, Griffith, Kallicharran, Majid Khan, Murray, Mushtaq Mohammed, Ramadhin, Rowe, Umrigar, Walcott

Gilchrist (26) Abdul Qadir, Benaud, Botham, Danish Kaneria, De Silva, Dravid, H. Gibbs, Gough, Hughes, Inzamam, Kallis, Kapil Dev, Kumble, Mohammed Yousuf, Mushtaq Ahmed, Ntini, S. Pollock, B. Richards, Saqlain Mushtaq, Slater, Stewart, Thorpe, Trescothick, Walters, Wasim Akram, Willis

Goddard (1) Waite

Gower (2) Holding, Kirmani

Graveney (2) Chandrasekhar, Prasanna

Greenidge (26) Asif Iqbal, Azharuddin, Boon, Botham, Chandrasekhar, G. Chappell, De Silva, Donald, Dujon, Hughes, Hunte, Jones, Kallicharran, Kirmani, Kumble, Marshall, B. Richards, Richardson, Roberts, Saeed Anwar, Slater, Stewart, Thorpe, Underwood, Vengsarkar, Waqar Younis

Grimmett (3) Bradman, Brown, Walters

Grout (2) Griffith, Murray

Gupte (4) Prasanna, Ramadhin, Rowe, Umrigar

Hadlee (19) Azharuddin, Bedi, Boon, Chandrasekhar, De Silva, Donald, Garner, Hazare, Holding, Hughes, Hunte, Kapil Dev, Ranatunga, Saqlain Mushtaq, Snow, Taylor, Willis, Wright, Zaheer Abbas

Hall (7) Danish Kaneria, Griffith, Prasanna, Ramadhin, Rowe, Umrigar, Walcott

Hammond (6) Bailey, Appleyard, Brown, Edrich, McKenzie, Trueman

Hanif Mohammed (5) Gupte, Majid Khan, Mushtaq Mohammed, Sutcliffe, Umrigar

Harvey (9) Adcock, Appleyard, Davidson, Graveney, Tyson, Umrigar, Waite, Walcott, Walters

Hayden (5) H. Gibbs, Inzamam, Kallis, Shastri, Trescothick

Haynes (4) H. Gibbs, Greenidge, Stewart, Wasim Akram

Headley (7) Boycott, L. Gibbs, Majid Khan, Murray, Roberts, Rowe, Valentine

Healy (7) Bailey, Bland, Boon, Hazare, Jones, Marshall, Taylor

Hobbs (14) Bailey, Bedi, Benaud, Boycott, M. Crowe, Gavaskar, L. Gibbs, Goddard, Hadlee, Illingworth, Jones, McKenzie, Mudassar, Valentine

Holding (10) Asif Iqbal, Bailey, Harvey, Illingworth, Kirmani, Majid Khan, Marshall, Procter, Roberts, Rowe

Hunte (3) Garner, Griffith, Murray

Hutton (21) Appleyard, Bedi, Bedser, Boycott, Brown, Davidson, Edrich, Gavaskar, Goddard, Graveney, Hanif Mohammed, Harvey, Illingworth, Lloyd, Ramadhin, Sutcliffe, Trueman, Tyson, Umrigar, Waite, Walcott

Imran Khan (21) Abdul Qadir, Benaud, De Silva, Hanif Mohammed, Holding, Hughes, Inzamam, Kapil Dev, Kirmani, Marshall,

Mohammed Yousuf, Mudassar, Mushtaq Ahmed, Mushtaq Mohammed, Saeed Anwar, Saqlain Mushtaq, Shastri, Vengsarkar, Waqar Younis, Wasim Akram, Willis

Javed Miandad (12) Abdul Qadir, Asif Iqbal, Botham, De Silva, Garner, Hazare, Kirmani, Marshall, Mudassar, Ranatunga, Saqlain Mushtaq, Wasim Akram

Kallis (4) Croft, Ntini, Stewart, Trescothick

Kanhai (2) Gupte, Ramadhin

Kapil Dev (8) Azharuddin, Dravid, Hazare, Jones, Kirmani, Kumble, Prasanna, Vengsarkar

Kirmani (3) Azharuddin, Chandrasekhar, Kirmani

G. Kirsten (1) Ntini

Knott (34) Asif Iqbal, Bedi, Boycott, Croft, M. Crowe, Edrich, G. Pollock, Gavaskar, L. Gibbs, Gooch, Greenidge, Gupte, Hadlee, Holding, Hunte, Illingworth, Kallicharran, Lloyd, Majid Khan, Mudassar, Mushtaq Mohammed, Prasanna, Procter, Roberts, Rowe, Saeed Anwar, Shastri, Smith, Snow, Trueman, Underwood, Vengsarkar, Wright, Zaheer Abbas

Laker (12) Bailey, Bedi, Bedser, G. Chappell, Davidson, Edrich, Graveney, Gupte, Hanif Mohammed, Lloyd, Sutcliffe, Valentine

Lara (25) Abdul Qadir, Asif Iqbal, Croft, De Silva, Donald, Dravid, H. Gibbs, Hazare, Inzamam, Kallis, Kapil Dev, Mohammed Yousuf, Mushtaq Ahmed, Ntini, S. Pollock, Saeed Anwar, Smith, Stewart, Thorpe, Trescothick, Walters, Waqar Younis, Wasim Akram, Willis, Zaheer Abbas

Larwood (3) Danish Kaneria, McKenzie, Valentine

Lawry (1) Griffith

Lillee (53) Asif Iqbal, Bedi, Benaud, Boon, Botham, Boycott, Bradman, G. Chappell, Croft, M. Crowe, Dujon, Edrich, G. Pollock, Garner, Gavaskar, L. Gibbs, Goddard, Gooch, Gough, Greenidge, Hadlee, Hanif Mohammed, Healy, Holding, Hughes, Hunte, Jones, Kallicharran, Kapil Dev, Lloyd, Majid Khan, Marshall, McKenzie, Mudassar, Murray, Mushtaq Mohammed, Prasanna, Procter, B. Richards, Richardson, Roberts, Rowe, Shastri, Slater, Smith, Snow, Taylor, Thomson, Underwood, Walters, Warne, Wright, Zaheer Abbas

Lindwall (14) Bedser, Bland, Bradman, Brown, Davidson, Goddard, Graveney, Gupte, Harvey, Ramadhin, Trueman, Tyson, Waite, Walcott

Lloyd (6) Chandrasekhar, Danish Kaneria, Greenidge, Hughes, Marshall, G. Pollock

McCabe (1) Brown

McGlew (1) Adcock

McGrath (8) Kallis, Ntini, Snow, Stewart, Trescothick, Warne, Wasim Akram, Willis

McKenzie (3) Chandrasekhar, Griffith, G. Pollock

Mankad (1) Umrigar

Marsh (6) Dujon, Garner, Ranatunga, Richardson, Thomson, Warne

Marshall (35) Azharuddin, Boon, M. Crowe, Danish Kaneria, Donald, Dravid, Dujon, Garner, H. Gibbs, L. Gibbs, Gooch, Gough, Greenidge, Healy, Hunte, Inzamam, Kumble, Lloyd, Mohammed Yousuf, Mudassar, Richardson, Roberts, S. Pollock, Saqlain Mushtaq, Shastri, Slater, Smith, Stewart, Thomson, Thorpe, Underwood, Vengsarkar, Waqar Younis, Wasim Akram, Wright

May (7) Adcock, Davidson, Edrich, Gupte, Illingworth, Waite, Walcott

Miller (13) Bedser, Brown, G. Chappell, Davidson, Graveney, Gupte, Harvey, Healy, Illingworth, Tyson, Valentine, Walcott, Walters

Morris (7) Bedser, Bradman, Brown, Davidson, Harvey, Tyson, Walters

Muralitharan (7) Croft, Ntini, Ranatunga, Saqlain Mushtaq, Trescothick, Wasim Akram, Zaheer Abbas

O'Reilly (4) Bradman, Brown, Tyson, Warne

G. Pollock (10) Bland, G. Chappell, Kallicharran, Procter, S. Pollock, B. Richards, Smith, Snow, Underwood, Waite

S. Pollock (1) Greenidge

Ponting (7) H. Gibbs, Inzamam, Kallis, Mushtaq Ahmed, Ntini, Stewart, Trescothick

Prasanna (2) Hazare, Vengsarkar

Procter (1) G. Pollock

W. Rhodes (2) Bedi, Trueman

B. Richards (17) Bland, Bradman, M. Crowe, G. Pollock, Gooch, Hadlee, McKenzie, Prasanna, Procter, Rowe, Smith, Snow, Taylor, Thomson, Underwood, Warne, Wright

V. Richards (64) Abdul Qadir, Asif Iqbal, Azharuddin, Bailey, Benaud, Boon, Botham, G.

Chappell, Croft, M. Crowe, Danish Kaneria, De Silva, Donald, Dravid, Dujon, Garner, Gavaskar, H. Gibbs, L. Gibbs, Goddard, Gooch, Gough, Greenidge, Hadlee, Hanif Mohammed, Healy, Hughes, Hunte, Illingworth, Inzamam, Jones, Kallicharran, Kapil Dev, Kirmani, Lloyd, Marshall, B. Richards, McKenzie, Mohammed Yousuf, Mudassar, Mushtaq Ahmed, S. Pollock, Prasanna, Procter, Richardson, Roberts, Saeed Anwar, Saqlain Mushtaq, Shastri, Slater, Smith, Snow, Taylor, Thomson, Thorpe, Underwood, Vengsarkar, Walters, Waqar Younis, Warne, Wasim Akram, Willis, Wright, Zaheer Abbas

Roberts (5) Chandrasekhar, Gavaskar, Kallicharran, Murray, B. Richards

Saeed Anwar (1) Saqlain Mushtaq

Sehwag (4) Kapil Dev, Kumble, S. Pollock, Trescothick

Simpson (1) Ramadhin

Sobers (73) Asif Iqbal, Bailey, Bedi, Bedser, Benaud, Bland, Boon, Boycott, Bradman, Chandrasekhar, G. Chappell, Croft, M. Crowe, Danish Kaneria, Davidson, Dravid, Dujon, Edrich, G. Pollock, Garner, Gavaskar, H. Gibbs, L. Gibbs, Goddard, Gough, Graveney, Greenidge, Griffith, Gupte, Hadlee, Hanif Mohammed, Harvey, Healy, Hunte, Illingworth, Inzamam, Kallicharran, Kumble, B. Richards, Lloyd, Majid Khan, McKenzie, Mohammed Yousuf, Mudassar, Murray, Mushtaq Mohammed, Prasanna, Procter, Ramadhin, Richardson, Roberts, Rowe, Saeed Anwar, Shastri, Slater, Smith, Snow, Sutcliffe, Taylor, Thomson, Thorpe, Trueman, Tyson, Umrigar, Underwood, Valentine, Walcott, Walters, Warne, Wasim Akram, Willis, Wright, Zaheer Abbas

Statham (1) Sutcliffe

Sutcliffe (2) Appleyard, Willis

Tallon (8) Bradman, Brown, G. Chappell, Davidson, Harvey, Healy, McKenzie, Tyson

Tayfield (3) Adcock, Bland, Waite

Taylor (1) Donald

Tendulkar (42) Abdul Qadir, Asif Iqbal, Azharuddin, Bailey, Bedi, Benaud, Bradman, Croft, M. Crowe, De Silva, Donald, Dravid,

Dujon, Gavaskar, Gooch, Gough, Hadlee, Harvey, Hazare, Healy, Kallis, Kapil Dev, Kumble, Mohammed Yousuf, Mushtaq Ahmed, Ntini, S. Pollock, Prasanna, Ranatunga, Shastri, Smith, Stewart, Taylor, Thorpe, Trescothick, Vengsarkar, Waqar Younis, Warne, Willis, Wright, Zaheer Abbas

Trueman (9) Adcock, Appleyard, Boycott, Edrich, Gavaskar, Hadlee, Hanif Mohammed, Ramadhin, Sutcliffe

Trumper (1) McKenzie

Underwood (2) G. Pollock, Graveney

Verity (2) Appleyard, Valentine

Waite (1) Adcock

Walsh (2) Mushtaq Ahmed, Ntini

Warne (61) Asif Iqbal, Azharuddin, Bailey, Benaud, Appleyard, Bland, Boon, Botham, Boycott, G. Chappell, Croft, M. Crowe, Danish Kaneria, De Silva, Donald, Dravid, Dujon, Edrich, H. Gibbs, L. Gibbs, Goddard, Gooch, Gough, Greenidge, Hadlee, Hanif Mohammed, Harvey, Hazare, Healy, Hughes, Hunte, Inzamam, Jones, Kallis, Kapil Dev, Kumble, McKenzie, Mohammed Yousuf, Mudassar, Murray, Mushtaq Ahmed, Ntini, Procter, B. Richards, Richardson, S. Pollock, Saeed Anwar, Shastri, Slater, Smith, Snow, Stewart, Taylor, Thomson, Thorpe, Trescothick, Underwood, Walters, Waqar Younis, Wright, Zaheer Abbas

Wasim Akram (27) Abdul Qadir, Azharuddin, Botham, Danish Kaneria, De Silva, Dravid, H. Gibbs, Gooch, Gough, Hunte, Inzamam, Kallis, Kapil Dev, Kumble, Marshall, Mohammed Yousuf, Mushtaq Ahmed, S. Pollock, Ranatunga, Saeed Anwar, Saqlain Mushtaq, Slater, Stewart, Thorpe, Trescothick, Waqar Younis, Zaheer Abbas

S. Waugh (6) Kallis, Kumble, Ntini, Saeed Anwar, Saqlain Mushtaq, Waqar Younis

Weekes (9) Bedser, Boycott, Davidson, Graveney, Griffith, Gupte, Ramadhin, Sutcliffe, Walcott

Worrell (6) Graveney, Gupte, Murray, Ramadhin, Valentine, Walcott

Zaheer (2) Holding, Underwood

RESULTS BY COUNTRY

AUSTRALIA

30 players selected (337 votes of possible 1,100 for 30.6% of total vote)

Openers: Morris (7), Hayden (5), Lawry (1), Simpson (1), Taylor (1), Trumper (1).
Middle-order: Bradman (53), Border (16), G. Chappell (12), Harvey (9), Ponting (7), S. Waugh (6), I. Chappell (1), McCabe (1).
All-Rounders: Miller (13), Benaud (4), Davidson (3).
Wicketkeepers: Gilchrist (26), Tallon (8), Healy (7), Marsh (6), Grout (2).
Spinners: Warne (61), O'Reilly (4), Grimmett (3), Dooland (1).
Fast Bowlers: Lillee (53), Lindwall (14), McGrath (8), McKenzie (3).

AUSTRALIA ALL-TIME XI:

Comments: The openers and bowlers were way ahead in the voting with all-rounder Miller. Healy would have been more popular if it were not for the emergence of Gilchrist who, in one player's words, 'changed the landscape for wicketkeepers'. After Bradman and Border, places in the middle-order were tight, but Greg Chappell squeezed out Harvey. Reserve fast bowlers McKenzie and Davidson had three votes each, while reserve spinners Benaud and O'Reilly each had four.

1) Arthur Morris – played 46 Test matches, 1946–1955
2) Matthew Hayden – played 103 Test matches, 1994–2009
3) Donald Bradman – played 52 Test matches, 1928–1948
4) Allan Border – played 156 Test matches, 1978–1994
5) Greg Chappell – played 87 Test matches, 1970–1984
6) Keith Miller – played 55 Test matches, 1946–1956
7) Adam Gilchrist – played 96 Test matches, 1999–2008
8) Shane Warne – played 145 Test matches, 1992–2007
9) Ray Lindwall – played 61 Test matches, 1946–1960
10) Dennis Lillee – played 70 Test matches, 1971–1984
11) Glenn McGrath – played 124 Test matches, 1993–2007

Reserves: Neil Harvey (9 votes), Don Tallon (8 votes), Bill O'Reilly (4 votes), Richie Benaud (4 votes), Graham McKenzie, Alan Davidson (3 votes each)

ENGLAND

25 players selected (187 votes of possible 1,100 for 17 % of total vote)

Openers: Hutton (21), Hobbs (14), Boycott (3), Sutcliffe (2).
Middle-order: Compton (10), May (7), Cowdrey (6), Hammond (6), Barrington (2), Gower (2), Graveney (2), Dexter (1).
All-Rounders: Botham (18), Rhodes (2), Flintoff (1).
Wicketkeepers: Knott (34), Evans (10).
Spinners: Laker (12), Underwood (2), Verity (2).
Fast Bowlers: Barnes (10), Trueman (9), Bedser (7), Larwood (3), Statham (1).

ENGLAND ALL-TIME XI:

Comments: The openers, the bowlers, all-rounder Ian Botham and wicketkeeper Alan Knott were unrivalled. The one area open to debate is between Hammond and Cowdrey in the middle-order. Hammond makes this team on the basis that Sir Donald Bradman named him in his XII. Current star Kevin Pietersen may have been ignored because he was up against modern greats like Tendulkar, Lara and Ponting. A lack of success in recent years for the team may also have cost modern England players. Rhodes is reserve all-rounder and spinner.

1) Leonard Hutton – played 79 Test matches, 1937–1955
2) Jack Hobbs – played 61 Test matches, 1908–1930
3) Denis Compton – played 78 Test matches, 1937–1957
4) Peter May – played 66 Test matches, 1951–1961
5) Walter Hammond – played 85 Test matches, 1927–1947
6) Ian Botham – played 102 Test matches, 1977–1992
7) Alan Knott – played 95 Test matches, 1967–1981
8) Fred Trueman – played 67 Test matches, 1952–1965
9) Alec Bedser – played 51 Test matches, 1946–1955
10) Jim Laker – played 46 Test matches, 1948–1959
11) Sydney (S.F.) Barnes – played 27 Test matches, 1901–1914

Reserves: Godfrey Evans (10 votes), Colin Cowdrey (six votes), Geoffrey Boycott (3 votes), Harold Larwood (3 votes), Wilfred Rhodes (2 votes)

WEST INDIES

20 players selected (305 votes of possible 1,100 for 27.7% of total vote)

Openers: Greenidge (26), Haynes (4), Hunte (3).
Middle-order: Richards (64), Lara (25), Weekes (9), Headley (7), Worrell (6), Lloyd (6), Kanhai (2).
All-Rounders: Sobers (73).
Wicketkeepers: Dujon (2).
Spinners: Gibbs (11).
Fast Bowlers: Marshall (35), Holding (10), Hall (7), Roberts (5), Ambrose (4), Garner (4), Walsh (2).

WEST INDIES ALL-TIME XI:

Comments: As several greats included Lara in their World XI as an opener, a position he batted in one-day cricket on occasions, he is positioned here, due to the middle-order batsmen polling more votes than the next specialist opener Desmond Haynes. The three-man pace attack and spinner Lance Gibbs were out on their own in the voting. Reserve Rohan Kanhai, who polled two votes, would also be the back-up wicketkeeper, having played in this position in three Test matches.

1) Gordon Greenidge – played 108 Test matches, 1974–91
2) Brian Lara – played 130 Test matches, 1990–2006
3) George Headley – played 22 Test matches, 1930–54
4) Viv Richards – played 121 Test matches, 1974–91
5) Everton Weekes – played 48 Test matches, 1948–58
6) Garfield Sobers – played 93 Test matches, 1954–74
7) Jeffrey Dujon – played 81 Test matches, 1981–91
8) Malcolm Marshall – played 81 Test matches, 1978–91
9) Michael Holding – played 60 Test matches, 1975–87
10) Lance Gibbs – played 79 Test matches, 1958–76
11) Wes Hall – played 48 Test matches, 1958–69

Reserves: Frank Worrell, Clive Lloyd (6 votes), Andy Roberts (5 votes), Desmond Haynes (4 votes), Rohan Kanhai (2 votes).

INDIA

11 players selected (130 votes of possible 1,100 for 11.8 % of total vote)

Openers: Gavaskar (58), Sehwag (4).
Middle-order: Tendulkar (42), Dravid (1).
All-Rounders: Kapil Dev (8), Vinoo Mankad (1).
Wicketkeepers: Kirmani (3).
Spinners: Bedi (5), Gupte (4), Chandrasekhar (2), Prasanna (2).
Fast Bowlers: (Kapil Dev, see all-rounders list)

INDIA ALL-TIME XI:

Comments: The top four would seemingly appear unquestionable. It may then be argued that the others thereafter are a place too high in the order, but Mankad was good enough to score 231 against New Zealand in a Test, while Kapil did score a Test hundred at six. There is an obvious lack of a second seamer, but this only reflects India's struggles in this regard through history. The four-man spin attack, plus Mankad, would seem to be the best bowling they have to offer, as opposed to picking a lesser seamer for the sake of it. Anil Kumble is clearly an unlucky omission from the team but he did not poll a vote, no doubt a victim of the dominance of Shane Warne in many teams.

1) Sunil Gavaskar – played 125 Test matches, 1971–87
2) Virender Sehwag – played 75 Test matches, 2001–10
3) Rahul Dravid – played 138 Test matches, 1996–2010
4) Sachin Tendulkar – played 166 Test matches, 1989–2010
5) Vinoo Mankad – played 44 Test matches, 1946–59
6) Kapil Dev – played 131 Test matches, 1978–94
7) Syed Kirmani – played 88 Test matches, 1976–86
8) Erapalli Prasanna – played 49 Test matches, 1962–78
9) Bishan Bedi – played 67 Test matches, 1966–79
10) Subhash Gupte – played 36 Test matches, 1951–61
11) Bhagwath Chandrasekhar – played 58 Test matches 1964–79

Reserves: Gundappa Viswanath and Anil Kumble (as Indian players to merit mentions as 'almost selected' players)

PAKISTAN

7 players selected (70 votes of possible 1,100 for 6.3 % of total vote)

Openers: Hanif Mohammed (5), Saeed Anwar (1).
Middle-order: Javed Miandad (12), Zaheer Abbas (2).
All-Rounders: Imran Khan (21).
Spinners: Abdul Qadir (2).
Fast Bowlers: Wasim Akram (27), (Imran Khan, see all-rounders list)

PAKISTAN ALL-TIME XI:

Comments: As just seven Pakistan players polled votes in the book, the four additional players of Inzamam-ul-Haq, Wasim Bari, Waqar Younis and Saqlain Mushtaq have been added to this side on the basis that all of them were mentioned as players who narrowly missed out on selection in certain Greatest XIs. For example, India's great all-rounder Kapil Dev toyed with the idea of picking Inzamam in his team but, in the event, just named him in his 14-man squad. Players like Mushtaq Mohammed, Fazal Mahmood, Imtiaz Ahmed, Younis Khan, Mohammed Yousuf, Shoaib Akhtar and Danish Kaneria might be considered unlucky for failing to warrant a mention in the selections.

1) Hanif Mohammed – played 55 Test matches, 1952–69
2) Saeed Anwar – played 55 Test matches, 1990–2001
3) Zaheer Abbas – played 78 Test matches, 1969–85
4) Javed Miandad – played 124 Test matches, 1976–93
5) Inzamam-ul-Haq – played 119 Test matches, 1992–2007
6) Imran Khan – played 88 Test matches, 1971–92
7) Wasim Akram – played 104 Test matches, 1985–2002
8) Wasim Bari – played 81 Test matches, 1967–84
9) Saqlain Mushtaq – played 49 Test matches, 1995–2004
10) Waqar Younis – played 87 Test matches, 1989–2003
11) Abdul Qadir – played 67 Test matches, 1977–90

SOUTH AFRICA

12 players selected (44 votes of possible 1,100 for 4% of total vote)

Openers: Barry Richards (17), Gary Kirsten (1), Jackie McGlew (1).
Middle-order: Graeme Pollock (10).
All-Rounders: Jacques Kallis (4), Trevor Goddard (1), Mike Procter (1).
Wicketkeeper: John Waite (1).
Spinners: Hugh Tayfield (3).
Fast Bowlers: Allan Donald (3), Neil Adcock (1), Shaun Pollock (1).

SOUTH AFRICA ALL-TIME XI:
Comments: Modern players such as Graeme Smith, Mark Boucher, Makhaya Ntini and Dale Steyn may be considered unlucky but might have had a greater chance if these selections been made some time in the future, because of the growing success of the current team. Further, the likes of Bruce Mitchell, Dudley Nourse and Aubrey Faulkner from previous eras would be considered by many to be greats in South Africa's history. However, the players below were named in World XIs in the book and such tributes should not be undermined. Keeper Waite, for instance, faced the new ball against greats like Lindwall and Miller, and Bedser and Statham. Adcock is reserve on the basis that his vote came from himself, while the others were voted by other players.

1) Barry Richards – played 4 Test matches, 1970
2) Gary Kirsten – played 101 Test matches, 1993–2004
3) Jackie McGlew – played 34 Test matches, 1951–62
4) Jacques Kallis – played 136 Test matches, 1995–2010
5) Graeme Pollock – played 23 Test matches, 1963–70
6) Trevor Goddard – played 41 Test matches, 1955–70
7) Mike Procter – played 7 Test matches, 1967–70
8) John Waite – played 50 Test matches, 1951–65
9) Shaun Pollock – played 108 Test matches, 1995–2008
10) Hugh Tayfield – played 37 Test matches, 1949–60
11) Allan Donald – played 72 Test matches, 1992–2002

Reserve: Neil Adcock

NEW ZEALAND

Only Richard Hadlee was selected (18 votes).
Played 86 Test matches, 1973–90

SRI LANKA

Only Muttiah Muralitharan (7 votes) and Aravinda De Silva (1) polled.
Played 132 Test matches, 1992–2009 and 93 Test matches, 1984–2002

WORLD XI RESULTS

108 players selected from eight different countries

30 players were from Australia, representing 27.7% of the total vote
25 players were from England for 23.1% of the total vote
20 players were from West Indies for 18.5% of the total vote
11 players were from India for 10.1% of the total vote
12 players were from South Africa for 11.1% of the total vote
 7 players were from Pakistan for 6.4% of the total vote
 2 players were from Sri Lanka for 1.8% of the total vote
 1 player was from New Zealand for 0.9% of the total vote

Openers: (20) Gavaskar, Greenidge, Hutton, B. Richards, Hobbs, Haynes, Morris, Hanif Mohammed, Sehwag, Boycott, Hayden, Hunte, Taylor, Saeed Anwar, G. Kirsten, Lawry, McGlew, Simpson, H. Sutcliffe, Trumper.

Middle-order: (29) V. Richards, Bradman, Tendulkar, Lara, Border, G. Chappell, Weekes, Javed Miandad, Compton, S. Waugh, G. Pollock, Harvey, May, Cowdrey, Headley, Lloyd, Hammond, Worrell, Ponting, De Silva, Graveney, Zaheer Abbas, Barrington, Gower, Kanhai, I. Chappell, Dexter, Dravid, McCabe.

All-Rounders: (16) Sobers, Wasim Akram, Botham, Imran Khan, Hadlee, Miller, Kapil Dev, Benaud, Kallis, Davidson, Rhodes, Flintoff, Goddard, Mankad, S. Pollock, Procter.

Wicketkeepers: (10) Knott, Gilchrist, Healy, Evans, Tallon, Marsh, Dujon, Kirmani, Grout, Waite.

Spinners: (15) Warne, Laker, Gibbs, Bedi, Muralitharan, O'Reilly, Grimmett, Gupte, Abdul Qadir, Verity, Chandrasekhar, Dooland, Prasanna, Tayfield, Underwood.

Fast Bowlers: (18) Lillee, Marshall, Lindwall, Holding, Ambrose, Trueman, Barnes, Bedser, Hall, Garner, Roberts, Donald, McGrath, Larwood, McKenzie, Adcock, Statham, Walsh.

THE ALL-TIME WORLD XI

1) Sunil Gavaskar (58 votes)
Many greats from all eras showed their respect, especially for his runs against an all-conquering West Indies. The figures show he was voted the best opener ever by a long way.

2) Gordon Greenidge (26 votes)
It was close between him and fellow West Indian Brian Lara, but his contribution to a champion West Indies team edged it. He polled the same number of votes as Adam Gilchrist, but Alan Knott was the most popular wicketkeeper with 34 votes.

3) Donald Bradman (53 votes)
While some players chose to ignore his stats because they didn't see him play, it is reassuring that someone so dominant from the 1920s to 1940s still made a World XI in 2010.

4) Viv Richards (64 votes)
For batsmen alone, this man received the most votes from the greats, trailing only the great Garfield Sobers in the entire voting list.

5) Sachin Tendulkar (42 votes)
His remarkable and prolonged supremacy at the top level has astounded. His record-breaking feats were duly recognised by the greats who voted in this book.

6) Garfield Sobers (73 votes)
By far the most popular choice in the book, as players noted how he was good enough to make this team with either bat or ball, as well as being a supreme fielder.

7) Alan Knott (34 votes)
Deemed the best specialist wicketkeeper as opposed to the best batsman-keeper that many regarded as Gilchrist.

8) Shane Warne (61 votes)
The fact that great spinners like Muralitharan, Kumble, Underwood, Qadir and Vettori were largely ignored in the book is because of Warne. He was not only a great bowler; he has been the finest ambassador of spin bowling, making it popular with youngsters. Jim Laker was the next-highest spinner with 12 votes.

9) Wasim Akram (27 votes)
He has been recognised as the bowler with the box of tricks; unpredictable and skilful.

10) Malcolm Marshall (35 votes)

There have been faster bowlers, though not many, but players in the book recognised Marshall's ability to swing the ball both ways; he was a real handful for batsmen.

11) Dennis Lillee (53 votes)

The highest-ranking fast bowler in these pages and rated by so many as the undisputed king of pace bowling.

Reserves:

Adam Gilchrist (26 votes), Brian Lara (25 votes), Len Hutton (21 votes), Imran Khan (21 votes), Jim Laker (12 votes).